THE LIFE AND STORIES OF THE JAINA SAVIOR PARCVANATHA

THE LIFE AND STORIES OF THE JAINA SAVIOR PARCVANATHA

By
MAURICE BLOOMFIELD

GYAN

ISBN : 978-81-212-0001-1

Published, 2018

Published by

Gyan Publishing House
5, Ansari Road
Daryaganj, New Delhi-110002
Phone: 011-47034999, 9811692060
www.gyanbooks.com
E-mail: books@gyanbooks.com

Printed at: G. Print Process, Delhi.

CONTENTS

SARGA THE SIXTH

SARGA THE SEVENTH

PREFACE

The publication in India, in the year 1912, of Bhāvadevasūri's Pārçvanātha Caritra opens out, for the first time, a more connected and complete account of the life and supposed teachings of the penultimate Jaina Tīrthaṁkara, or Savior, Pārçva or Pārçvanātha. The lives of the twenty-two Saviors preceding Pārçva are pure myth. The last Tīrthaṁkara, Vardhamāna or Nirgrantha Jñātṛputra,[1] best known as Vīra or Mahāvīra, presumably a historical personage, regarded by the Jainas as the real founder of their religion, is supposed to have lived either in the last half of the sixth, or in the first half of the fifth century B. C. Pārçvanātha is said to have preceded Vīra by only 250 years,[2] a passably moderate time, as Hindu time conceptions go. But beyond the persistent and, on the whole, unitarian character of his story and his teaching, there is little to show that he was an historical personage. Be this as it may, the doctrines ascribed to Pārçva are fundamental in Jaina religion, and Pārçva's personality figures large in the Jaina legend and in Jaina consciousness. The life of Pārçva, including his nine pre-births, as presented in Bhāvadeva's work, is the first complete account of Pārçvanātha published to the Western world. And his account of Pārçva's life, along with the many stories woven into it, adds to the chain of Hindu fiction books a jewel of no mean price.

[1] Prākrit Nātaputta or Nāyaputta, turned erroneously into Sanskrit Jñātaputra or Jñātiputra; in Sanskrit the correct Jñātṛputra does not figure. See Jacobi, Indian Antiquary, ix. 158 ff.

[2] The Jainas say that he was born 817 B. C.

Were it not for the other chronicles of Pārçvanātha, whose manuscripts are scattered thru Indian and European libraries,[3] the text which I treat here would call for a complete translation and elaboration. Yet such a treatment, undertaken without reference to the parallel versions, would remain not much less fragmentary than that presented here. For these versions, in the light of other experience, would not only clarify one another reciprocally, but they suggest a synoptic edition of the Pārcvanātha Caritras as the only ultimately satisfactory scholarly end.

Operations along this line are precluded by the present world conditions. In lieu thereof it has seemed to me well to promote a preliminary familiarity with the Pārçvanātha cycle. The body of this essay consists of a full digest of the frame story and the illustrative stories which are boxed in, in the usual exigent Hindu fiction manner. The frame story contains the fullest extant account of the Jain Savior Pārçvanātha's life, preceded by a series of nine pre-births, beginning with the two hostile brothers Marubhūti (the ultimate Pārçva) and Kamaṭha (the ultimate Asura Meghamālin). These pre-births are described with the meticulous care of a chronicle of real life, and with the sincerity of a devout believer. The hostility of the two brothers is carried on thru all pre-births; in each of them the incarnation of Kamaṭha kills the incarnation of Marubhūti, until Marubhūti's soul ripens into that of the Savior Pārçva, and until Meghamālin is converted to the worship of Pārçva.

The intercalated stories count among the best of Jaina fiction. One of these, namely, 'Vikrama's adventures in the body of a parrot,' I have translated in full and elaborated on pp. 22-43 of my paper, 'On the art of entering

[3] See p. 1 ff.

INTRODUCTION

This essay is based upon Çrī Bhāvadevasūri's Pārçvanātha Caritra, edited by Shravak Pandit Hargovinddas and Shravak Pandit Bechardas (çrāvakapaṇḍita-haragovindadāsa-becaradāsābhyāṁ saṁçodhitam). Benares, Vīrasaṁvat, 2048 (A. D. 1912). Professor Leumann, in his List of Digambara Manuscripts in Strassburg, WZKM. xi, p. 306, mentions an Oxford MS. of a Pārçvanātha Caritra by Sakalakīrti.[1] A manuscript of the same work by the same author is also catalogued by R. G. Bhandarkar, in his Report on the search for Sanskrit manuscripts in the Bombay Presidency (Bombay, 1887), in the list of Digambara MSS. (pp. 91-126, nr. 12). A third Pārçvanātha Caritra, by Udayavīragaṇi, is cataloged by Rājendralālamitra, in his Catalog of Sanskrit Manuscripts in the library of the Mahārāja of Bikāner (Calcutta 1880), nr. 1502; and a fourth, by Māṇikyacandra, on pp. 157-164 of Peterson's Third Report on search of Sanskrit Manuscripts in the Bombay Circle (Bombay 1887). J. Burgess, Indian Antiquary, ii. 139, note, has the following statement: " It (namely, the Pārçvanātha Caritra) was written by ' Briddha Tapa Gacha ' in Saṁvat 1654, and occasionally calls this Jaina by the name of Jagannātha.—Delamaire, Asiat. Trans. vol. i, pp. 428-436." As the Asiatic Transactions are not accessible, I

[1] According to C. M. Duff, The Chronology of India, p. 260, one Sakalakīrti probably composed in 1464 the Tattvārthasāradīpaka; cf. Leumann's List, p. 302. Sakalakīrti is also author of one of several Çāntinātha Caritras; see Guerinot, Essai de Bibliographie Jaina, p. 90, and cf. pp. 75, 84, 399. See also Weber, Berlin Handschriftenverzeichnisse, vol. ii, pp. 903, 1091-2.

do not undertake to appraise this statement. The name given the author (Vṛddhatapagacha) does not conform, but there is no reason why there should not exist a Pārçvanātha Caritra of that date.

There is also a Pārçvanātha Kāvya by Padmasundara, listed by Aufrecht in his Catalog of the Bodleian Library nr. 70 (p. 392); and referred to by Weber in his Berlin Handschriftenverzeichnisse, vol. ii, p. 1016, note 2. Bhadrabāhu's Kalpasūtra 149-169 contains a very brief and jejune Life of Pārçva which does not touch upon the dramatic episode of his relation to Kamaṭha (Kaṭha, Meghamālin) and Dharaṇa (Dharaṇendra). And the 14th sarga of the Çatruṁjaya Māhātmyam, in its first 97 stanzas, gives a brief account of Pārçva's history which is evidently based upon previous Caritras; see Weber, in the Abhandlungen für die Kunde des Morgenlandes, vol. i, part 4, pp. 83 ff. (cf. pp. 37 ff.); also J. Burgess, Indian Antiquary, xxx, pp. 302 ff. For the very secondary 'Pārçvanātha Caritram' of the commentator Lakṣmīvallabha see below.

The Praçasti describes Bhāvadevasūri's spiritual descent or pontifical succession, beginning, as frequently is the case, with Sudharma, that disciple of Mahāvīra, who followed Gāutama Indrabhūti as spiritual leader of the Jains after Mahāvīra's and Gāutama Indrabhūti's death. Next comes Kālikasūri, belonging to the Khaṇḍillagacha.[2] In this form the name occurs in the list of Gurus in Dharmasāgaragaṇi's Gurvāvalīsūtra.[3] Since this text mentions his sister, the nun Sarasvatī; his conquest of King Gardabhilla; and his connection with the dispute about keeping the Paryuṣaṇa (Pajjusan),[4] Kālikasūri is

[2] The name of this Gacha is otherwise unknown. Is it connected with Çāṇḍilya?

[3] See Weber, Handschriftenverzeichnisse, vol. ii, p. 1001.

[4] See SBE. xxii. 296 ff.

identical with Kālakācārya or Kālikācārya who lived 453 years after Mahāvīra. The Çrīkālakasūriprabandha, fourth in the Prabhāvaka Carita (pp. 36 ff.), tells his life; see also Weber, Pañcadaṇḍachattraprabandha, p. 7, note 1 (Berlin Academy 1877); Jacobi in ZDMG. xxiv. 247 ff.;. Leumann, ibid. xxvii. 493 ff.; Stevenson, The Heart of Jainism, pp. 75 ff.

The succeeding Gurus are Vijayasiṁha, whose Prabandha is the sixth in Prabhāvaka Carita (pp. 69 ff.); then Vīrasūri, whose Prabandha is the twentieth in the same collection (pp. 272 ff.); next the Munīçvara Çrījinadevasūri (yo dharmam āropya guṇe viçuddhadhyāneṣuṇā moharipuṁ bibheda); after that other distinguished Sūris of the name Çrījinadeva (gurukrame punaḥ çrījinadevākhyā babhūvur varasūrayaḥ); then a teacher Yaças (= Yaçodevasūri); and finally Bhāvadevasūri who composed his work in Çrīpattanā in raviviçvavarṣa 1312.

Judging from the unitarian character of the Pārçva legend, systematic accounts of his pre-births and life, such as are likely to be given in the unpublished Pārçva Caritras listed above, probably do not diverge greatly. The following story of Pārçva's pre-births and life is based on Bhāvadevasūri's published 'History,' and a small prose Sanskrit account, incorporated in Lakṣmīvallabha's commentary to the Uttarādhyayana-Sūtra (Calcutta, Saṁvat 1936 = A. D. 1878), pp. 682, line 7 to 688, last line. This version also styles itself Pārçvanāthacaritram. Since it differs somewhat from Bhāvadevasūri, it is likely to be derived from one of the other Pārçva Caritras, but the differences are not such as to change the character of the story as a whole. The two accounts are hereafter designated as Bh and L.

The story opens in the city of Potana, where rules

under magnificent auspices King Aravinda with his wife Dhāraṇī. Aravinda has a Purohita, Viçvabhūti, whose wife, Anuddharā,[5] bears him two sons Kamaṭha and Marubhūti.[6] Kamaṭha has for wife Varuṇā; Marubhūti's spouse is Vasuṁdharā. Viçvabhūti retires from active life to pious contemplation, dies, and goes to heaven, followed there by his desolated widow, Anuddharā. Kamaṭha and Marubhūti remain behind, sorrowing for their parents. A great Sage, Hariçcandra, preaches the Law to such purpose, that Marubhūti is weaned from all terrestrial attachments and becomes a disciple, whereas Kamaṭha, whose heart is not pierced by the Sage's instruction, remains a slave of his passions. Owing to Marubhūti's abstention, his wife, Vasuṁdharā, lives in enforced chastity, and becomes love-mad. For a time she repels Kamaṭha's advances, but finally submits to his unbridled lust. Blinded by love, they live in incestuous adultery. Varuṇā, Kamaṭha's wife, observing, reports the affair to Marubhūti. Whereupon he goes to a distant village, returns in the guise of a holy beggar, and asks Kamaṭha for shelter. Kamaṭha permits him a nook in his house,[7] so that, while pretending sleep, he becomes witness to the misconduct of his brother with his own sister-in-law. He reports the affair to King Aravinda, just but stern monarch. The King has Kamaṭha mounted upon an ass, marked with many insignia of shame, and expelled from the city.

Kamaṭha, disgraced, deprived of wealth and relatives, roams solitarily in the forest, broods revenge, and bides his time. He happens upon a hermitage in the forest, takes sacred vows, and practices asceticism upon a moun-

[5] L: Anudarī.

[6] First pre-birth of the pair.

[7] For Bh.'s gṛhakoṇe L. has caturhastamadhye.

tain. In the mean time Marubhūti becomes despondent, because of the dire retribution he has brought upon his brother. Even tho restrained by King Aravinda, he goes to the forest to conciliate Kamaṭha. Throwing himself upon his knees, he begs forgiveness, but Kamaṭha takes up a stone, and with a single blow crushes his brother's head, and, with it, his own sacred vows. While in pain from that mortal blow Marubhūti harbors distressing thoughts (ārtadhyāna). As result, he is reborn as a wild elefant,[8] leader of a herd in the Vindhya mountains. Varuṇā, Kamaṭha's wife, blind with fury, also dies, is reborn as a she-elefant, and becomes his mate. Wildly they roam together in the forest.

King Aravinda, living on the pinnacle of worldly pleasures, one day contemplates a great storm. In the manner of a Pratyekabuddha,[9] he is reminded by the breaking of the clouds of the perishableness of all things in the saṁsāra, and decides to abandon the world. He takes vows with a teacher, and wanders alone thru towns and villages. In the course of these wanderings he succeeds in converting to the faith of the holy Jina Saints the merchant Sāgaradatta, head of a caravan. Going on his way, Sāgaradatta comes to the spot where the elefant chief (Marubhūti) is in the habit of disporting himself with his females. While he is camping on the banks of a lake, the elefant comes there to drink, and proceeds to attack his caravan, slaying and dispersing. Aravinda's spiritual insight tells him that the time to enlighten the elefant

[8] Second pre-birth of the Marubhūti soul.

[9] The meaning of this word is probably 'enlightened by some particular thing, circumstance, or occurrence,' as is the case each time in the Jain legends about the four kings in Jacobi's Ausgewählte Erzählungen in Māhārāṣṭrī, pp. 34 ff.; cf. Jātakas 378, 408. The word is rendered otherwise by translators and lexicografers.

has come. He places himself in kāyotsarga posture,[10] and reverently approaches him. Aravinda reminds him of his former high estate as Marubhūti, and bids him desist from his mad folly. Marubhūti, remembering his former existence, reverently signifies with his trunk that his faith is restored. Whereupon, after Aravinda has retired, the elefant lives piously on sun-warmed water and dry leaves, repenting his career of fright and destruction.

In the mean time, Kamaṭha, unchastened even by his murder of Marubhūti, loathed of men, dies in a troubled state of soul, and is reborn as a kurkuṭa-serpent.[11] Killing or endangering all living beings, he infests the forest, and finally bites the elefant Marubhūti, who then dies while contemplating the Law (dharmadhyāna), to be reborn as a god in the Sahasrāra heaven.[12] The kurkuṭa-serpent (Kamaṭha) on its death, is reborn as a hell-dweller in the Pañcamāvani hell,[13] suffering the tortures of that hell.

On the Vāitāḍhya mountain stands the sumptuous city of Tilakā, ruled by the Vidyādhara king Vidyudgati with his queen Tilakāvatī.[14] The soul of the elefant falls from the eighth Kalpa, to be reborn as prince Kiraṇavega.[15]

[10] 'Relaxation of the body': 'The ascetic stands immovable, his arms held stiffly downward, his knees pressed together, his feet four fingers' length apart; his toes stretched forward.' So according to R. G. Bhandarkar, Report on the search for Sanskrit Manuscripts, 1887-91, p. 98 note. The word is rendered 'statuesque posture' by Tawney in his Translations of Kathākoça, p. 54, and Prabandhacintāmaṇi, p. 137; 'hockende stellung,' Jacobi, Ausgewählte Erzählungen, vocabulary, under kāussagga. Stevenson, The Heart of Jainism, p. 250, describes the 'kāusagga' position, as with legs crossed and hands in lap; cf. also p. 257.

[11] Second pre-birth of the Kamaṭha soul.

[12] Third pre-birth of the Marubhūti soul.

[13] Third pre-birth of the Kamaṭha soul.

[14] Called Kanakatilakā in L.

[15] Fourth pre-birth of the Marubhūti soul.

Vidyudgati, taking the vow, makes over his kingdom to Kiraṇavega. Kiraṇavega also, in time, turns from concerns of the body to those of the soul, and makes over the kingdom to his son Kiraṇatejas. Kiraṇavega goes to Puṣkaradvīpa, and passes some time in penance on the mountain of Vāitāḍhya in company with an image of the Jina. The soul of the kurkuṭa-serpent is reborn as a great serpent (mahāhi).[16] Owing to their prenatal hostility the serpent bites Kiraṇavega, who dies forgivingly, and is reborn as a god in Jambūdrumāvarta.[17] The serpent is burned by a forest-fire, and goes to the Dhūmaprabhā hell.[18]

The soul of the former Kiraṇavega, in due time, falls from its high estate, and is reborn as Prince Vajranābha, son of Lakṣmīvatī,[19] queen of Vajravīrya, king of Çubhaṁkarā.[20] He grows into every bodily and mental perfection, so as to become fit mate for Vijayā, daughter of King Candrakānta of Baḍgadeça. While still heir-apparent, Vajranābha, together with an infidel cousin of his, Kubera, is converted by the sage Lokacandra. His father, King Vajravīrya, retires from the world; Vajranābha, after him, rules piously and righteously with his queen Vijayā, who presents him with a son, Cakrāyudha. Vajranābha, in turn, has misgivings as to stability of the world and its attractions; appoints Cakrāyudha his successor; takes the vow with the Jina Kṣemaṁkara; and wanders as a mendicant to Sukachavijaya. In the mean time the soul of the serpent, returning from hell,

[16] Fourth pre-birth of the Kamaṭha soul.

[17] Fifth pre-birth of the Marubhūti soul.

[18] Fifth pre-birth of the Kamaṭha soul. L. calls this stage, pañcamapṛthivīnāraka.

[19] L. corruptly, akṣimatāyā bhāryāyāḥ.

[20] Sixth pre-birth of the Marubhūti soul.

is reborn as a wild Bhilla, Kurañgaka,[21] infesting the mountain Jvalana. As Vajranābha happens to be present there in kāyotsarga posture, Kurañgaka, out of prenatal hatred, hits him with an arrow. Vajranābha, tho struck fatally, remains free from evil thought, merely remarking that he had been killed by the soul of the Bhilla in a former existence. He is reborn as a god, Lalitāñga.[22] Kurañgaka, when he dies, goes to the Saptamāvani hell.[23]

The soul of Vajranābha falls from heaven and enters the womb of Sudarçanā, wife of King Vajrabāhu[24] of Surapura. The queen dreams the fourteen great dreams which augur the birth of a Cakravartin (emperor). In due time a son, Suvarṇabāhu[25] is borne; he grows up with every accomplishment. The king takes the vow, leaving the kingdom to his son. One day Suvarṇabāhu is carried off by a horse of inverted training to a hermitage, where he meets a royal maiden and her companion, quite in the manner of the Çakuntalā story. He carries away with him this maiden, Padmā, daughter of Ratnāvalī, widow of the Vidyādhara king of Ratnapura, and becomes, by the aid of his wife's Vidyādhara relatives, a Cakravartin. In time he is converted by the Tīrthaṁkara Jagannātha. One day, as he stands with a Jain image in the forest of Kṣīragiri, he is attacked by a lion, inhabited by the soul of the Bhilla Kurañgaka, reincarnated in the lion's body,[26] after leaving hell. He dies forgivingly; is reborn as a god in the Mahāpra-

[21] Sixth pre-birth of the Kamaṭha soul.

[22] Seventh pre-birth of the Marubhūti soul.

[23] Seventh pre-birth of the Kamaṭha soul.

[24] L. Kuliçabāhu.

[25] Eighth pre-birth of Marubhūti soul. In L. the boy is named Kanakaprabha.

[26] Eighth pre-birth of the Kamaṭha soul.

bhavimāna heaven;[27] but the lion, at his own death, goes to the fourth hell.[28]

The soul of Marubhūti, after having passed thru nine existences as high-born man or god, finally is reincarnated in the womb of Vāmādevī, queen of the mighty Ikṣvāku king, Açvasena of Vārāṇasī. The events of this incarnation are described in the fifth sarga of our text with a degree of minuteness that reminds one of the Buddhology on the one hand, and of Mahāvīra's birth on the other hand. Not only the court of Benares, but also the entire Jaina Olympus is joyously interested in the gestation, birth, growth, and education of the future Lord of the World. Because the pregnant queen had seen in a troubled night a serpent by her side (pārçvataḥ), therefore he is called Pārçva. In accordance with a profesy he marries Prabhāvatī, the perfect daughter of Prasenajit, king in Kuçasthala. But, in order to fulfill this item of his destiny, he must first convert a truculent rival for Prabhāvatī's hand, Yavana, king of Kaliñga.

In the mean time the soul of the lion, the Kamaṭha soul, is reborn as Kaṭha,[29] son of a Brahman, named Rora. Owing to the death of his parents, he is brought up by charity; carries on a miserable existence begging from house to house, shy and given to fear. Disgusted with life he turns ascetic, and subsists on the roots of plants.

One day Pārçva sees Kaṭha, surrounded by a great

[27] Ninth pre-birth of the Marubhūti soul.

[28] Ninth pre-birth of the Kamaṭha soul.

[29] L. does not mention this name, but substitutes the original eponymic Kamaṭha. Çatrumjaya Māhātmyam 14. 12 has Kaṭha, but the variant Kamava points to the alternate Kamaṭha. Evidently the two names are interchangeable. This is the tenth pre-birth of the Kamaṭha soul, destined in the next birth, as the Asura Meghamālin, to be converted to Pārçva's belief.

concourse of people, performing the severe five-fire-penance (pañcāgnitapas). And he sees that Kaṭha has thrown a great serpent into a fire-pan which stands upon the fagots of the fire. He asks the reason for this pitiless practice, inconsistent with Kaṭha's own austerities. Kaṭha replies that kings might understand elefants and horses, but that sages alone understood religion. Pārçva has the fire put out; the agonized serpent comes out; and Pārçva makes his people show honor to him. Absorbing the essence of their worship, the serpent is reborn as Dharaṇa, the wealthy king of the Nāgas in Pātāla, the subterranean home of the serpents. Kaṭha, as the result of his false practice, is reborn as an Asura by name of Meghamālin.

Pārçva, happening to see on the wall of his palace a picture of the Arhat, Nemi,[30] who had taken the vow early in life, decides to do the same, and to undertake the enlightenment of the world. Preparatory to his consecration he distributes vast alms. To the songs and music of the people he goes to a hermitage where the very trees and plants rejoice over his presence. At the foot of an açoka-tree he renounces power and wealth, plucks out his hair, and, at the age of thirty, obtains the knowledge due to mental perfection. He wanders from place to place, instructing, and acclaimed as a Saint. While standing in the forest of Kāuçāmbī in the kāyotsarga posture, the serpent-king Dharaṇa comes in great state to do him honor, performs a mimic representation, and during three days holds an umbrella over his head

[30] L. calls him Ariṣṭanemi. This name also, e. g., in Merutuñga's Upadeçaçata or Mahāpuruṣacarita; see Weber, Die Handschriftenverzeichnisse der Kgl. Bibliothek zu Berlin, ii, p. 1025. It is in fact the fuller name of the 22nd Arhat; see Kalpasūtra 170 ff.; Uttarādhyayaṇa 22. 4 ff. The two names interchange in Jain literature, Nemi being hypocoristic.

to protect him from the sun. He wanders again, to many places, to find out where dwells the enemy Illusion. The Asura Meghamālin (the soul of Kamaṭha) attacks the Lord Pārçva with tigers, elefants, and scorpions, but, when he shows no fear, they slink off, as tho ashamed. Meghamālin then tries to submerge him in the waters produced by a fearful thunderstorm; even then the Lord does not budge from his place and his pious meditations. Dharaṇa, finding out by superior insight that Kamaṭha is attacking the Lord, fashions by means of his serpent hoods an umbrella over his head: the Lord stands there like a royal haṅsa bird, submerged in a deep trance, retaining his equanimity in the face of both Kamaṭha's attacks and Dharaṇa's devotion. Dharaṇa then excoriates Meghamālin's hatred of the Lord, pointing out that he had done him no injury, but on the contrary, had saved him from the sin of burning up Dharaṇa on the occasion of his uncanny practice. Meghamālin then repents, resorts to the Lord, and goes home, determined to devote himself to piety. Thus ends the drama of the persecution of the soul of Marubhūti by the soul of Kamaṭha, carried on thru ten existences.

Then Pārçva returns to his native city of Kāçī (Vārāṇasī), where he reaches the state of Kevalin with all its supernatural powers. His father, Açvasena; his mother, Vāmā; and his wife, Prabhāvatī, come out to honor him; Açvasena sings a hymn in his praise. Pārçva continues to wander and preach, until he realizes that Nirvāṇa is at hand. He then goes to the Sammeta mountain, and practices a month's asceticism. He attains to various forms of spiritual refinement, up to the point when his karma is destroyed. He dies and reaches the summit of heaven. Çakra bathes the body with the fluid of the ocean of milk, and adorns him with divine jewels. The gods place his body upon a pyre of sandal, and pour fragrant substances upon it. Cloud-youths (meghakumārakāḥ) quench the pyre. Over the bones of the Lord the gods erect a jewel stūpa, and then disperse to their various homes.

In the present Pārçvanātha Caritra the accounts of the pre-births, birth, life, and nirvāṇa of the Saint, being the frame of the Caritra, are interrupted by fiction episodes which make up the bulk of the work. It will be convenient to assemble here in succession the passages which deal with Pārçva himself, including the account of his pre-births:

1. 17-60: Story of the brothers Kamaṭha and Marubhūti.

1. 670-797: The enmity between Kamaṭha and Marubhūti.

1. 815-885: The enmity between Kamaṭha and Marubhūti, concluded.

2. 1-51: King Kiraṇavega.

2. 1027-1065: Kiraṇavega's conversion and death.

3. 1-104: King Vajranābha and his infidel cousin Kubera.

3. 1034-1108: Conversion of both, and death of Vajranābha.

4. 1-161: Cakravartinship of Suvarṇabāhu and his death.

5. 1-254: Early life of the Arhat Pārçvanātha.

6. 1-149: Marriage and later life of the Arhat Pārçvanātha.

6. 166-213: Life of Pārçvanātha, continued: Meghamālin's attack and conversion.

6. 214-279: Life of Pārçvanātha, continued: Sermon on the four-fold dharma.

6. 1343-1360: Life of Pārçvanātha, continued.
7. 1-7: Life of Pārçvanātha, continued.
7. 826-838; Life of Pārçvanātha, continued.
8. 358-393: Life of Pārçvanātha, concluded. His nirvāṇa.

* * *

The prenatal history of Pārçva (Marubhūti) and Kamaṭha represents a type of fiction in which a pair of souls are held in relation to one another by the tie of love or hatred, thru a succession of parallel births. Professor Leumann has elaborated the story of Citta and Saṁbhūta (the Prākrit Bambhadatta story) in two articles in vols. v and vi of the Vienna Journal of Oriental Studies. Here a pair of fond souls pass thru successive existences, until, in the end, one of them makes an abortive attempt to save the other from perdition. A faint suggestion of the same motif is found in the story of Brahmadatta, Kathās. 3. 27 ff.; 114. 17 ff. An impressive example of hatred in successive births is contained in the story of Sanatkumāra (Prākrit Sanaṁkumāra) in Pārçvanātha Caritra 6. 1011 ff.; Kathākoça, pp. 31 ff.; and Devendra's Prākrit version:[31] King Vikramayaças falls in love with Viṣṇuçrī, beautiful wife of the merchant Nāgadatta. The king's jealous wives kill her by sorcery. The king is grieved to the point of madness, until his chief men show him the festering, evil-smelling body of Viṣṇuçrī. He turns ascetic, is reborn in heaven, falls thence, and is born again as the merchant Jinadharma. In the mean time Nāgadatta, dying in sore affliction, is reborn as the Brahman Agniçarman. Agniçarman, having turned ascetic, wanders to Rājagṛha, the city of King Naravāhaṇa. There also arrives Jinadharma. Agniçar-

[31] See Jacobi, Ausgewählte Erzählungen, pp. 20 ff.

man sees him, and, goaded on by his prenatal enmity, says to the king: 'Sire, if I may be allowed to eat a pudding of rice and milk off the back of this merchant, I will break my fast, but not otherwise.' The ascetic eats from a red hot dish placed on the back of Jinadharma; when the meal is finished, the dish is wrenched from his back together with blood, sinews, flesh, and fat. But the victim bears patiently the fruit of his actions in a former life, turns ascetic, and is reborn as Indra. Agniçarman is reborn as Āirāvaṇa, the elefant on which Indra rides. The latter falls from that position and, after various animal rebirths, comes into existence again as the Yakṣa Asita. Indra, too, falls, to be reborn as the emperor Sanatkumāra. The two finally meet in a great combat, in which the Yakṣa is conquered, but, being immortal, his final discomfiture takes the form of flight.

The Prākrit Samarāïccakahā and its Sanskrit digest, Pradyumnasūri's Samāráditya Saṁkṣepa, deal with nine existences (bhava) of the Prince Guṇasena and the Brahman Agniçarman. In each of these the soul of Agniçarman is controlled by hatred of the soul of Guṇasena, and in each existence the reincarnation of Guṇasena is destroyed by that of Agniçarman, until Guṇasena reaches final emancipation.

Anent Dhammapada 291 ('Not hatred for hatred'), Buddhaghoṣa's Dhammapada Commentary, 21. 2, tells how a girl eats the eggs of a hen, whereupon the hen prays that she may be reborn as a Rākṣasī, or ogress, fit and able to devour the children of her enemy. In 500 successive existences they return hatred for hatred. In time the girl is reborn as a young woman of Sāvatthi, and the hen is reborn as an ogress. The ogress devours two children of the young woman, and is about to seize the third, when the young woman seeks refuge in the monastery. The Buddha admonishes them to return good for evil.[32]

In Kathākoça, pp. 8 ff., two Brahmans, Devadharma and Devaçarman, obtain two urns of gold, which they agree to bury on the bank of a river, and then seek more wealth. Coming to a well, the elder brother tells the younger to see if there is water, pushes him over while he is looking, but is himself also dragged in by the younger. They both perish; are reborn as pairs of animals, until, in their fifth birth, they again rise to the position of Brahman brothers. Whenever they come over the spot where the two urns are buried, they fall to quarreling, but at home they are on the best of terms. A Saint explains the phenomenon as due to their prenatal quarrel, whereupon they are converted, die, and go to the world of the gods.

In addition to 'successive birth in pairs' the story exploits another well-established fiction motif, namely 'hostile brothers.' The last illustration contains both motifs. The motif 'hostile brothers' begins with Mahābh. 1. 209. 1 ff.: Two brothers, Sunda and Upasunda, obtain thru ascetic practices control of the world. Brahman grants them immunity from death, except at one another's hands. They proceed to drive the gods from heaven, and to extirpate the Brahmanical caste. Viçvakarman fashions a woman, Tilottamā, so entrancing that, at the sight of her, Sthāṇu Mahādeva develops four faces, and Indra a thousand eyes. The two brothers, as soon as they see Tilottamā, both fall in love with her, and slay one another as the result of their rivalry.[33]

[32] See Burlingame, in the Introduction to his Translation of this work, p. 127.

[33] This story is repeated in Kathās. 15. 135 ff. (45. 382), and retold of a pair of Asuras, Ghaṇṭa and Nighaṇṭa, Kathās. 21. 229. Tawney, in a note to his Translation of Kathāsaritsāgara, vol. ii, p. 629, draws attention to

In Pārçvanātha 4. 53 ff., at the death of the king of Ratnapura, his two sons quarrel over the succession, so that the widowed queen Ratnāvalī finds it advisable to take her daughter Padmā for safety to the hermitage of her uncle Gālava. Similarly in Dharmakalpadruma ii, the princes Çūra and Vīra fight for the sovereignty of Kāuçāmbī, so that their sister Jayamālā has to be placed in safety with her uncle, King Candraketu of Ratnapura. In Pārçvanātha 6. 280 ff. the destiny of two princes, Vijaya and Candrasena is determined by their hostility.

In Ralston's Tibetan Tales, p. 279, two princes, the older Kṣemaṁkara, the younger Pāpaṁkara, go on an expedition to a jewel island, fill their ship with jewels, but are shipwrecked. They get to shore; Pāpaṁkara robs Kṣemaṁkara of jewels which he has fastened to his girdle, puts out his eyes with a thorn, and leaves him on the shore. Pāpaṁkara returns home, succeeds to the throne, and is desired for son-in-law by a neighboring king who had previously offered his daughter to Kṣemaṁkara. The daughter refuses, and asks for a svayaṁvara. Kṣemaṁkara, now a blind vagabond musician, stands at the svayaṁvara, to one side. The princess throws the garland upon him, thus marrying him to the remonstrances of the people. Thru saccakiriyā [34] ('truth declaration') Kṣemaṁkara regains his sight, and is reinstated as rightful heir to the throne.

* * *

As regards other versions of the Pārçva legend, the Çatruṁjaya Māhātmyam (14. 1-97) treats Pārçva's life briefly, but in essential accord with our Caritra account.

the story of Otus and Ephialtes (Preller's Griechische Mythologie, vol. i, p. 81), and cites Grohmann's Sagen aus Böhmen, p. 35.

[34] For this important motif see Burlingame, 'The Act of Truth,' JRAS., 1917, p. 449.

It omits, however, all pre-births, beginning with his descent from the Prāṇata Kalpa (Caritra 5. 29). This text, however, alludes to the enmity of Pārçva and Kaṭha (Kamaṭha) during the course of ten prebirths and birth (14. 42, daçabhavāratiḥ Kaṭhāsuraḥ). There are minor differences; e. g. Prabhāvatī, Pārçva's wife, is the daughter of a King Naravarman, instead of Prasenajit, Naravarman's son (Caritra 5. 145 ff.). But, in general, personal as well as geographical references agree with those of the present text.

The Kalpasūtra (149 ff.) not only disregards the prenatal history of the Saint, beginning with his descent from the Prāṇata Kalpa, but, furthermore, omits all reference to Kamaṭha (Kaṭha) and the serpent king Dharaṇa. We may suspect that Kamaṭha has a historical kernel, being some sectarian, hostile to Pārçva's Jina doctrine. The Kalpasūtra agrees with the Caritras as to his birth-place, Benares, and his family: his father King Açvasena; his mother Vāmā (Vāmādevī).[35] The story of his marriage to Prabhāvatī, daughter of Prasenajit, king of Kuçasthala, is ignored in the Kalpasūtra, but it is stated that he lived thirty years as a householder; more precisely the Caritra, 6. 105; 8. 377, has it that he was thirty years old when his niṣkramaṇa took place. The Kalpasūtra points out at the beginning of its sketch that the five most important moments of Pārçva's life happened when the moon was in conjunction with the asterism Viçakhā. Any suspicion that this statement is artificially systematic passes away in the light of Pārçvanātha Caritra 5. 30, 43; 6. 108, 217; 8. 370, where are described, in order, the Saint's conception; his birth; his wandering out into houselessness and pluck-

[35] Pārçva has the metronymic Vāmeya in 5. 106.

ing out his hair; his attainment to the state of Kevalin; and his final salvation. All authorities agree explicity as to this chronology; they also state that Pārçva lived a hundred years: Kalpasūtra 168; Çatruṁjaya Māhātmyam 14. 96; Caritra 8. 377. The texts agree that the chief of Pārçva's Çramaṇa following was the Gaṇabhṛt Āryadatta; see Kalpasūtra 161; Çatruṁjaya Māhātmyam 14. 68 [36]; Caritra 6. 1352; 7. 1; the systematized list of the early followers of Pārçva in their total, as given in the Caritra 6. 1352, 1363 differs a good deal from that of Kalpasūtra 160 ff.

In one matter the Kalpasūtra does not seem to be on all fours with an important point of tradition, or, at least, is very inexplicit. The name of the Saint, Pārçva, 'Side,' is explained irrelevantly in the Kalpasūtra, but the Commentator remarks that the name was given him because his mother, before his birth, while lying on her couch, saw in the dark a black serpent crawling about. This accords with the other authorities, especially our Caritra 5. 125, 126: 'While the Saint was in his mother's womb, she saw by night, tho it was dark, a serpent moving about. At once she told her husband, who bore it in mind, decided that the serpent was the embryo's power (garbhasya prabhāvaḥ), and, therefore, named his son Pārçva.' [37] Now it is worth while to point out, in this connection, that serpent lore or mythology figures to an extraordinary extent in the Pārçva legend. Jain tradition, especially iconografic tradition, assigns to each Arhat or Tīrthaṁkara two attendant geniuses, or servitors; see of recent literature, J. Burgess in the Appendix to his Translation of Bühler's Indian Sect of the Jainas,

[36] This text mentions ten unnamed Sūris, led by Āryadatta.

[37] On name-giving in deference to a dream see additional note 10, on p. 189.

pp. 66 ff.; Stevenson, Heart of Jainism, p. 313. In our Caritra, 7. 827 ff., Pārçva's servants are described verbally:[38] 'A black, four-armed Yakṣa, Pārçva by name, who was born at that Tīrtha, who carried as an umbrella the hood of a cobra, who had the mouth of an elefant, who had a tortoise as chariot, who held an ichneumon and a serpent in his two right arms, bhaktaḥ pārçve 'bhavad vibhoḥ (became a devotee at the side of the Lord).' According to Hemacandra, Abhidhānacintāmaṇi 43, Pārçvanātha has a servant bearing his own name. This is the Çvetāmbara view of Pārçvanātha's male attendant; see particularly, Burgess, Indian Antiquary, xiii. 276.

According to another tradition, current among the Digambaras, Pārçva's male attendant is the serpent-prince Dharaṇa (Dharaṇendra) whom Pārçva saver from the cruelty of Kamaṭha or Kaṭha (see 6. 50-68); cf. Burgess, Indian Antiquary, xxxii, pp. 459-464. The Pārçva group reproduced there shows Dharaṇendra (riding on a tortoise). Burgess remarks on p. 463: 'Among the Digambara Jainas in the Kanarese district in Southern India, there appear to be differences in the iconography, especially of the attendant Yakṣas and goddesses (Yakṣiṇīs), compared with that of the Çvetāmbaras, as described by Hemacandra.' Of course, the present Caritra text takes the Çvetāmbara view.

Pārçva's female attendant, or Yakṣiṇī,[39] is named Padmāvatī. She is described in our Caritra 7. 828 as golden-complexioned; of distinguished might; having a kurkuṭa-serpent as chariot; holding in her two right hands a lotus and a noose, in her two left hands a fruit

[38] This is, as far as I know, the first verbal description published.

[39] Such female divine aids are known familiarly in Jaina literature as Çāsanadevī, Çāsanadevatā, or Çāsanasundarī; see p. 167 of this work.

and a hook; cf. the figure of Padmāvatī, sitting on a cock (-serpent), in Burgess' reproduction.[40] The same group shows a serpent underneath the figure of Pārçvanātha himself, that being the cognizance or symbol of that Saint thruout Jaina tradition. Pārçva's head is covered with seven cobra hoods[41] in the group mentioned, as well in a statue of the Saint at Elūra, reproduced in Ferguson and Burgess, Cave Temples of India, plate lxxxvi. Pārçva's attendants have each five cobra hoods over their heads. All this, together with the role which the Serpent King, Dharaṇa, plays in the life of the Saint, Pārçvanātha Caritra 6. 50 ff.; 6. 143 ff.; especially Dharaṇa's dramatic part in the final reconciliation between Pārçva and Kamaṭha, shows that the legend connects Pārçva definitely with serpent mythology. The account of his name accords with this feature of the Pārçva story.[42]

There are other minor points of difference between the Kalpasūtra and the Caritra, but both the precision and the moderation observed by the writers in the matter of Pārçva's life history warrant a settled tradition and after all, perhaps, a modicum of historical foundation. See Jacobi, Indian Antiquary, ix. 160 ff.; Tawney in his Translations of Prabandhacintāmaṇi, p. 133, note 2; Kathākoça, p. viii.

Some of the features of the Pārçva legend occur not only in connected legends, but also incidentally in such

[40] Burgess' explanation (l. c.) of Padmāvatī's cognizance (cihnā) as a haṅsa is not in accord with the present description, nor with his reproduction which shows distinctly a cock under the figure of Padmāvatī.

[41] The Gaṇadharasārdhaçatakam of Jinadattasūri speaks of Pārçva wearing nine serpent's hoods, pārçvanāthanavaphaṇadhāraṇa; see Weber, Verzeichnisse, vol. ii, p. 982. Rāuhiṇeya Carita, stanza 422, states distinctly that Dharaṇendra, here called 'Nāga king of Pātāla,' covers him with seven hoods.

[42] Cf. Oldham, JRAS. 1891, pp. 384-386.

texts as deal with, or allude to the 23d Arhat. Thus, in the Kalyāṇamandira Stotra of Siddhasenadivākara,[43] the congenital hostility to the Lord on the part of Kamaṭha is alluded to. In stanza 2 Pārçva is designated as kamaṭhasmayadhūmaketu, which Jacobi, with the aid of the commentary, renders by, 'verfinsterer des liebesgottes' (Comm. kamaṭhasmaya = smara). It seems to mean primarily, 'he who clouds (obscures) the smile of Kamaṭha, i. e., 'changes his smile to grief,' or the like. More in accord with the legend is stanza 31: rajāṅsi roṣād utthāpitāni kamaṭhena çaṭhena yāni chāyāpi tāis tava na nātha hatā, 'the dust which the rogue Kamaṭha from anger cast up did not as much as hit thy shadow,' alluding to Kamaṭha's (Meghamālin's) final efforts against the Lord, when he attacked him with a great storm, from which he was saved by the serpent-king Dharaṇa. Again, in the Kathāmahodadhi of Somacandra the story of Kamaṭha's unholy fire-practice with the serpent[44] is told briefly, along with Meghamālin's conversion, to wit (with some corrections): vārāṇasyāṁ nagaryām pañcāgnisādhanarūpaṁ tapaḥ Kamaṭhas tapati | anyadā gavākṣasthena çrī-Pārçvakumāreṇa tāpasapūjāvyāpṛtaḥ pūrjano bahir dadṛçe avadhinā | kāṣṭhamadhye prajvalan bhujaṁgaç ca | tatra gatvā prajvalakāṣṭhamadhyāt sarpo bahir karṣitaḥ | namaskāro dattaḥ | sa (sc. sarpo) Dharaṇendro jajñe | re mūrkha kim ajñānaṁ tapas tapasi | dayādharmaṁ na jānāsī 'tyādivākyāis tāpaso janasamakṣaṁ dhikcakre | svāmino dīkṣāgrahaṇānantaraṁ kāyotsargasthasya tāpasajīvo Meghamālī musalapramāṇadhārābhir nīropasargaṁ cakāra | taṁ sahamānasya Dharaṇendraphaṇāmaṇḍapādhaḥsthitasya svāminaḥ ke-

[43] See Jacobi, Ind. Stud. xiv. 376 ff. for this collection of perfervid bhakta-stanzas.

[44] Extracted in Weber, Handschriftenverzeichnisse, vol. ii, p. 1102 ff.

valajñānam utpede | Dharaṇendrabhayabhīto Meghamālī prabhupādayor lagnaḥ | mithyā duḥkrtaṁ dadāu.

Dharaṇa or Dharaṇendra, king of the serpents, continues a lively existence in Jain writings as saint and thaumaturge. In Merutuñga's Prabandhacintāmaṇi, p. 311, the king of Pātāla, Dharaṇendra, cures the Jain doctor Abhayasūri by licking his body with his tongue, afterwards showing him Stambhanaka, the holy place of Pārçva. In Kathākoça, p. 184, he saves King Ceṭaka, when he falls into a well while holding an image of the Jina in his hand. See also Weber, Bhagavatī, p. 211. Dharaṇa continues in relation with and is worshiped by Vardhamāna,[45] the 24th Arhat; see Weber, Berlin Handschriftenverzeichnisse, vol. ii, pp. 991, 1036; he is mentioned together with Padmāvatī, Pārçva's Yakṣiṇī, ib. 1039, being the alternate of the above mentioned Yakṣa (Pārçva) as attending genius of the Arhat.

Many holy places connected with Pārçva's career of self-culture or evangelism, as mentioned in this Caritra, seem to have enjoyed wide fame among the Jains. Thus, in 6. 140, and in the first stanza of the Praçasti at the end of the book, Kalikuṇḍa, a tīrtha on lake Kuṇḍa, so called, because it was near the Kali mountain (kaleḥ kuṇḍasya āsannabhāvitvāt), is quoted Çatruṁjaya Māhātmyam 14. 25 ff.; in Haṅsaratna's Ullekha (prose version) of the same work (see Weber, l. c., p. 1073); and in Vīraprabandha, çloka 9 (Prabhāvaka Carita, p. 206). Two other tīrthas or towns of our text, Ahichatrā, 6. 145, and Kurkuṭeçvara, 6. 167, whose names are explained by legends, are mentioned in the Çatruṁjaya Māhātmyaṁ 14. 34-40, and in the same Ullekha. A tīrtha named Stam-

[45] Or Mahāvīra, who is understood to have been in the beginning of his career a Çramaṇa follower of Pārçva; see Āyārañga-Sutta 2. 15. 16.

bhanaka, which I do not remember to have seen in our Caritra, but which is mentioned in the first verse of the Praçasti, is closely associated with Pārçva in Prabandhacintāmaṇi, pp. 311, 312, 'the Jina Pārçvanātha of Stambhanaka,' and 'Stambhanaka, a holy place of Pārçvanātha'; see also the same text, p. 275, and Weber, ibid., 992, 1039. The Praçasti in its first stanza mention in addition, a number of tīrthas: at Mathurā, Çañkhapura, Nāgahrada, Lāṭahrada, and Svarṇagiri; they may be connected with the Pārçva legend in general, but do not occur in our Caritra. Presumably, as coming from a later time, Merutuñga, Prabandhacintāmaṇi, p. 309, mentions an image of the Saint set up in the temple of Dvāravatī, which remains unharmed after Dvāravatī was burned and overwhelmed by the sea.[46] The Caritra has no occasion to take account of this later legend, any more than of the late tradition that King Kumārapāla (circa 1125 A. D.) erected an image of the Saint in the name of his father in the Tribhuvanapāla temple in Vāgbhaṭapura; see Merutuñga, p. 219.[47] Images or cāityas of the saint are frequently mentioned in Jain literature; see Pārçvanātha Caritra 6. 137, 166; Prabandhacintāmaṇi, p. 34; Weber, Ind. Stud. xv. 290; Handschriftenverzeichnisse, pp. 1039, 1047, 1049, 1050, 1053, 1076. Stotras, such as Indra sings in honor of the newly born Saint in 5. 105 ff.; or such as Pārçva's father himself sings in honor of the Saint in 6. 247 ff., continue to be sung; see ibid., 471, 928, 938, 943, 992, 1012, 1033, 1039, 1001. Processions (yātrā) and mimic representations (nāṭyavidhi), such as our text mentions in 6. 134, 143, continue to be performed in honor of the Lord; see Weber, ibid., 274, 1054-56.

[46] See Jacobi, ZMDG. xlii. 493 ff.

[47] Cf. Bühler, Ueber das Leben des Jaina Mönches Hemachandra, pp. 40, 41.

DIGEST OF BHĀVADEVASŪRI'S PĀRÇVANĀTHA CARITRA

Sarga the First

Invocation of Arhats and Divinities

Author's proemium in praise (mañgala) of the Jaina Arhats, Nābheya, Çāntinātha, Nemi, Pārçvanātha, and the collective Jinendras that liberally bestow holy knowledge.[1] Adoration of Vāgdevī (Sarasvatī), the Moon, and other divine personifications, closing with a statement of the purpose of the book, namely the history (carita) in eight chapters (sarga), describing the ten existences (pre-births and birth) of the holy Jina, Lord Pārçva, whose superlative qualities are praised beforehand in ecstatic language (1-16).

Frame Story: The brothers Kamaṭha and Marubhūti

Flowery description of the city of Potana. There ruled magnificently King Aravinda with his Queen Dhāraṇī, endowed with every womanly virtue (25). He had a wise Purohita,[2] Viçvabhūti, whose virtuous wife Anuddharā bore him two sons, Kamaṭha and Marubhūti. Kamaṭha's wife was Varuṇā; Marubhūti's, Vasuṁdharā.

[1] Analogous to the stotras, stavas, or stutis which play a more important role in Jaina religion than in Buddhism, or even Brahmanical sectarianism; see as specimens the Çobhanastutayaḥ of Çobhanamuni (Jacobi in ZDMG. xxxii. 509 ff.); or the Bhaktāmarastotra, and the Kalyāṇamandirastotra (the same author in Indische Studien, xiv. 359 ff.) Cf. Guerinot, Essai de Bibliographie Jaina (Annales du Musée Guimet, vol. xxii), pp. 203 ff.

[2] Combination of chaplain and chancellor.

They passed their lives in the pleasures of the senses. Viçvabhūti, in time, made over the care of his house to his sons, lived in fast under the direction of a holy Teacher, pondered with his whole soul the mantra of the Parameṣṭhinamaskāra,[3] and, abandoning his body, was reborn as a god in the Sāudharma heaven. Also his bereaved wife Anuddharā, desolated over the loss of her husband, thinking that for her there was no further happiness, practised profound penance and died (17-37).

Kamaṭha and Marubhūti performed in sorrow the funeral rites for their parents. Then the great Sage Hariçcandra, compassionate and generous, arrived in a park outside the city. The citizens, singing songs of praise, swarmed about him like bees, attracted by the fragrance of his virtues. The two brothers also went there, anxious to dispel their grief for the loss of their parents thru the consolations of religion. The Sage preached the Law (dharma), winding up with the following illustration: Devotion to religion leads to success, as in the case of Lalitāñga; the reverse leads to destruction, as in the case of his servant, Sajjana (38-60):

Story of Lalitāñga and his servant Sajjana[4]

In the city of Çrīvāsa ruled Naravāhana, whose wife Kamalā bore him a son, Lalitāñga, endowed with many engaging qualities, prominent among them munificence, which he carried on to the point of passion (73). With

[3] Mantra addressed to the five Parameṣṭhins, Yugādīça (Ṛṣabha), Çānti (Çāntinātha), Nemi (Ariṣṭanemi), Pārçva, and Vīra (Mahāvīra); see Weber, Über das Çatruṁjaya Māhātmyam, p. 15. The prayer is used by Jains as last resort in danger, and before death; see, e. g. Kathākoça, pp. 104, 124, 214, and often in this book.

[4] This story in briefer form in Kathākoça, p. 160 ff.; and in Suvābahuttarīkathā, nr. 72 (see Hertel in Festschrift an Ernst Windisch, pp.

him grew up a servant named Sajjana, by nature evil (durjana). Tho people spoke adversely of this attachment, Lalitāñga would not discard Sajjana. One day the king presented a valuable ornament to the prince, who gave it away, because he questioned a gift from one who imposed burdens. Sajjana informed the king. He flew into a rage, but, after citing Lalitāñga into his presence, because of his youth, merely chided him gently, pointing out the virtue of thrift with a view to preserving the resources of the kingdom. Even tho liberality be the greatest of virtues, moderation is the best norm: 'when one eats too much camfor the teeth fall out' (102). He must not destroy his possessions, for some day he will have to shoulder the responsibilities of the kingdom (61-110).

Lalitāñga, impressed by his father's expostulations, checked his excessive generosity. His petitioners, in their turn, blamed him, because he, the crest-jewel of the princes of liberality had, now, without apparent reason, and contrary to his practice, become an ordinary stone. The world can not live if the moon withdraws her digit,[44] the giver his tribute, or the cloud its water. They added many other arguments (131), until Lalitāñga, tho still torn by conflicting emotions, again began to give. The king angrily had the doors of the palace shut upon him. Lalitāñga then decided that he could not remain where liberality, which secured people's love, was construed as

149 ff.). According to Leumann, in a note on p. 239 of Tawney's Translation of the Kathākoça, the story is found also among the Āvaçyaka tales. Ralston, Tibetan Tales, p. 279; Kingscote, Tales of the Sun, pp. 65 ff., present some of the traits of this story. More remotely, ZMDG. lxi. 49; Jātaka 417. The allegory of Lalitāñga in Pariçiṣṭaparvan 3. 214 ff. has no connection with the present story.

[44] See Böhtlingk, Indische Sprüche, nr. 1576.

a sin. In the secrecy of the night, he set out in a certain direction, mounted on a beautiful horse (111-141).

Sajjana, knowing from certain signs what the prince was about, was prompted by his evil nature to follow him on foot. Lalitāñga bade him tell something diverting. Sajjana embarked upon an argument as to the relative merits of virtue and vice, in which he, of course, took the side of vice. He advised Lalitāñga to practice vice, and to acquire wealth by robbery. The latter replied that fortune obtained thru unrighteousness, like a lamp, illumines objects for a while, but, when it goes out, there is nothing but darkness. They agreed, on a bet, to lay their dispute before arbiters, Lalitāñga engaging to become Sajjana's servant, in case the arbiters decided that vice procures success. On arriving at a village, Sajjana asked the elders in the assembly house whether success arises from virtue or vice (158). Taken unawares, they decided in favor of vice. Sajjana then made Lalitāñga give up to him his horse, which he spurred on, so that Lalitāñga had to run after him, as a servant, bathed in sweat, to the jeers of Sajjana. Lalitāñga, in turn, told him that he was badly named Sajjana ('good man') since there was no evil man (durjana) like unto him: 'You are worse than the hunter who spreads havoc, for he who advises evil is worse than he who does it' (111-167):

Parable of the hunter who was moved to compassion

A certain hunter in a forest, his bow at the point of his ear, was implored by a gazelle facing death to be spared, until she had nursed her young, otherwise sure to perish from hunger. She would take upon herself the consequence of the great five sins, if she did not return after having nursed them.[5] When the hunter still doubted her, she agreed to take upon herself the yet greater sin of him that gives evil advice to one that asks, or practices mischief upon one that confides. The hunter let her go. When she returned and asked the hunter how she might escape from his arrow, the latter became disgusted with continuously threatening the lives of animals, and bade her avoid his right side and live[6] (168-176).

Story of Lalitāñga, continued

Lalitāñga continued his arraignment of Sajjana with pious saws and illustrations, until the latter exclaimed: 'O wise man and counselor of perfection, why do not your virtues grant you your wishes? You are like the villager whose mother told him that he must under no circumstances give up wealth once acquired. Then he caught hold of a bull by the tail, and was dragged and killed by him, because, tho people called to him, "let go, let go," the fool would not let go.[7] Like that fool you have but one idea. If you want to make another bet as to the merits of virtue and vice, there is nothing left but that you should pluck out your eyes.' The prince, in passion, agreed (168-191).

They arrived at Çākhāpura and submitted their dispute to some people, who again, as destiny would have it, decided as before. Sajjana then addressed Lalitāñga: 'O thou, that are drunk with truth, king among princes, expert in doing good to others, treasury of righteous deeds, tell what you will do now!' Lalitāñga, goaded

[5] See additional note 1 on p. 183.

[6] This passage contains the root chuṭ: see Lexical notes, p. 232.

[7] This suggests loosely the anecdotes about letting go the bear, told by Swynnerton, Romantic Tales from the Panjāb, pp. 174, 293.

by his mockery, as if by a knife fresh from the whetstone, went to the forest, stood under a banyan tree and, called the Forest-divinities (vanadevyaḥ) and the World-protectors (lokapālāḥ) to witness that Truth alone is victorious. The divinities showered flowers upon him. He then plucked out his eyes,[8] and gave them to Sajjana, who rode off, recommending him to live on the fruit of the tree whose blossoms destroy all prosperity, whose branches endow with virtue. The prince, in great despair and want, still clings to virtue: 'Virtue alone is permanent, there is no other road to success in the three worlds!' (191-207).

After sunset Lalitāñga, alone under the banyan tree, overheard[9] some Bhāraṇḍa-birds asking a certain old bird in their midst to report the news. He narrated, to wit: 'In the city of Campā rules Jitaçatru who has a daughter Puṣpāvatī, dearer than life. Her charms of person are perfection itself, but a trick of destiny has rendered all vain, since she is blind.[10] On a certain occasion the king sat in the assembly-hall, his daughter on his lap, reflecting that she could not be married on account of her bodily defect. He then proclaimed, by beat of drum,[11] that he who would furnish sight to the princess should obtain her as wife together with half the kingdom.'[12] Then a young bird asked the old bird: 'Father, is there any means by which her eyes may be restored?' The old bird first answered evasively,

[8] Pāpaṁkara takes out his brother's, Kṣemaṁkara's, eyes, Ralston, Tibetan Tales, p. 282; they are later restored. Loss and restoration of eyes also ZMDG. lxi. 50; Parker, Village Folk-Tales of Ceylon, vol. i, p. 386, bottom.

[9] See additional note 2 on p. 185.

[10] See Benfey, Pañcatantra i. 370.

[11] See additional note 3 on p. 185.

[12] See additional note 4 on p. 186.

'because by night, surely, trees have ears,'[13] but finally was cajoled into betraying his secret. He told that, upon that very tree there was a creeper whose sap, when extracted, restored sight (208-235).

Lalitāñga felt with his hands for the creeper, cut a branch off with his knife, and poured its sap into his eye-sockets. At once, tho it was night, he could see every object.[14] Then he took more of the potent herb, and crawled in among the tail-feathers of the old bird[15] who had previously announced that he would fly to Campā in the morning. In this way he arrived in a park of that city. He bathed, went into the city, and announced his purpose. He was cited to the presence of the king, who inquired after his family and country, but Lalitāñga pressed his mission. Having filled the princess' eyes with the sap of the creeper, her sight was promptly restored, whereupon she expressed her devotion to the prince. The king arranged a sumptuous marriage, gave Lalitāñga half his kingdom, so that henceforth he lived like a Dogundaka immortal,[16] in great splendor (236-268).

One day, Lalitāñga, standing at a window of his palace, beheld Sajjana in a wretched plight: ragged, disheveled, his veins standing out like serpents, repulsive as a skeleton, like one who has come up from hell. Sajjana was

[13] See additional note 5 on p. 186.

[14] See additional note 6 on p. 187.

[15] Traveling in the tail-feathers of a gigantic bird of the nature of a vulture brings Çaktideva to the golden city, in Kathās. 26. 34. In Devendra's story of Udāyaṇa (Jacobi, Ausgewählte Erzählungen, p. 29. lines 12 ff.) Kumāranandī fastens himself to the middle legs of two three-legged Bhāruṇḍa birds, which carry him to the siren island of Pañcasela. In Kathās. 117. 81 Manohārikā mounts a bird which carries her to the city of the Vidyādharas. In Çatruṁjaya Māhātmyam 10. 88 the draught from the wings of Bhāraṇḍa birds set afloat a foundered ship. Cf. Weber in the note on p. 31 of his essay on the last mentioned text.

[16] For this term see p. 226.

begging alms from door to door. Overcome by pity, Lalitāñga had him cited to his presence, and asked whether he knew him. Sajjana did not recognize him, but taking him to be a strange king, replied: 'Who does not know the sun, or the cloud high in heaven?'[17] Lalitāñga then recalled himself to his memory, by telling how he had plucked out his eyes, whereupon Sajjana stood with his face downcast, as if desirous to escape even into hell. But the king made him bathe, take food, and put on becoming clothes, saying: 'To-day my kingdom has borne fruit, since in it you, my comrade in misfortune,[18] have arrived. Therefore enjoy happiness with a mind free from care!' Sajjana then, in pretended humility and contrition, told a hard-luck story: how, after leaving Lalitāñga, he had been attacked by thieves, robbed, and beaten; and how he had come to realize with his own eyes the fruit of sin. He did not consider himself fit to associate with the king. But Lalitāñga generously pointed out that he would not have attained his own exalted and happy state, but for Sajjana's companionship. Sajjana had been the touchstone wherewith the gold of Lalitāñga's virtue had been tested (269-295).

Queen Puṣpāvatī, suspicious of Sajjana, advised Lalitāñga to treat him generously, but to keep him at a distance. They should no more associate than the swan and the crow (296-305):

Fable of the swan and the crow[19]

A crow, while hunting fish, tumbled into a pool, and was rescued by a hañsa-bird and his mate on the plan

[17] For this trait see my paper on Mūladeva, Proceedings of the American Philosophical Society, vol. lii, p. 649.

[18] Cf. this text 3. 321, and Mūladeva, l. c., p. 643.

[19] See additional note 7 on p. 187.

of the tortoise on the stick.[20] The crow invited the haṅsa for a visit, and he accepted in the teeth of the remonstrances of his mate. The crow and the haṅsa went into the forest, and perched amicably upon the branch of a nimba-tree.[12] There the crow defecated upon the head of a king who had come to rest under that tree, and then flew away. The haṅsa was shot down with a sling-shot [22] by one of the king's men, and, when they expressed surprise at seeing a crow in the shape of a haṅsa, the latter recited: 'I am not, great king, a crow, but a haṅsa who lives in limpid water. Addiction to the society of the vile brings death, without doubt' (306-322).

Story of Lalitāṅga, continued

Puṣpāvatī continued to describe Sajjana keenly, as a conch-shell, white outside, full of tortuosities inside. But the prince would not abandon Sajjana, for fate has it that noble men tend to associate with villains, just as camfor loves charcoal. Sajjana then sowed suspicion and dislike for Lalitāṅga in the mind of his father-in-law, and finally betrayed to him with feigned reluctance the supposed secret of their relation. Sajjana pretended that he himself was the son of King Naravāhana (Lalitāṅga's father), and that Lalitāṅga was the son of a mahīyasya kāurikasya.[23] Of attractive person, but

[20] See the author in JAOS. xxxvi. 60. Two birds take each the end of stick into their bills: the animal to be rescued catches hold of the stick by mouth.

[21] The acrid fruit of this tree is no good, except to be eaten by crows; see Böhlingk's Indische Sprüche 3733. The snuhi tree is similarly despised, Pārçvanātha 7. 14.

[22] dhanurgulikā: the word recurs as dhanurgolikā in 3. 189.

[23] The translation of the Kathākoça has 'potter' in the place of this group of syllables. For low, cunning types (barber and potter) see additional note 23 on p. 202.

ashamed of his caste, he had left his home to roam in strange lands. The king then ordered some servants of his to slay that night any man who came alone by a certain route to the palace. When night came he sent a call to Lalitāñga to come to him in the palace, by that route. But Puṣpāvatī, alert and suspicious, induced Lalitāñga to send Sajjana in his place, whereupon the latter was duly slain by the king's men.[24] Puṣpāvatī heard the uproar, and bade Lalitāñga flee outside the city with an army. His father-in-law threatened war, but his ministers checked him with wise cautions, illustrating by the following story the folly of hasty action (323-381):

Story of the parrot that brought the fruit of immortality. Strike but hear [25]

In a great forest in the Vindhya mountains, on a banyan-tree, lived a pair of parrots. Theirs was a beloved young parrot. One day it flew off, but being very young, it fell upon the ground. A hermit picked it up, took it to his hermitage, fed it, educated it, and treated it like a son. One day the young parrot overheard the abbot of the hermitage tell his pupils that in the middle of the sea there was an island, Harimela, in whose north-east corner stood a large mango-tree, bedewed with ambrosia; and that the fruit of this tree restored youth by curing deformities, diseases, and old age. The young parrot, remembering his decrepit parents, considered that he

[24] See additional note 8 on p. 188.

[25] See the author, in Festgruss an Ernst Windisch, p. 359 (with note). In addition to the parallels there given see also Siamese Pakṣi Pakaranam, in Hertel, Das Pañcatantra, p. 350 (nr. xvii); Taylor, Catalogue Raisonné of Oriental Manuscripts, vol. iii, p. 615; Kingscote, Tales of the Sun, p. 350. Cf. Benfey, Pañcatantra i, 416. Parrot and poison-tree in different application, Mahābh. 13. 5. 1 ff.

might now pay the debt of their love. He flew to the magic tree and fetched one of the mangoes, but, on returning, grew tired and fell into the ocean, keeping the fruit in his bill (406). A merchant by the name of Sāgara picked him up; the parrot, out of gratitude, presented him with the fruit, after which he flew away to get another. The merchant decided to make the virtue of the fruit universally accessible. When he arrived at Jayapura, he presented it to the king then ruling, who had it planted, in order to reproduce the fruit for the benefit of his people (435). But a serpent, carried in the beak of a bird, happened to drop poison [26] upon one of the mangoes, so that it ripened and fell to the ground. The keeper of the garden joyously took it to the king who gave it to his chaplain, and he ate of it and died. The king in rage had the tree cut down. But a host of men, afflicted with incurable diseases, ate of its fruit for euthanasia (sukhamṛtyave), and became thereby like unto the God of Love. The king, discerning the true state of things, regretted his rash act, and lost pleasure in his kingdom (382-454).

Story of Lalitāñga, continued

On hearing this illustration of the evil effects of hasty action King Jitaçatru sent one of his ministers to Lalitāñga, and obtained from him the true account of his life. The king, in mixed joy and sorrow, sent trusty messengers to report everything to Lalitāñga's father, King Naravāhana in Çrīvāsa. Naravāhana, delighted and grateful to Jitaçatru, asked him to send back Lalitāñga. Jitaçatru apologized humbly to his daughter and his son-

[26] For snakes spitting venom into food see Tawney's note in his Translation of Kathāsaritsāgara, ii. 296; Çatruṁjaya Māhātmyam 14. 207.

in-law for the wrong he had done them, made over his entire kingdom to Lalitāñga, and retired to the forest (484). Lalitāñga returned with Puṣpāvatī to his father Naravāhana, who joyfully proposed to him the succession to the throne, and his own retirement from the world (512). After a polite and lengthy discussion between the two, Lalitāñga accepted the responsibility, and ruled his dual kingdom in prosperity and happiness (455-538).

Naravāhana, now a Royal Sage (rājarṣi) arrived at a park near the city, to visit Lalitāñga. The latter in great joy went out with zenana and retinue to greet him. Naravāhana preached the Law with particular reference to the Jain virtue of samyaktva (perfection), illustrating by the following story (539-569):

Story of the Çrāvaka[27] *Gandhāra who rejected magic art*

In the city of Vasanta lived a Jain disciple, pious and virtuous, named Gandhāra. Once, when he was honoring the gods in a Jain temple, a Vidyādhara,[28] named Mahājāina, admiringly offered him the choice of magic arts (vidyā). Gandhāra refused, because he was not interested in successes limited by particular conditions (āupādhika), since these result only in pain. But finally he was induced to accept a certain magic charm, which he, in turn, imparted to a friend of his, Skandila by name, because he himself had no use for it (584). Skandila went to a cemetery to execute the charm, filled a basin with live coals, and placed it under a tree. He then

[27] Designation of Jaina lay disciples.

[28] Literally, 'Science-holder,' a species of demigods, famed for their knowledge of magic art, especially the art of travelling in the air (khecara).

started to climb a rope which he had fastened to a branch of this tree. This rope he had to cut while hanging upon it. But, when he had cut one strand of it, he became afraid of falling into the basin, and came down again to the ground. While gathering courage to try the charm once more, a thief came along with a jewel-casket which he had stolen from the palace of the king. The thief, frightened by the knowledge that he was pursued by the king's men, asked Skandila what he was about. Skandila told him all, and the thief proposed to barter the charm in exchange for the jewel-casket.[29] Skandila agreed, and taught the thief the charm. The latter climbed the rope, cut successively its four strands, whereupon the Science[30] named Adhiṣṭhāyinī, 'Floating,' delighted with his courage, furnished him with a car on which he ascended to heaven (599). In the morning the king's men, shouting on all sides,[31] 'Catch him, bind him, the thief has been caught with the goods,' ran up to Skandila. Thereupon the thief in the role of a Vidyādhara produced a big stone, and cried out in heaven, 'Whosoever shall injure my Teacher Skandila, upon him will I cast this rock.' The bailiffs, frightened, reported the occurrence to the king, who came and asked the thief reverently how Skandila came to be his Teacher. He told the story which they all absorbed in astonishment (570-604).

[29] The thieves' trick of dropping loot or presenting loot to an innocent person, so as to avert suspicion from one's self, belongs to the refinements of the steyaçāstra: see this text 2. 452 ff., 652 ff.; 8. 124 ff.; Kathās. 10. 167; Dhammapada Commentary 5. 8; 12. 5 and 9; Jātaka 444; Samarādityasaṁkṣepa 2. 188 ff., 492 ff.; 6. 102, 465 ff.; 8. 518 ff.

[30] For these 'Sciences,' or vidyās see my paper, 'On the Art of Entering another's Body,' Proceedings of the American Philosophical Society, vol. lvi (1917), pp. 4 ff.

[31] Read in 600 viṣvagvyāhārakā for viṣvag vyāhārakā.

Story of Lalitāñga, concluded

Naravāhana continued his panegyric on the virtue of samyaktva which remains valid even if good conduct is infringed upon (cāritrayāne bhagne'pi). Lalitāñga greatly honored Naravāhana, and received further instruction. He built a magnificent Jaina temple, in which he set up an image of Nābheya (Ṛṣabha). Under the influence of his father's teaching he renounced his kingdom, entered upon the vow of complete resignation (samastavirati-vrata), died, and went to heaven. Falling from thence he will obtain final perfection (siddhi) in Videha (605-669).

Frame story: The enmity between the brothers, Kamaṭha and Marubhūti [32]

The story returns to the Sage Hariçcandra (see verse 40), thru whose influence many people were converted, among others Marubhūti, who was weaned from passion, devoted himself to the Law, and practiced many virtues. Kamaṭha, whose heart was not pierced by the Sage's instruction, remained unenlightened. Owing to Marubhūti's chastity his wife Vasuṁdharā became love-mad, and, after first repelling Kamaṭha's advances, finally submitted to his unbridled lust. Blinded by love, they constantly indulged in incestuous adultery (683). Varuṇā, Kamaṭha's wife, observing, reported the affair to Marubhūti. Thereupon he went to a distant village, but returned in the guise of a holy beggar (kārpaṭika), and asked Kamaṭha for shelter. The latter assigned to him a corner of his house, where, pretending to sleep, he became witness to the misconduct of his brother with

[32] See Introduction, p. 13 ff.

his own wife. He reported the affair to the king, Aravinda, just but stern monarch, who had Kamaṭha forcibly mounted upon an ass,[33] marked with many insignia of shame, and expelled from the city (700).

Kamaṭha, disgraced, deprived of wealth and relatives, roaming solitary in the forest, brooded revenge against his brother. He decided to bide his time. Consumed by wrath, yet unable to retaliate, he happened upon a hermitage in the forest, took sacred vows (dīkṣā), and practiced asceticism on a mountain. In the mean time Marubhūti became despondent on account of the dire retribution he had brought upon his brother. Even tho restrained by the king, he went to the forest to conciliate Kamaṭha (717). He threw himself upon his knees and begged forgiveness, but Kamaṭha took up a stone and with a single blow smashed his brother's head, and at the same time his own ascetic vow. While in pain from that mortal hurt Marubhūti harbored distressed thoughts (ārtadhyāna); he was, therefore, reborn as a wild elefant,[34] leader of a herd in the Vindhya mountains. His sister-in-law Varuṇā also, blinded by anger, was born as a she-elefant, and became his mate. Wildly they roamed together in the forest (727).

King Aravinda, living at the pinnacle of worldly pleasures, one day contemplated a great storm. The breaking of the clouds reminded him of the perishableness of all things in Saṁsāra. Disgusted with his own excessive indulgences, he decided to abandon the world and its pleasures. His wives begged him not to abandon them, nor to expose the kingdom to danger. Nevertheless he took the vow in the presence of a teacher, and

[33] See additional note 9 on p. 188.

[34] Second pre-birth of the future Pārçva.

wandered about solitarily thru towns and villages. During these roamings he met a merchant, Sāgaradatta, who asked him where he was going. He replied that he was going to Mount Kāilāsa, to honor the gods. Sāgaradatta asked whether there was any profit in honoring these hand-made gods. Aravinda replied that his gods were the twenty-four Arhats, Ṛṣabha, etc., who had surmounted passion, were omniscient, were honored by Çakra. By their teaching of the Law, they had become the saviors of every being. These Arhats must be worshipped, and alms must be given without doubt or question, as is illustrated by the following parables (670-797):

Two parables

Two merchants, Nandaka and Bhadraka, occupied adjoining shops. Bhadraka steadily attended to his business in the morning; Nandaka, on the other hand, went to a temple to worship. Bhadraka became jealous, thinking that Nandaka must be rich to be able to neglect his business. Nandaka, in his turn, thought that Bhadraka, in the absence of competition, would be making hay while the sun shines that is, that Bhadraka would be doing business while he was spending his time in worshiping the Prince of Jinas. Owing to his evil doubts (kuvikalpa) he lost the fruit of his merit in worshiping the Savior (805).

A rich merchant's soṇ, while sitting in his shop, was accosted by a mendicant Sage who asked for alms. Gladly he poured ghee into his bowl in an unbroken stream (akhaṇḍadhārayā). The Sage, out of fear that he would curtail the merit of the merchant which grew as fast as he poured, did not withdraw his bowl. Then the giver became dubious, thinking, 'What will the solitary ascetic do with so much ghee, if he does not even now let up? ' As fast as he was thus doubting, he kept falling step by step from the world of gods which he had been reaching thru his good deed. The Sage, who knew this, explained to him the wonderful virtues of giving, and the injurious effects of doubt (798-814).

Frame Story: The enmity between the brothers Kamaṭha and Marubhūti, continued

In consequence of the instruction of the Royal Sage Aravinda, Sāgaradatta became a Jain disciple (çrāvaka). Going on his way, Sāgaradatta arrived at the place where the elefant king, Marubhūti, was in the habit of disporting himself with his females. Sāgaradatta camped on the banks of a beautiful lake. The elefant Marubhūti came there to drink, and proceeded to attack Sāgaradatta's caravan, slaying and dispersing. Aravinda knew thru his profound insight (avadhi) [35] that the time to enlighten the elefant had now come. He placed himself in kāyotsarga position; the elefant came to his side and revered him. Aravinda reminded him of his former state as Marubhūti, and exhorted him to abandon his mad folly. Marubhūti then remembered his former birth as a Çrāvaka, paid his respects to the Sage, and signified with his trunk that his faith was restored. Varuṇā, his mate, as well as many people, including Sāgaradatta, accepted the faith. Then Aravinda retired to the mountain Kāilāsa; the elefant Marubhūti lived piously on sun-warmed water and dry leaves, repenting that he had inflicted destruction and terror upon living beings (815-857).

[35] See for this term, Leumann in Tawney's Translation of Kathākoça, p. 241 note.

In the mean time Kamaṭha, unchastened even by the murder of Marubhūti, ignored by his teacher, despised by other ascetics, had died in a troubled state of mind (ārtadhyāna), and was reborn as a kurkuṭa-serpent.[36] Killing or endangering all living beings, he infested the forest, and finally bit the elefant Marubhūti. The latter died in the thought of the Law (dharmadhyāna), therefore was reborn as a god in the Sahasrāra heaven,[37] where he was acclaimed by celestial females. Varuṇā also was reborn in heaven as Marubhūti's wife; they lived there in the highest enjoyment of the pleasures of the senses. The kurkuṭa-serpent (Kamaṭha) was reborn as a hell-inhabitant in the Pañcamāvani hell,[38] suffering all the tortures of that hell (858-885).

---

[36] This is the second pre-birth of the future Asura Meghamālin. The fabulous serpent, called kurkuṭoraga, kurkuṭāhi, kukkuṭoraga, kukkuṭāhi, kukkuṭābha, occurs here for the first time in literature. It is likened in stanza 860 to a winged Yama (jātapakṣo yama iva), and, therefore, is conceived as a winged dragon. But it figures as a mere cock in the sculpture described on p. 19 ff.

[37] This is the third pre-birth of the future Pārçva.

[38] This is the third pre-birth of the future Asura Meghamālin.

Sarga the Second

Frame Story: King Kiraṇavega

On the Vāitāḍhya mountain stood a sumptuous city, Tilakā, in which ruled a Vidyādhara king, Vidyudgati, with his beloved wife Tilakāvatī. The soul of the elefant (Marubhūti) fell from the eighth Kalpa (aṣṭamāt kalpāt) into the womb of Tilakāvatī, to be reborn as prince Kiraṇavega.[1] In due time that prince was married to Padmāvatī, daughter of an important vassal of the king. The king, after giving instructions to his ministers and preaching royal wisdom to his son, made over to him his kingdom, and took vows with the celebrated Guru Sāgara (34). Kiraṇavega had a son, Kiraṇatejas, who grew up finely. A Sage, Suraguru by name, arrived at a park outside the city, and delivered a sermon culminating in the five-fold vow (pañcavrata [2]), being the duties in lighter form (aṇu) of the householder (gṛhin) in distinction from the ascetic (yati). The five duties are: ahiṅsā, 'non-injuriousness'; satya, 'truth'; asteya, 'non-theft'; brahmacarya, 'chastity'; and aparigraha, 'non-acquisition.' Ahiṅsā, or 'non-injuriousness,' is described and illustrated by the following story (1-51):

[1] This is the fourth pre-birth of the future Pārçva.

[2] For these vows see e. g. Āyāranga-Sutta 2. 15; Tattvārthādhigamasūtra 7. 1 (Bibl. Ind.); V. S. Ghate, The Indian Interpreter, vol. x, p. 31, where the fifth vrata is styled ākiṁcanya (ākinichanya!). These five vows are in accordance with the teaching of Mahāvīra, rather than the reputed teaching of Pārçva, which postulates only four vows, omitting the brahmacarya. Thus, explicitly, Uttarādhyayana Sūtra 23. 12; cf. Bühler, Über die Indische Secte der Jaina, p. 101; Stevenson, The Heart of Jainism, p. 49.

Story of Prince Bhīma and his friend Matisāgara

In Kamalapura ruled king Harivāhana. His queen, Mālatī, dreamed that she had a lion in her lap.[3]. The king called in a Brahman skilled in the Science of Dreams, which he explained in a brief 'Traumschlüssel' (67). Next, he interpreted the particular dream of the queen: she would be delivered of a noble son. In due time a prince was born, and named Bhīma. Simultaneously the king's minister, Buddhila, had a son, Matisāgara, who became Bhīma's friend and adviser.[4] One day, while the prince was sitting in the lap of his father, the gardener of the Campaka park announced the arrival of the Sage Abhinanda. Greatly rejoiced, the king, the prince, and the court went there to greet him, and hear his sermon. Bhīma and his friend Matisāgara were converted, and enjoined especially not to injure innocuous living things. This the Sage illustrated by the following parable (52-106):

Parable of the six men who started to destroy a hostile village

The first of the six men proposes to kill both men and beasts; the second advises that the human beings be killed, but why the beasts? The third says, the men alone must be killed, not the women; the fourth narrows it down still further by proposing that only men in arms are to be slain; and the fifth proposes that even of those in arms only they that actually fight should be slain.

[3] See additional note 19, on p. 189.

[4] This relation between prince and minister's son, or prince and other youthful friend, is constant and fundamental in fiction; e. g. Kathās. 28. 115: Jacobi, Ausgewählte Erzählungen, p. 5, l. 18.

Finally the sixth says, 'He who is without enemies does not have to kill any one' (vinā çatrūn ghātaḥ kāryo na kasya cit). The six men are designated respectively as Black, Blue, Grey, Brilliance (tejas), Lotus (padma), and White. But the best of all is he by whom all persons are protected from enemies (107-112).[5]

Story of King Naladharma and the deer

The Sage continues his illustration of ahiṅsā, to wit: King Naladharma of Vijaya and his minister Tilaka, while hunting, came upon a deer with long and strong horns. As the king was about to cast his arrow, the deer told him not to slay, since it was a Kṣatriya's business to protect (trā) from injury (kṣatāt).[6] A king must not kill grass-eaters: even enemies that eat grass must be spared[7] (123). When the king was surprised at the deer's speech, the minister explained that the animal must be an Avatar of a god or demon. They followed the animal which led them to a young Sage, and bade them make obeisance to him. They did so, and were rewarded with a sermon. The king then, surprised at the youth of the Sage, asked him why he had retired from the world. The Muni told the following parable (113-136):

Parable of the illusory deluge

King Bhuvanasāra of Siddhapura rules under the guidance of his minister Mahāmati. One day players from the Dekkhan are permitted to present a spectacle

[5] For the spirit of this parable cf. Mahābhārata 12. 95.

[6] This pun is as old as Mahābhārata 12. 59. 127. It recurs in Pārçva 3. 600. Jacobi, Das Mahābhārata, p. 131, and Hertel, Das Pañcatantra, p. 6, translate kṣatāt by, 'from loss.' This seems to me to slip by the point.

[7] See additional note 11, on p. 191.

and concert at the court. In the midst of the festivity the door-keeper announces an astrologer who desires an audience. The king is impatient at the disturbance, but the minister points out that the astrologer is more important than the spectacle. The astrologer is then admitted; he is robed in white, and holds a book in his hand. After exchange of courtesies, the astrologer predicts that on that very day a deluge shall arise, turning that city into an ocean (153). At once a vividly described storm and deluge break out, which drive the king and the minister to the seventh story of the palace.[8] After reproaching himself for neglect to attend to his spiritual welfare, the king makes the five-fold obeisance (pañcanamaskṛti [9]) in his mind, when, all at once, a ship arrives (168). As he starts to board the ship, lo, there is no water, no cloud, no ship, no thunder. When the king asks the alleged astrologer to explain, he says that he is no astrologer, that he is a magician who has exhibited hocus-pocus (indrajāla). The king then draws the moral that life and its attractions are also illusory; happiness, like a candle, sputtering in the wind, is impermanent. He makes over his kingdom to Prince Harivikrama and turns Ascetic (çramaṇa) (137-182).

[8] The seventh story of a palace is a cliché of Hindu fiction. See this text 2. 339; 5. 204; 6. 610, 1118; Jacobi, Ausgewählte Erzählungen, p. 8, l. 1; p. 48, l. 33; Kathākoça, pp. 130, 185; Pariçiṣṭaparvan 2. 674; Jātakas 62 and 458; Samarādityasaṁkṣepa 4. 391; Pañcatantra 1. 5; Pañcadaṇḍachatraprabandha 2 (p. 31). For the uses of the higher stories of Hindu palaces, see Weber's and Jacobi's remarks on p. 68, note, of the former's translation of Pañcadaṇḍachatraprabandha, Transactions of the Berlin Academy, 1877.

[9] Made in succession to the different grades of Jaina Saints and Teachers; see, e. g. Kalpasūtra 1.

Story of King Naladharma and the deer, continued

King Naladharma complained that, unlike the Sage then teaching, he was, because of his sins, unripe for emancipation. Thereupon the Sage taught him to cultivate perfection (samyaktva). The king asked who was the deer that had brought about his purification. The Sage replied that the deer in a former birth was Naladharma's friend and spiritual adviser; he had practiced wrong asceticism, had died, and had been reborn in that place as a Yakṣa. He had then become pious by constant association with himself, and, out of his love for Naladharma in the previous life, had changed into a deer in order to bring about his enlightenment. The deer now appeared in the form of a Yakṣa; told that he, like the king, had reached perfection (samyaktva); received additional instruction from the Sage; and returned to his Yakṣa home. The king also returned to his capital; erected an image of the Arhat; became a Great Disciple (mahāçrāvaka); and will in future attain perfection (siddha) (183-194).

Story of Prince Bhīma and his friend Matisāgara, continued. The Wicked Kāpālika [10]

At the end of these illustrations the Sage Abhinanda (verse 75) continued to instruct Bhīma (here called Bhīmasena) in piety, and in the duty of enlightening others. Bhīma returned home, and devoted himself to dharma (religion), happy in the worship of the gods. A certain Çāiva ascetic (kāpālika), a rogue, arrived into the presence of Bhīma and his friend Matisāgara. He told them that he was in possession of a Science, called 'Earth-

[10] See additional note 12, on p. 191.

Shaking' (bhuvanakṣobhiṇī),[11] which he had cultivated for twelve years, but that it still required a final performance in a cemetery. For this he needed Bhīma as his aid. Matisāgara warned Bhīma not to mix himself up with a rogue, but the prince, confident of his own virtue (dharma), persisted in coöperating with the rogue (213). They arrived at the cemetery, where the Kāpālika, after drawing a circle and adoring some divinity, attempted to prepare Bhīma's hair-lock, intending to cut off his head. Bhīma saw thru the deceit; told him that courage alone was his top-lock (mama sattvam eva çikhābandhaḥ); and to proceed with his business. The rogue then, realizing that his trick would not work, prepared to cut off Bhīma's head by force, and, by way of preliminary, made the whole world shake by his terrible doings. Bhīma stood undaunted. The rogue then told him, that, if he would freely yield his head, he would be born to bliss in another birth. After further give and take, Bhīma jumped upon the shoulders of the Kāpālika; the latter flew up in the air, threw Bhīma off, and, as he fell, a Yakṣiṇī (Siren) received him in her folded hands, and took him to her house (228).

He found himself sitting upon a divine throne, and was addressed by the Yakṣiṇī. She told him that he was in the Vindhya mountain, in her magic pleasure-house; that her name was Kamalākṣā; that she was living a licentious life with a retinue of gods; and that she had seen him falling, as he was hurled down by the Kāpālika. She had taken care of him out of love; moreover she put herself and her retinue at his service. Bhīma playfully described her condition, as showing that not only earth-dwellers, but also the wise gods were subject to the lure of love.

[11] For these 'Sciences' see my article, 'On the Art of Entering another's Body,' Proceedings of the American Philosophical Society, vol. lvi, pp. 4 ff.

He recommended her to call to mind the Jina who destroys the serpent's poison of Kandarpa (the God of Love), and who acts like the Great Gāruḍa charm [12] (mahāgāruḍamantrābhaṁ jinam). Kamalākṣā declared that Bhīma's mere speech has cured her of the poison of illusion, and asked him to teach her the salvation which destroys all pain (195-244).

While they were thus communing, sweet sounds arose, which Kamalākṣā explained as coming from the chants of Munis. Bhīma rejoiced; Kamalākṣā showed him the way to the Munis, and then proceeded to her own home, promising to return with her retinue. While Bhīma was paying his respects to the Munis, headed by their Guru, a great she-serpent (mahābhujā) appeared from heaven, and alighted before him. Wondering what she was, and whither she was going, he sprang upon her back. Desiring to cross the heavens, he shone there like Acyuta (Kṛṣṇa), mounted upon the Kāliya-serpent, like a mariner whose ship is wrecked and who desires to save himself upon a plank [13] (261). After traversing many rivers, forests, and mountains, they came upon a temple of Kālikā (Durgā), built, or adorned with men's bones, skulls, etc. In the centre of that temple stood a frightful image of Kālikā, in front of which he saw the wicked Kāpālika holding a beautiful man (who turns out to be Matisāgara) by the hair. Bhīma hid himself, in order to

[12] A charm that cures snake poison.

[13] The phalaka or kāṣṭhaphalaka, 'wooden board,' represents the stenciled method by which shipwrecked mariners save themselves and get to shore; see, e. g. Pārçvanātha 2. 261; 2. 925; 8. 21; Kathās. 25. 46; 36. 99; 52. 328; 67. 61; Daçakumāracarita i, p. 9; Samarādityasaṁkṣepa 4. 98; 5. 155, 218, 269, 278, 360; 6. 106; 7. 508. This is one of the features of 'naufragium,' 'shipwreck,' one of the most prized devices of Hindu fiction. This links itself with the motifs, 'Treasure-Island,' 'Jonah,' and 'Sirens.' Of all this elsewhere.

see what the Kāpālika would do, and that he might then suit his actions to the occasion. The Kāpālika addressed his victim: 'Unhappy wretch, think quickly of thy favorite divinity, before I cut off thy head in honor of this Kālikā!' In this plight Matisāgara resorted first to the Jina, and then to Bhīma. The Kāpālika told him that in attempting to sacrifice Bhīma, who had, as he thought, the proper characteristics, he had lost him; that the latter was at this time with Bhikṣus in the Vindhya mountains; therefore he had brought him, Matisāgara, to be sacrificed in his stead. Bhīma then sprang upon him, threw him upon the ground, and put his foot upon him. As he was about to kill him, Kālikā bade him not to slay her child, that was ever collecting skulls for her. That he was just about to furnish the 108th skull, by whose means she would fulfil her purpose. Moreover, pleased with Bhīma's heroism, she bade him ask a gift. Bhīma entreated her to desist thenceforth from the slaughter of living beings and other crimes, in order that she might thus obtain perfection (siddhi). Ashamed, because a mere man, even tho of noble mind, was the source of her enlightenment, she consented to his wish, and then vanished from sight (295). Matisāgara related how he happened to have gotten into the power of the Kāpālika. When Bhīma had disappeared, the court was in despair. The house-divinity then showed herself, told what had happened to Bhīma, and predicted that Bhīma would return in time. Yet Matisāgara, after consulting sundry omens,[14] went in search of Bhīma, was seized by the Kāpālika, and saved by Bhīma. At the end of his report the Kāpālika also underwent change of heart, and resorted to the protecting grace of Bhīma (245-314).

[14] In the present text, as in all fiction texts, omens are both consulted intentionally, or deferred to when they happen incidentally; see 1. 324;

Story of Prince Bhīma and his friend Matisāgara, continued. Çibi motif

While they were thus conversing, a great elefant appeared, placed Bhīma and Matisāgara upon his back, flew up into heaven, and deposited them outside a deserted city.[15] Bhīma, leaving Matisāgara outside, fearlessly entered alone the empty but wealthy city. He saw there a lion with a man in his paws, about to eat him. He requested the lion to release the man, and the lion, in turn, asked him how then he was to subsist. Bhīma, taking the lion to be a god, told him that the gods were not in the habit of eating morsels,[16] and that he should be ashamed of himself. But, if he really could not still his desire for human flesh, he would give him some from his own body[17] (328). The lion refused, because his victim had inflicted injuries upon him in a former birth which would keep alive anger, yea even thru a hundred existences. Bhīma then took the man from the lion by force, and threw him over his back. The man became invisible, but held Bhīma by the hand, and led him into a palace. Bhīma ascended

[15] Deserted cities figure frequently in fiction: Pārçvanātha 6. 314; Bambhadatta (Jacobi, Ausgewählte Erzählungen, p. 7, l. 28); Kathākoça, p. 129; Kathāsaritsāgara 43. 46; Hertel, Das Pañcatantra, p. 109, note 4; Pañcadaṇḍachatraprabhanda 2 (p. 27); Swynnerton, Romantic Tales from the Panjāb, p. 87.

[16] See also 2. 202. This is an addition to the usual signs of the gods: they do not sweat; are dustless; do not wink their eyes; cast no shadow, and do not touch earth with their feet. See the author in Proceedings of the American Philosophical Society, vol. lvi, p. 28, note 60. In Valāhassa Jātaka (196) the bodies of Yakkhinīs turn cold after eating human flesh. The signs of the gods are freely exploited in Fiction as well as in Epic. Additional examples: Pārçvanātha 7. 503; Daçakumāracarita, ii. 15; Ralston, Tibetan Tales, p. 16. Even Rākṣasas participate in these characteristics; see Parker, Village Folk-Tales of Ceylon, i. 145, and Jātaka 1.

[17] See additional note 13, on p. 192.

to its seventh [18] story, was greeted by sweet sounds from çāla-wood statutes which descended from their postaments and conducted him to a golden throne.[19] The statues offered to bathe him, whereupon he requested them to fetch Matisāgara. Both were then bathed and feasted. Bhīma fell into a sleep, and heard in his dream the voice of a god who told him that he was pleased with his prowess, and, therefore, bade him choose a gift. Bhīma asked him what city that was, and why it was devoid of life (346).

The god told: This is the city of Hemapura; its king was Hemaratha, who had a Purohita, named Caṇḍa, hated of all men. The king also was cruel by nature, and, on mere suspicion, inflicted severe punishment. An enemy of Caṇḍa, spread a report that he was intimate with a low-born woman [20] (mātañgī). The king consulted an ordeal, and, tho he did not determine the truth, had Caṇḍa wrapped in hemp and boiled in oil. Caṇḍa had no chance before he died to wear away his sins, and therefore, was reborn as a Rākṣasa, named Sarvagila ('All-devourer'). He remembered the hostilities of his former birth, came to that city, hid away all its people, and, having assumed the shape of a lion, carried off King Hemaratha. He had been greatly surprised when Bhīma, in heroic pity, had released Hemaratha, but, nevertheless had arranged for Bhīma's entertainment, and had again brought out the people of the city. No sooner had he said this than all the people put in their appearence (315-355).

Then Bhīma's teacher (v. 251) arrived by the road of heaven. All four, namely Bhīma, Matisāgara, the Rāk-

[18] See note 8, on p. 46.

[19] See additional note 14, on p. 192.

[20] See additional note 15, on p. 195.

ṣasa (sc. Caṇḍa), and Hemaratha went to pay their devotions to him; this he rewarded by a longish sermon on the futility and destructiveness of wrath, in consequence of which Caṇḍa was converted (370). While the Muni was still speaking a great elefant came rushing on with a roar that scattered the assemblage. Bhīma tamed him, whereupon he also paid his respects to the Sage. The elefant then changed his form to that of a Yakṣa, declared that Hemaratha was his son in a former birth, and that he himself, thru evil associations, had ruined his perfection (samyaktva), and had become a Vyantara. The Sage then preached on samyaktva. Afterwards Bhīma visited Hemaratha's palace where he was received as an honored guest. They exchanged fair and pious speeches (390). Kāli (Kālikā, vv. 145-244) arrived, accompanied by the Kāpālika. The goddess informed Bhīma that his family was distressed at his absence, and that she herself had promised that he would return shortly. Bhīma was seized by a longing for his home. The gods came upon the scene and announced the arrival of the Yakṣiṇī Kamalākṣā, who told of her conversion by Bhīma and the Sages. The Yakṣa then produced a car by magic; Bhīma and Matisāgara mounted it for their homeward journey. In due time they arrived at a park near Kamalapura, their native city (414). There Bhīma adored the gods and the Jina, the Lord of the world (425). King Naravāhana, his father, heard of his arrival; the king and the queen went to greet Bhīma, who threw himself at their feet. Bhīma and Matisāgara returned in triumf on a state elefant. Matisāgara, on request, narrated Bhīma's adventures. Naravāhana gave many princesses in marriage to Bhīma, consecrated him as king, and himself took the vow (dīkṣā). Bhīma also in the end took to the forest. Because he abstained from killing, teaching others also to abstain, he obtained the highest success in the two worlds (355-438).

Story of mother and son punished for cursing one another by implication[21]

The narrative here passes from ahiṅsā (injury by deed) to the demonstration that injury by words also is reprehensible: In Vardhanāgapura lived a man of good family, Sadvaḍa, with his wife Candrā, and a son Sarga. Sadvaḍa died poor. Candrā subsisted by doing chores in other people's houses, while Sarga gathered wood in the forest. One day, when Sarga was away at the forest, Candrā was called to carry water to a merchant's house. Before leaving she fondly hung up an excellent meal for her son in a hammock, and went to the merchant's house. In the evening Sarga returned, threw down his wood, but, not seeing his mother, hungry and thirsty, as he was, waxed exceeding wroth. When the mother finally arrived, worn out from her day's work, Sarga said to her roughly: 'How long, wretched woman, will you stand there, *impaled on a stake?*' Thereupon she retorted petulantly: '*Are your hands cut off,* that you can't take your supper out of the hammock and eat it?' In due time both became Jain ascetics, died, and went to the heaven of the gods (451). Falling from that state, the soul of Sarga was reborn as Aruṇadeva, the son of Kumāradeva, a merchant of Tāmaliptī; the soul of Candrā, as Deviṇi,[22] the daughter of a rich merchant Jasāditya

[21] The same story, with less obvious application, in Samarādityasaṁkṣepa 7. 492 ff. Cf., remotely, Pariçiṣṭaparvan 2. 316 ff.; and Hertel, Das Pañcatantra, p. 108, note 4.

[22] In the sequel also Devinī. Samarādityasaṁkṣepa has the Prākrit form, Deīṇī, taken over from the Samarāïccakahā.

in Pāṭalāpura. A marriage was arranged for the pair, but Aruṇadeva, not being ready to marry, started on a mercantile expedition with a friend of his, Maheçvara. Their ship was wrecked, but they reached the shore near Pāṭalāpura. Maheçvara left his friend in a ruined temple, to get food, before the latter should put in appearance as bridegroom. Aruṇadeva, worn out by fatigue, fell asleep. Then the former Sarga as well as his former mother Candrā were both overtaken by their karma in their previous birth. A robber *cut off Deviṇī's hands*, while she was promenading in the garden, in order to steal her bracelets. Beadles took up his pursuit; he fled into the ruined temple where Aruṇadeva was sleeping. There he dropped the bracelets and his sword.[23] Aruṇadeva woke up; thought that the divinity of the temple had made him a present; hid away the bracelet; and was just wondering what the sword meant, when the beadles arrived in pursuit, took him for the thief, and beat him, until the bracelets fell from him. They brought him before the king by whose command *he was impaled upon a stake*. Maheçvara returned, missed Aruṇadeva, and, on inquiry, learned that a thief had been captured there. Suspecting disaster, he soon came upon Aruṇadeva impaled, and at the sight broke into terrible lamentations, falling down in a faint. When he came to he explained that the victim was Aruṇadeva. In his despair he attempted to kill himself with a rock, but was restrained by the spectators (476). Jasāditya also heard of the occurrence, went there with Deviṇī; and at the sight fell in a faint. On recovering he begged to enter the funeral fire. The king heard of the affair, went there, and consoled Jasāditya by pointing out the irresistible power of

[23] See note 29, on p. 37.

karma. The Sage Amareçvara came along and instructed them all. The king was taken with remorse at his hasty action; he himself and Jasāditya took the dīkṣā; and even the thief repented. Aruṇadeva, Deviṇī, and the thief went to heaven (439-499).

Parable of the impatient beggar who went to hell

The text passes from the theme of injurious words to that of injurious thoughts, illustrating: A certain wandering beggar came into the neighborhood of the Vāibhāra mountain. Because he got no alms, he conceived the following evil thought: 'There is plenty to eat and drink, and yet no one gives me alms. Therefore I shall seize all.' In deep dudgeon and fierce thought he climbed to the mountain top, tore off a huge rock, and pitilessly cast it down; in its downward course all the world was destroyed. He himself was ground to pieces and went to hell as a dramaka [24] (499-505).

Story of King Vasu who violated the truth [25]

The text turns to the second of the five light vows (aṇuvrata), namely truth-telling (verse 46), and illustrates: King Abhicandra of Çuktimatī had a son named Vasu. A teacher, Kṣīrakadamba, had a son Parvata. Vasu, Parvata, and another boy, named Nārada went to school with Kṣīrakadamba. Once, while they were studying by night on the top of the palace, sleep overcame the pupils, but the teacher overheard two ascetics who were wandering in the heavens and observing the school, say to one another: 'One of these three boys will go to

[24] See p. 233.

[25] Cf. Mahābhārata 12. 337. 1 ff.

heaven; the other two to hell' (519). The teacher, grieved, desired to find out which was which. So he gave to each of them a cock made of dough (piṣṭakurkuṭa),[25a] saying: 'These are to be slain where no one sees.' Vasu and Parvata 'slew' theirs in lonely places, but Nārada, looking about in every direction, reflected: 'Yonder Sun sees; I see; the birds see; the Protectors of the World see; and all that are gifted with higher knowledge see. There is no place where no one sees. Therefore I must not slay the cock; the Teacher has merely desired to test our intelligence.'[26] They reported what they had done to the teacher, who rejoiced at Nārada's insight, but grieved because his teaching had failed in two out of three cases. He therefore retired to the forest. Parvata took his place as teacher; in due time, Nārada became expert in all knowledge, and returned home (546).

Then King Abhicandra took vows; Vasu ruled as his successor, and became famous all over the earth for his love of truth. It happened that a certain hunter of deer cast an arrow which was lost in the ridge of the Vindhya mountain. When he went to investigate why the arrow was lost he found, by feeling about, an atmosferic crystal.[27] He then understood that this had seemed to him a

[25a] See the additional note 16, on p. 195.

[26] Analog to this story, Sīlavīmaṅsana Jātaka (305): 'There is no such thing as secrecy in wrong doing'; cf. Morris, Folk-Lore Journal iii. 244. The motif is as old as Mahābhārata 13. 42. 17 ff.: 'Nothing can be hidden from the two dancers (day and night) and the six dice-players (the six seasons).'

[27] ākāçasphaṭikā, or khasphaṭikā 'atmosferic cryṣtal,' is either candrakānta, 'moon-stone,' or sūryakānta, 'sun-stone.' Apparently one of their qualities is to be invisible and to make anything into which they are fixed float in the air. In general acceptance the moonstone is formed from the coagulation of the rays of the moon, and dissolves under the influence of its light.

gazelle, as does the shadow of the earth in the moon,[28] and that, without touch, he would nowise have found out what it was. He decided to make a present of it to King Vasu, who accepted it and rewarded the hunter; had it secretly fixed into the base of his throne; and then had the workmen who did this killed. The crystal had the effect of making the throne float in the air; this the people thought was due to the power of his truthfulness. The report was spread that the gods hovered about him on account of his truthfulness; in consequence he obtained the reputation called Ūrjasvinī (' Mighty '), so that kings in fear of him became his vassals (558).

It came to pass that Nārada visited Parvata, who had become Kṣīrakadamba's successor as a teacher of the Vedas. He overheard the teacher explain the expression, ajāir yaṣṭavyam, by meṣāir yaṣṭavyam, i. e., ' one should sacrifice goats.' Nārada was scandalized.[29] He insisted that ajāir in the phrase meant ' three-year old grain,' because that cannot be born again.[30] Parvata referred to the authority of the Nighaṇṭu,[31] and insisted that Kṣīrakadamba had interpreted it the other way. They finally bet that he who was wrong should have his tongue cut out, and that their former fellow-pupil, King Vasu should decide the controversy (567). Parvata's mother

[28] The moon is mṛgāñka ' having the figure of the deer,' or çaçāñka, ' having the figure of the hare.'

[29] Such practice, as, indeed, all slaughter, is heinous in the eyes of Jains and Buddhists; e. g. Prabandhacintāmaṇi, pp. 93, 320; Mattakabhatta Jātaka (18); also Jātakas 20, 50. The idea is by no means strange to Brahmanism; see, e. g., how Mahābh. 14. 28. 6 ff. decries goat sacrifice as hiṅsā, ' injury.' Cf. Bühler, Über das Leben des Jaina Mönches Hemachandra, p. 39.

[30] trivārṣikāṇi dhānyāni na hi jāyanta ity ajāḥ. The same pun argument occurs Mahābh. 12. 337. 1 ff.; Pañcatantra, 3. 2.

[31] Cf. Yāska's Nirukta 4. 25; 6. 4.

knew that he was wrong. In distress she went to King Vasu and begged him to save Parvata,[32] by deciding that ajāḥ meant 'goats.' Vasu at first refused to take part in this act of perfidy, but in the end succumbed to the specious argument that his first duty was to protect the son of his former Teacher. A great assembly of wise men was called together; over it presided Vasu, floating in the air on his magic throne, like the moon in the sky (584). Nārada and Parvata presented their contentions, each calling upon Vasu to decide in accordance with the truth. The wise men at the assembly also solemnly conjured Vasu by all the gods and the laws of the universe to speak the truth. Nevertheless Vasu ruled that ajāḥ meant 'goats.' Then the gods angrily shook his throne, so that he fell to the ground. Nārada refused to look any longer upon the face of the 'dog-cooker,'[33] who gave false witness. Vasu went to hell. The gods kept on destroying his successors, until eight of them had perished (598). The story is concluded with an impressive panegyric on truth, which must not be violated even in a dream or in jest (506-608).

[32] dīyatāṁ putrabhikṣā mahyaṁ mahīpate, 'Give my son to me as alms, O ruler of the earth!'

[33] çvapāka, çvapaca, çvapācika, Prākrit suṇahapāya, primarily designation of a Pariah, and thence standard term of opprobrium; see Pārçvanātha 3. 619, 858; Daçakumāracarita ii, p. 30; Mūladeva, in Jacobi, Ausgewählte Erzählungen, p. 63, l. 21. In Mahābh. 12. 141. 1 ff., Viçvāmitra, during a famine, tries to steal the leg of a dog from a Cāṇḍāla, an act so degrading that the Cāṇḍāla himself tries to dissuade him. In Kathās. 13. 148, 189 branding a dog-foot on the forehead is a sign of degradation. Cf. Benfey, Das Pañcatantra, vol. i, pp. 439, 445.

Story of the thief who was destined to die like Absalom. Unavertable fate[34]

The text turns to the third of the five light vows (aṇuvrata), namely abstention from theft (verse 46), picturing forcibly its wickedness. Worse than murder, it causes death alive; it defiles as the touch of a Mātañga even with a finger, and so on. Then follows illustration by story: In Çrīpura ruled a king, Mānamardana. A young man of good family and well educated, Mahābala by name, gradually lost his relatives, began to lead a dissolute life, and, from a gambler, became a thief. Once he went by night to steal in the house of a merchant named Datta. As he peeked into the house thru a lattice-window, he saw Datta quarrelling bitterly with his son over some trifling disagreement of accounts.[35] Out of decency he reflected, that a man who would abandon sleep in the middle of the night, and quarrel with his diligent and proper son over such a trifle, would die of a broken heart, if he were to steal his property. So he went to the house of a hetaera, Kāmasenā. He saw her lavish her professional ministrations upon a leprous slave, as tho he were a god. He decided that he could not afford to steal from any one as greedy for money as all that (626). Then he went to the house of a Brahman and saw him sleeping with his wife on a couch.

[34] The notion that specific fate, or fate imposed by supernatural power, is unavertable is a fruitful psychic motif of fiction: Mahābhārata 1. 41. 1 ff.; Hitopadeça in Braj Bhākhā 4. 3 (Hertel, Das Pañcatantra, p. 56, with parallels.; Nirmala Pāṭhaka 2. 6 (Hertel, ib., p. 283); Kathākoça, pp. 147-157; Dhammapada Commentary 9. 12; Ralston, Tibetan Tales, pp. 273 ff. Cf. ZDMG. lxv. 434 ff., 440, 441, 449.

[35] Unintelligible words: viçopakāikasyā 'melato lekhyake, 'an account not agreeing by a single viçopaka (?). The word viçopaka occurs in Rāuhiṇeya Carita; see p. 233.

A dog[36] urinated into the Brahman's hand, who said, 'Thank you!', as he rose with a start. The thief reflected that such was the Brahman's greed (for alms) that it persisted even while he was asleep; he, therefore, must not steal there (639).

He then decided to eschew mean folks; and broke into the king's palace. There he saw the king resting with his queen on a couch. As he stood there, intending to rob, a serpent came thru a hole in the door, bit the hand of the queen that hung outside the bed, and glided away. Greatly astonished, he forgot his own business, and silently followed the serpent to the ground floor. There the serpent took on the form of a great bull, and with a roar proceeded to kill the keeper of the main door of the palace.[37] The thief caught hold of the bull's tail, and asked him who he was, why he had come here, and what he would do next. The bull replied in a human voice, that he was the servant of Yama;[38] that he had come, at his command, to kill the queen and the doorkeeper; and that on the next day the architect of the new palace of the king would fall from one of its turrets. The thief then made the bull tell him how he himself would die. Reluctantly the bull informed him that he would die hanging on the branch of a banyan tree which stood on the king's highway. The thief then let go the bull's tail. Next day the architect died, as predicted; the thief, afright over his own impending death, went to a distant village, and

[36] The text reads khunā for çunā.

[37] pratolī means 'the main street of a town'; pratolī-dvāra, 'the gate opening upon that street.'

[38] See the story, 'Lord of Death,' in Steel and Temple, Legends of the Panjāb, pp. 207 ff. (same as Wide-Awake Stories, pp. 219 ff.); R. S. Mukharji, Indian Folk-Lore, pp. 92 ff.; McCulloch, Bengali Household Tales, pp. 1 ff. Serpent as messenger of death as early as Mahābh. 13. 1. 35.

took the dīkṣā (initiation) with an ascetic that lived near by (650).

While the former thief, Mahābala, was preaching asceticism in the forest, a thief who had stolen a jewel casket from the king's palace came running up, pursued by the king's beadles, dropped the casket in front of Mahābala,[39] and fled. No sooner had Mahābala taken up the casket, which was like a 'poison-maiden,'[40] than the beadles came along, surrounded him, and accused him of the theft. They beat him with their fists and with staffs, fettered him, and led him to execution. Then Māhabala recited a çloka, which described the grip of his fate. His captors wondered what he meant, and brought him before the king, in whose presence he repeated his çloka, narrating all his experiences. The king determined that he should escape his impending doom. Mahābala asked to be removed from the fateful banyan, but the king succeeded in allaying his apprehensions. In due time Mahābala rode out with the king upon a mettlesome horse, which became unmanageable, and dashed under that very banyan. Mahābala (Absalom-like) was caught in the throat by a thorn in a branch of that tree. The horse ran off, and he hung there dying, but reciting his çloka at the very end[41] (668). The king mourned Mahābala piteously, had him cremated in sandal-wood, and retired broken-spirited to his palace (699). Two Munis came along, and enlightened the king, so that, by the road of justice, he reached a state of imperishableness (padam avyayam) (609-722).

[39] See note 29, on p. 37.

[40] See additional note 17, on p. 198.

[41] See additional note 18, on p. 199.

Story of the chaste royal pair Sundara and Madanavallabhā

The text turns to the fourth of the five light vows (aṇuvrata), namely chastity (verse 46): one should see, and yet not see others' wives; even the gods extol the glories of the chaste. The theme is illustrated by the following story: Good King Sundara of Dhārāpura had but a single wife, Madanavallabhā, crest-jewel of good women. The pair had two exemplary sons, Kīrtipāla and Mahāpāla. The king regarded all other women as sisters (sodaryavrata),[42] wherefore his reputation reached to heaven. Once, in the middle of the night, the house divinity of the king told him, sad-faced, that his would be a rude fate, but that she herself might be able to postpone his troubles until after his youth had passed. The king, however, realizing that his trials must be due to his karma, chose to shoulder them without delay (740). He placed his kingdom in charge of his minister Subuddhi, took his wife and children, and, in garb suitable to his prospective humble life, went forth, appraising his past grandeur at the value of a blade of grass. A thief promptly robbed him, while he was asleep on the road, of the provisions he had taken with him, and also took his signet-ring. Plagued by hunger and thirst, guarding his daintily reared wife, and cajoling his crying boys, he arrived at the city of Pṛthvīpura (750).

Outside the walls of that city camped a merchant, named Çrīsāgara. He allowed the exiles a place in his camp to live. The king was unaccustomed to work, his two boys too small. But the queen, by feminine instinct (strīsvabhāva), showed skill in house-work, and earned

[42] See the note on 6. 773 ff.

their living by doing chores in neighboring houses, such as sweeping away cow-dung, and so on. They were treated kindly, and were given cast-off clothing, and coarse, cold food. Near there camped another caravan where she did some work. Its head, Somadeva, became enamored of Madanavallabhā, but she rejected him scornfully. He then affected to treat her honorably, but in the end carried her off with him on a journey to his own city (768). Even then his designs were foiled by her virtue and regard for her husband (772).

King Sundara, much afflicted by his separation from his beloved queen, chided his fate, but remained there awaiting developments. A merchant, Çrīsāra, happened where he was, pitied his sad condition, and offered him shelter and food, in exchange for which he and his boys were to tend a temple which the merchant had built. This he did to the satisfaction of the merchant, until one day the merchant noticed the two boys hunting birds. In punishment for this childish offence,[43] he beat them, broke their bows and arrows, and told the king, father of such boys, that he could no longer live with him. Together with his boys he again started to wander, crossed a wild and dangerous forest, and arrived at an unfordable river. He put one of his boys on his shoulder, crossed the river, and left him there. But, on returning to fetch the second, he was carried off his feet by the flood, and barely saved himself by means of a log of wood which came floating his way. Thus all three were separated. Racked by despair, he finally gathered courage to move on (813). He managed to reach a village, was entertained by a householder, but the housewife made improper advances to him[44] (821). Leaving this forbidden

[43] The offence from the Jain point of view, however, is grave.

[44] See additional note 19, on p. 199.

ground, he came to Çrīpura, in the outskirts of which city he went to sleep under a mango tree. The king of Çrīpura having just died sonless, the five oracle method (pañcadivya-adhivāsana[45]) of finding a successor was employed. The procession of elefant, horse, chowries, umbrella, and water-jug, headed by the court arrived at the spot where Sundara slept. The horse then neighed, the elefant roared, the water-jug emptied itself on the king, the umbrella stood over his head, and the two chowries waved. He was carried in triumf on the back of the elefant to the city, and received the homage of the ministers and vassals. Not even in all this glory did King Sundara, devoted to his own most beloved wife, think of marriage, for sooner than have two wives a man should go to prison, or exile, or hell (838).

The king's two sons separately wandered far, but in time each arrived at Çrīpura and met at the watch of the town. The merchant Somadeva also, having Madanavallabhā, their mother, in his caravan, came to that city, and asked the king for watchmen for his caravan. The two boys were assigned to this duty. By night, in order to pass the time, the younger asked the older to tell him a story, whereupon he told him his own story. Their mother, Queen Madanavallabhā, still attached to Somadeva's camp as woman of all work, lying awake sadly, overheard[46] the boys, recognized them as her long-lost children, came out, and embraced them with tears. Somadeva was angered by this occurrence, and had the boys brought before the king. Him they told what had happened between them and the woman from the camp. The king then questioned Somadeva, who told him that the woman had been carried with his caravan from Pṛthvī-

[45] See additional note 20, on p. 199.

[46] See additional note 2, on p. 185.

pura, and that she had conducted herself unexceptionably as a woman of good family (850). The king sent for her, but she would not go out alone. Then he himself went to the camp, found her meanly clad, and ailing. He addressed her tenderly, but she stood with her eyes cast upon his feet, struggling with conflicting emotions. The king, after humbly blaming himself for his shortcomings, had her conducted on an elefant to the palace, and they entered the state chamber. Then the king appointed his sons provincial rulers, after which the entire family, as the result of their virtue and courage, lived together happily (866).

In the meantime the minister Subuddhi, whom Sundara had left in charge of his kingdom in Dhārāpura, had placed the king's shoes on the throne,[47] and kept faithful charge of his trust. When he heard of the events that happened to his king Sundara in Çrīpura, he sent a messenger to report the continued homage of his subjects, and their intense longing to see him again in their midst (876). The king left his older son in charge of Çrīpura, and returned with his wife and other son to Dhārāpura, where he was acclaimed jubilantly by ministers, vassals and citizens (881).

The next day a profetic Sage arrived at a park outside the city. The king went out to pay his respects, and asked him to describe his previous karma. The sage told him that he and his queen had existed in a previous birth in Campā as the merchant Çañkha and his wife Çrī. They had lived piously, but on account of their youth had fallen

[47] Signifying that the king still ruled. So in the Rāmāyaṇa, Bharata places his exiled brother Rāma's shoes upon the throne, as a sign that Rāma is the true king of Ayodhyā. See also the two pādukas, symbolizing the dominion of Yugādīça (Ṛṣabha) in the Çatruṁjaya Māhātmyam, Indian Antiquary xxx. 243 top.

from grace. They were then born into their present state, had fallen into misfortune, but had been saved by their virtue. Sundara and his wife continued to live pious and virtuous lives, died peacefully, and went to heaven (723-890).

Story of the miserly merchant Dhanasāra

The text turns to the fifth and last of the light vows (aṇuvrata), namely greedlessness (aparigraha[48]), illustrating by story: In the city of Mathurā lived a merchant, named Dhanasāra, who counted his wealth by lakhs and crores, but was exceedingly stingy. The sight of any of his people giving alms would make him shut his eyes and fall in a faint. If his neighbors gave alms, a thing which he did not see, but heard of, the mere report of that would make him flee. If urged to give for religious ends, he would shut his teeth, and stand motionless. He changed the first syllable of the word dāna, 'giving' (namely, *da*) to *na*, namely 'not.'

The ill repute of his stinginess became so great that no one would mention his name (906). Once upon a time he dug for treasure and made a find, but, as he looked at it, it turned to living coal. Another time he found treasure, but it turned to vermin, serpents, and scorpions.[49] Just as he was beating his breast in grief over this disappointment, he was told of the wreck of one of his ships. Almost choked with grief, he stood like a stone fence. Then he determined to go to sea to retrieve his wealth. Remembering the city of Mahākṛpaṇa ('Stingytown'), which he had once visited, he set out for that. His ship,

[48] Otherwise known as akiṁcanatva or ākiṁcanya.

[49] Gold turns to scorpions, Indian Antiquary xix. 311; Manwaring, Mahratti Proverbs, p. 217 (note on nr. 1675).

laden with precious wares, encountered a fierce gale and was smashed into a hundred pieces (924). But he saved himself upon a plank,[50] landed in a forest, and reflected upon the folly of his greed. In that forest he saw a Sage, paid his respects to him, and asked him why he had become a miser, and why he had lost his wealth. The Sage narrated (891-930):

Story of the two brothers, one stingy, the other generous

In Dhātakīkhaṇḍabhārata lived two brothers, Dhanāḍhya and Gṛhasaṁbhūta. At the death of their father the older, as head of the family, was upright and generous; the younger was stingy, and hated to see his older brother practise generosity. Yet Çrī ('Fortune') attended the older, so that he prospered notwithstanding his openhandedness, whereas the younger was abandoned by Çrī.[51] In time the older brother abandoned the world, died, and was reborn as a distinguished god in the Sāudharma heaven; the younger, having done scant penance, also died, and was reborn as an Asura (941); 'You (namely, Dhanasāra of the preceding story) are derived from the Asuras, but the older, having fallen from Sāudharma, was born in Tāmaliptī as the son of a wealthy merchant, and attained the wisdom of a Kevalin: I am he. This accounts both for your stinginess, and the loss of your wealth' (945). The Sage then continued to discourse on generosity and stingines, illustrating by story (931-958):

[50] See note 33, on p. 49.

[51] See additional note 21, on p. 202.

Story of the merchant Kubera and Çrī, the goddess of fortune: The gold-man [52]

In the city of Çrīviçāla ruled King Guṇāḍhya. There lived Kubera, a wealthy merchant. Once upon a time Çrī, the goddess of fortune, who is like a fickle woman [53] (verse 953), spoke to him in a dream: 'I have lived here in your house for seven seasons (paryāya); now I wish to go; I have come to take leave of you.' He asked for a delay of four days, which she granted. Kubera then gave away his entire property to the unprotected, poor, wretched, and to his own relatives. On the fourth day he joyously lay down upon an old bed, feigning sleep. The goddess arrived, he pretended to be aroused, and told her that he had been lying in deep, pleasurable sleep, because he no longer had any of the cares of wealth (972). He then asked Çrī what he should do, whereupon she suggested that he might find some means of checking her waywardness. When Kubera did not react upon this, but bade her go as she desired, Çrī confessed that his pious acts had renewed her attachment to him. In order to make it possible that she should stay with him (that is to say, in order that he should be rich again), she advised him to go to her temple, where he would find a man in ragged clothes. Him he should invite and feed; then touch his foot with a staff, whereupon he would turn into a gold-man (svarṇapuruṣa) (978).

In this way he obtained the gold-man. No matter how much gold he broke off him, he did not grow less. Then a barber [54] came to serve him, found out what had happened, and decided to try the same game. In due course

[52] See additional note 22, on p. 202.
[53] See additional note 21, on p. 202.
[54] See additional note 23, on p. 202.

he saw such a man standing in the temple of the divinity, invited and fed him, and then struck his foot with a cudgel. But the man fell at the blow, cried aloud, armed police arrived on the spot, and took the barber before the king. He told of the gold-man in Kubera's house, and how everything had happened differently when he had tried it. Whereupon Kubera was cited into the royal presence, and told the entire marvel from beginning to end. The king rejoiced that so pious a man as Kubera resided in his kingdom, honored him, and dismissed the barber. Others followed Kubera's example and led generous lives (959-989).

Story of the miserly merchant Dhanasāra, continued

Upon hearing these sermons and stories Dhanasāra told the Sage that henceforth he would keep for himself only one-fourth of such wealth as he might acquire, and distribute the rest in the cause of religion. The Sage accepted his declaration, and instructed him still further.

Later on Dhanasāra went to Tāmaliptī on business, but also passed some time in honoring the Jina. In the town there was a house which had been depopulated by a Vyantara demon. There Dhanasāra lived in the company of a Jina image. By night, until sunrise, the demon angrily haunted him, assuming terrible forms. But Dhanasāra kept calm, so that the demon was much impressed, and told him to ask a favor. Dhanasāra asked nothing; so the god, of his own accord, advised him to return home to Mathurā, and there become rich again. Dhanasāra accepted this advice, in order to purge himself of stinginess. He returned to Mathurā, found there his former property, in due time became enormously rich, built a lofty Jaina temple, made other benefactions, and retained only a fourth part of his wealth (1001). He died in fast, and became a god in the Sāudharma heaven. He will obtain salvation in Videha (990-1014).

Brahman and dish of grits[55]

The text proceeds to show that greed, even if only in thought (atilāulyatā-dhyāna), is reprehensible, illustrating by a version of ' The Brahman in the Potter's Shop ': A certain mendicant obtaining a dish of grits, settled to sleep in a temple with the dish at his feet. There he ruminated as follows: ' I shall sell these grits and buy a she-goat with the money; sell the goat and her kids and get a milch-cow; sell the milch-cow and get a she-buffalo; sell the she-buffalo and get a noble mare, whose superb colts will procure great wealth. Then I shall build a lovely palace with a couch of state, gather a retinue, invite my relatives, marry the beautiful daughter of a most distinguished Brahman, and have by her a son with all the perfect characteristics. He will gradually grow up, until one day I shall see him in the courtyard crying, whereupon I shall, in a rage, strike my wife with my foot —thus! ' Then he saw his dish smashed, his grits scattered—and greatly grieved (1015-1026).

Frame Story: Kiraṇavega's conversion and death

The Sage thus finished the exposition of the five light vows (aṇuvratāni) of the house-holders, which correspond to the great vows (mahāvratāni) of ascetics. Many people were converted. King Kiraṇavega turned from

[55] See my article, 'On recurring Psychic Motifs in Hindu Fiction, JAOS. xxxvi. pp. 26 ff. See also Dhammapada Commentary 3. 4; Parker, Village Folk-Tales of Ceylon, vol. i, pp. 197, 304, 306.

concerns of the body to concerns of the soul, and became as one who has attained salvation while yet alive (jīvan-mukta). There are four different grades of men who according to their various characters are influenced differently by stories. They are connected with the three so-called guṇas, or 'qualities': tamas, 'darkness'; rajas, 'passion'; and sattva, 'goodness,' culminating in sāttvikā narottamāḥ, 'most excellent men of sattva character[56] (1038). Kiraṇavega then thanked the Sage, resorted to his protection, and made over his kingdom to his son Kiraṇatejas. With the permission of the Guru he went to Puṣkaradvīpa, and passed some time on the mountain of Vāitāḍhya, in austere penance, carrying an image of the Jina. The soul of the kurkuṭa serpent (1. 858 ff.) came from hell, being reborn there as a great serpent.[56a] Owing to their prenatal enmity the serpent bit Kiraṇavega. The later regarded this as the result of his karma, died contentedly and forgivingly, and was reborn as a god in Jambūdrumāvarta.[57] The serpent was burned by a forest-fire, and went to the Dhūmaprabhā hell,[58] which is vividly described. Final blessing (1027-1065).

---

[56] The same classification in 6. 544, and a similar application of the guṇas in Mahābhārata 14. 36. 1 ff.

[56a] Fourth pre-birth of the future Meghamālin.

[57] Fifth pre-birth of the future Pārçva.

[58] Fifth pre-birth of the future Meghamālin.

Sarga the Third

Frame story: King Vajranābha and his infidel cousin Kubera

Kiraṇavega fell in due time from his high estate of god, and was reborn as Prince Vajranābha,[1] son of Lakṣmīvatī, the wife of Vajravīrya, king of Çubhaṁkarā. He grew into every bodily and mental perfection, so as to become the fitting mate of Vijayā, daughter of Candrakānta of Baḍgadeça, with whom he lived wisely and piously (20). It happened that he had a visit from a cousin (mātulanandana), by name of Kubera, an infidel, hated even by his own father. Kubera mocked Vajranābha's piety, advising him to 'fulfil every desire of his mind, speech, and body.' While Vajranābha was trying to reform Kubera, the great Sage Lokacandra arrived in a park outside the city. They both went to hear him preach a lengthy sermon on a variety of topics (58). Kubera remained sceptical, upheld the advantages of a sensual life, and supported his position by rationalistic arguments (65). The Sage gently reproved and refuted him, and, in the course of exposition of the Jaina doctrine, arrived at the four worldly (lāukika) virtues, which are the theme proper of this Sarga. These are vinaya, 'tact'; viveka, 'discernment'; susaṁga, 'association with good people'; and susattvatā, 'resolute courage'[2] (98). The text next defines the first of these virtues, illustrating by the following story (1-104):

[1] Sixth pre-birth of the future Pārçva.

[2] See Çālibhadra Carita 1. 21; 2. 2.

Story of King Vikrama as a parrot[2a]

In the city of Avantī, in the land of Avanti, ruled the mighty and accomplished King Vikrama, by the side of his noble and lovely queen Kamalāvatī. One day he addressed the people assembled in his hall of audience: 'Ah, tell me! Is there anywhere any accomplishment, science, wealth, or intelligence, so marvelous as not to be found in my kingdom?'[3] A stranger in the assembly rose up and declaimed aloud: 'Long have I roamed the treasure-laden earth, but I have not beheld a union of the rivers of glory and knowledge like unto thee. In Pātāla (Hades) rules Vāsuki (the beautiful king of the serpents); in heaven Çakra (Indra). Both these, invisible as they are, are realized by the mind thru thy majesty, O Ruler of the Earth!' He then went on to praise the ministers, warriors, and wives of the king, but found just a single shortcoming in the king, namely, that he was ignorant of the 'Art of entering another's body.' The king asked: 'Where is this to be found? Tell me quickly!' The other replied: 'On the mountain of Çrī, in the keep of a man Siddheçvara.'[4] The king dismissed the assembly, put his minister in charge of his kingdom, and, eager to obtain this science, went out from the city by night, without regard to danger or hardship. In due time he

[2a] This is, perhaps, the most interesting and original story of the book. It has been treated in relation to its congeners, and translated in full, by the author in his essay, 'On the art of entering another's body,' Proceedings of the American Philosophical Society, vol. lvi (1917), pp. 1 ff. The translation with annotations is on pp. 22-43.

[3] For this sort of boastful inquiry see, e. g., Jacobi, Ausgewählte Erzählungen aus dem Māhārāṣṭrī, p. 39; Leumann, Die Āvaçyaka-Erzählungen, ii. 8. 3 (p. 15).

[4] The name means 'Lord of Magic.'

reached the mountain of Çrī, beheld Siddheçvara, obtained his favor, and was accepted as a pupil (127).

Now a certain Brahman had been on the spot a long time ahead of Vikrama, hoping to acquire the same science. But the very devotion he showed became a plague, because of his constant importunity. On the other hand, the Master was pleased with the king's devotion, which was coupled with tact and disinterestedness, so that he begged Vikrama to accept from him the 'Art of entering another's body,' in discharge of the debt imposed by the king's devotion (133).

Upon hearing this, Vikrama, indifferent to his own interests, perceiving the disappointment of the Brahman, begged the Teacher rather to confer the science upon the Brahman. The Teacher said: 'Do not give a serpent milk to drink! He is unworthy, and with an unworthy person the science works great mischief. Think how, once upon a time, a Master of Magic, seeing the bones of a lion, made the body of the lion whole, and undertook to give him life; how, warned by his people, he nevertheless, in his madness, gave him life; then the lion slew him.[5] Notwithstanding this warning the king fervently embraced the Master's feet, and prevailed upon him to bestow the science upon that Brahman. After that, out of respect for the command of the Master, he also accepted it himself (144).

Vikrama, in the company of the Brahman, returned to Avantī, confiding to him on the way his own history. Leaving the Brahman outside the city, he entered alone, in order to observe the state of his kingdom. Noticing that the people within the palace were upset, because the

[5] This refers to a familiar fable: see Benfey, Das Pañcatantra i. 489; ii. 332; Hertel, Das Pañcatantra, p. 131.

state elefant had died, he returned to the Brahman and said to him: 'Friend, I have a mind to disport myself by means of my science; I shall enter into the elefant, so as to see something of what is going on in the city. Do you act as guardian beside my body, so that, with your help, I shall not fail to recognize it.' Thus he spoke, there left his own body, and entered into the carcass of the elefant, which then, as before, disported itself blithely. Then that base-souled Brahman, violator of faith, betrayer of friend, reflected: 'Of what use to me is my own wretched body, plagued by racking poverty; I will enter Vikrama's body, and serenely rule the kingdom!' Thus he did. The fake king entered the palace quivering like an animal of the forest, because he did not know how to behave, and where to go. Holding on to the arm of the minister, he sat down on the throne; the king's retinue bowed before him. The assembled multitude cried, 'Fate has restored to life the king of the elefants, and the king of men has returned again. This is indeed sugar falling into milk'[6] (160).

But the fake king continued to act strangely, so that the people wondered whether some god or demon, in the guise of the king, had not taken possesion of the vacant throne; or whether the king's mind was not wandering. The minister decided that the king's mind was sure to be restored by the nectar of Kamalāvatī's speech, and had him conducted to her. The queen rose in confusion, and, when she looked at him, fell to the ground in a faint. On being restored, and hearing his voice, she was greatly grieved and thought, 'He looks like my beloved, yet afflicts me like an enemy.' When the king asked her to explain her perturbation, she answered artfully: 'Your

[6] The same figure, çarkarādugdhasaṁyogaḥ, in 6. 1349.

Majesty! At the time when you started upon your journey, I uttered a fond prayer to Caṇḍī for your safe return, vowing not to look upon my beloved before adoring her. Now, having failed to do so, Caṇḍī felled me to the ground. Therefore I shall let you know myself, O king, the time for paying devotion to the goddess.' The king then retired (173).

At this time the minister was adorning the state elefant[7] for the royal entry, so that the people should see their sovereign, at length returned. Now the menials who were painting the ornamental marks on the elefant discussed the fake king's strange conduct, and Vikrama saw thru the treachery of the Brahman. Bitterly regretting his misplaced confidence, he decided to escape, lest the rogue should mount as a tuft upon his wretched person. This he did, escaping hot pursuit in a distant forest, where he took rest in the shade of a banyan tree. There he perceived a man standing between the trunks of the tree, engaged in killing parrots with a sling-shot.[8] The king, worried by his great and unwieldy body, decided to make a change, and entered into the body of a parrot. Then this parrot said to the hunter, 'Friend, what do you want to be killing so many parrots for? Take me to Avantī, and you will surely get a thousand ṭanka coins for me; you must, however, give me assurance of personal safety.' This the hunter did, and went with the parrot to Avantī, where he stood on the king's highway, offering the parrot for an exorbitant price, and justifying that price on the ground that the parrot could recite whatsoever Çāstras people asked for (195).

At this juncture some attendant maids of queen Kama-

[7] Now inhabited by Vikrama.

[8] dhanurgolikā: the word recurs in our text, l. 317, in the form dhanurgulikā. Neither compound is in the Lexicons.

lāvatī arrived. The parrot who knew well their dispositions, as soon as he was accosted by one of them, recited in a sweet voice: 'Pierced by the arrow of thine eyes, O graceful lady, one deems oneself happy and lives; not pierced, one dies: here is a marvelous Science of Archery.' After some further give and take, the maid reported to the queen, and she promptly commissioned her to buy the parrot. This she did; the hunter went to his home. When the parrot saw Kamalāvatī joyfully coming to meet him, he extended his right wing, and chanted sweetly: 'O queen, in order to uphold thy weight, as thou restest on his left arm, Vikrama holds the earth as a counter-balance on his right arm.' The queen replied smiling: 'O parrot! what you say amounts to this, that one cannot, unless he rules the earth, drag the load of a woman. Very pointedly you have stated that we impose a great burden: what wise person would not be pleased with a statement of the truth?' She put him into a golden cage, tended him in person, fed him upon every delicacy, and constantly regaled herself with the nectar flow of his conversation (209).

As time went by, the queen and the parrot engaged in a contest of riddles and charades, both simple and intricate,[9] on the whole counting among the most interesting of that species of jeux d'esprit in Hindu literature (227). Again, the queen asked the parrot to recite some well-spoken words, devoted to salutary instruction (hitopadeça). The parrot complied, discoursed on deliberation in speech and action; on rectitude and kindness; on wrath, envy, and malice; winding up with the simile of the three skulls, illustrating the value of discretion (233):

[9] They are expounded on pp. 31-35 of my translation of this story, cited above.

Simile of the three skulls, illustrating discretion[10]

A certain king of yore caused his wise men to make the test of the three skulls, that had been brought by a stranger from another land. On that occasion, a thread put into the ear of one of the skulls came out of its mouth: the price of that skull was a farthing (kaparda), because it would blab what it had heard. Again, a thread put into the ear of the second skull came out at the other ear: the price of that skull was a lakh, because it forgot what it had heard. But the thread inserted into the ear of the third skull went straight down its throat: that skull was priceless, because what it heard remained in its heart. 'Conforming with this, O queen, who, that has ears and hears reference to another's guilt, does not become discreet in mind?' (238).

Story of King Vikrama as a parrot, continued

Kamalāvatī's soul was so delighted with the parrot's discourse, that she promised to live and die with him. But the wise parrot answered: 'Say not so, beloved wife of a king! Of what account am I, a wee animal, beside thee, beloved of King Vikrama?' The queen said: 'My eye tells me that my beloved has returned, but my mind says not; I shall devise some means to dismiss the king. But you, as a husband, shall afford me delight, that do I here declare.' The king-parrot then realized that his science had been of profit to him, for how else could he have tested the heart of the queen? (245).

Next, the queen asked the parrot to instruct her on the

[10] This is named trikapālīparīkṣaṇam, for which see the citations in note 81 on p. 36 of the above-mentioned translation. See also Hertel, Das Pañcatantra, p. 46.

essence of religion, which the parrot did, in accordance with the familiar teaching of the Jaina vows, winding up with the superiority of mental purity as compared with ascetic practice. This he illustrates by the following story (252):

Episode, illustrating the superiority of soul purification over meritorious deeds

A wise king heard that his brother Soma, a Sage, was sojourning in a park outside his city. He went to pay his respects, listened to the law from his mouth, and returned to the palace. The chief queen then made the following vow: 'I shall in the morning salute this Sage, and not take food before he has feasted.' Now, on the road between the city and the park, there was a river. When she arrived there by night the river was in flood, too deep for crossing. In the morning she asked her husband how she might obtain her heart's desire. The king said: 'Go cheerfully with your retinue, adore the River goddess, and with pure mind recite, "O, Goddess River, if my husband has practised chastity, since the day on which he paid his devotions to my brother-in-law, then promptly give me passage."[11] The queen reflected in surprise: 'Why now does the king, fifth Protector of the World, say such an absurd thing? Since the day of his devotion to his brother, I have become pregnant by him with a son; that wifely state of mine he knows full well.' Nevertheless, out of wifely devotion, she went with her retinue to the bank of the river, honored the River goddess, and made the truth-declaration,[12] as told by her husband. At

[11] The notion that rivers may be induced by prayer to furnish passage is a very old one in India; see Rig-Veda 3. 33. 9; 4. 19. 6.

[12] satyaçrāvaṇā = the Buddhist saccakiriyā; see Burlingame, JRAS., 1917, pp. 429 ff.

once the river banked its waters to the right and to the left, became shallow, and the queen crossed.

After revering and feasting the Sage, she told him her story, and asked how her husband's inconceivable chastity could be valid. The Sage replied: 'When I took the vow, from that time on the king also became indifferent to earthly matters. But as there was no one to bear the burden of royalty, he kept on performing his royal acts, in deed, but not in thought. The king's chastity is valid, because his mind is unspotted, even as a lotus that stands in the mud.'

The queen then bade adieu to the Sage, and asked him how she was to recross the river. The Sage told: 'You must say to the Goddess River, "If that Sage, since taking the vow, has steadily lived in fast, then give me passage!"' The queen, in renewed surprise, went to the bank of the river, recited the words of the Sage, crossed, and arrived home. She narrated all to the king, and asked, 'How could the Sage be in fast, since I myself entertained him with food?' The king replied: 'You are simple, O queen, you do not grasp the spirit of religion: the lofty-minded Sage is indifferent to both eating or non-eating. Mind is the root, speech the crown, deed the branch-expansion of the tree of religion: from the firm *root* of that tree everything springs forth.' Then the queen understood (286).

Story of King Vikrama as a parrot, concluded

When the queen had heard this speech of the parrot, she recognized the parrot's true character: 'My faltering mind was under delusion; this is the king, here speaks his voice!' She went to sleep rejoicing. Then the parrot-king, noticing there a house-lizard, entered into it, that he might further test the queen. When the queen awoke, and saw the parrot still, she tried to rouse him with tender words and endearments. Failing to do so, she fell into a faint, and, when she came to, mourned the parrot piteously, but finally bathed and anointed his body, preparatory to his funeral rites, in the course of which she would, as a faithful wife, commit her body to the flames along with her spouse.

When the fake king heard this he exclaimed in consternation, 'Alas, alas, this kingdom, without Kamalāvatī, will be profitless to me: I must restore her to life.' He left the body which he had usurped, and entered that of the parrot. The king promptly left the lizard, and resumed his own body. Resplendent, like a mighty mass of glowing clouds, Vikrama quickly went to the presence of the queen (305). At the sight of him Kamalāvatī grew radiant as a garland of lotuses. Having perceived that his speech, his gait, his habit, and his regard were just as before, she fell at his feet and clung to him. The king teased her about her love for the parrot, but she averred that the parrot was now violently repulsive to her (312).

The king took the parrot in his hand and said: 'What have we here, O Brahman?' The parrot replied: 'That which befits them that deceive their teacher, their king, and their friend.' The king, recognizing his contrition, consoled him by pointing out that his companionship had enabled him to pass the troublous experience of the science.[13] Then the Brahman showed that he was fully penitent: 'Full well thou knowest, O king, what sort of companionship thou didst enjoy with me, that has strayed from my own house and body—tricker of friend, sovereign, and teacher. It does not befit thee to see and to

[13] See the note 18 above on p. 32.

touch me. Seize me by the left foot, and cast me somewhere, that I may devote myself to a better life. All this shall serve thee as a lesson in the wickedness of men!' The king's heart was still more softened; he dismissed him in peace to a life of religious devotion. Vikrama continued to rule his kingdom happily in Kamalāvatī's society. Thus the science, obtained by him thru tactful conduct, led to a happy issue, but the very same science imposed great misery upon the Brahman who was wanting in that virtue (105-324).

Story of Sumati, the evil-minded, whose vices were corrected by discernment

The Sage next expounds the second of the 'worldly virtues' (see verse 98), namely, viveka, or 'discernment.' Upon this he lavishes ecstatic praise, illustrating by the following story: King Çrīsena in Çrīpura had a Purohita, named Soma, who was childless. The king was worried, for fear that his successor should be deprived of spiritual support to his rule, in case the Purohita failed to have a son. He advised Soma to make an appeal for a son to his household divinity.[14] This he did, threatening to die of starvation,[15] in case she should not grant his wish (341). The goddess had no available child; there-

[14] See additional note 24, on p. 203.

[15] Threat of suicide, usually 'by entering the fire,' or by starvation ('hunger-strike') is one of the constant minor progressive motifs. The idea is closely related to the so-called dharṇa (Hopkins, JAOS. xxi. 146 ff.); so, e. g., in Jātaka 90. The point of the threat is, to exact some wish, which is then regularly granted. Thus in Prabhāvaka Carita, p. 9, çloka 138 (Vajraprabandha) Rukmiṇī tells her father that she wishes to marry Vajra, else she will enter the fire. In fact love-matters furnish the most frequent occasion for the threat. In Pārçvanātha the motif appears in 3. 606; 6. 568; 8. 96. The theme will furnish a substantial article for the Encyclopedia of Fiction.

fore, in her perplexity, she went to a Yakṣa who had attained perfection, and told him that Soma was threatening suicide. If he should happen to fulfil his threat, people would then cease to pay her devotion (pūjā). The Yakṣa advised her to trick the Purohita, by promising him a son, but that he should be a rake, gambler, and thief. The Purohita consulted the king, who advised him to accept her promise, but, with the additional stipulation, that the son should be gifted with discernment (viveka), the corrective of all shortcomings. He got the consent of his goddess to this proposition, and then mated with the second concubine of his household.[16] After that he reflected, remorsefully, that his son would be low-born, despised by his own family, and that the king also would become disgusted with him. Again he took counsel with the king, who reassured him, and pointed out that the 'sun of discernment' would dispel the darkness of guilt (361).

In due time, Soma had a son born him, and, when he grew up, the father himself instructed him. While teaching a group of pupils he placed him in an underground chamber, sitting the while on a bench over it expounding the Çāstras. In order to make sure that the boy understood what was being taught, Soma tied a string to his own thumb, passed the other end to his son, to shake whenever he did not understand. One day Soma recited the nīti-stanza:[17] 'Wealth is dissipated in three ways: by giving it away; by enjoying it; and by losing it. He who does not give it away, or does not enjoy it, his money is lost in the third way.' Sumati pulled the string; his

[16] See additional note 15, on p. 195.

[17] See Böhtlingk, Indische Sprüche, 2757, and the literature there cited. See also Bhojaprabandha, stanza 63, and compare Prabandhacintāmaṇi, p. 111.

father again expounded the çloka; the boy again pulled the string. Then his father dismissed the other pupils, and, calling his son out of his hiding, chided him for his failure to comprehend. But the boy pointed out that gifts fittingly bestowed, in truth, are never lost, or fruitless, whereas, the personal enjoyment of wealth is for the moment, for this world alone, and, therefore, lost (375). Soma rejoiced over his son's wisdom, and reported the occurrence to the king, who ascribed the boy's wisdom to his viveka. He had him brought in state to his court, and installed in the hereditary office of Purohita (386).

On some occasion the king asked Sumati what was the cause of the different stations which souls occupy in the world. Sumati skilfully met this test by pointing out that actions (karma), founded upon discernment or non-discernment, regulate fate in subsequent births. Thus the emperor Bharata, tho steeped in the mud of royal pleasures, obtained thru discernment release from saṁsāra,[18] but the fish Taṇḍula, owing to his guilt in eating other fish, went to the seventh hell.[19] The king acclaimed his wisdom (394).

However, the evil propensities which the family divinity had profesied, were bound to come out. One day, Sumati stole a necklace belonging to the king, and lived in fear of discovery henceforth. His discernment told him how little sense there was in his living the terror-stricken life of a thief, favorite of the king as he was. He restored the necklace (399). Another time he was tempted by one of the queens,[20] attracted by his charming person. But his discernment pointed out to him that the wife of his king must be regarded in the light of a mother, and

[18] Cf. Stevenson, Heart of Jainism, pp. 158, 170.

[19] Apparently alluding to some fable.

[20] See additional note 19, on p. 199.

that the punishment for intercourse with the wife of another is cutting off of one's head in hell, and infamy like that of Indra, because he violated Ahalyā, the wife of Gāutama.[21] He therefore managed to conserve his chastity (405). Again, he was attacked by the desire to gamble, but checked himself by realizing that gambling is the chief of passions, and that King Nala and others were by it plunged into misfortune. Thus his discernment overcame his third temptation (410). One day Sumati asked the king why he showed such implicit trust in him, tho it was not the habit of kings to be confiding. The king replied that there was no reason for distrust, because he, Sumati, came from the Purohitas of the royal family. Then Sumati again asked why he had been chosen while yet so young, and the king answered that he had desired to test the unfolding of his discernment. This he supported by the familiar punning allusion to the uselessness of a 'strong bow without string' = 'good family without virtue.'[22] The king then told him the story of his life, which he listened to with downcast face. In the end Sumati entered upon the path of virtue (325-419).

Story of Prabhākara and his king, wife, and friend

The sage then turns to the third worldly virtue (lāukika guṇa), namely, keeping good company (susaṁga, or susaṁsarga). By contact with a touchstone, brass becomes gold; by contact with gold, glass becomes a jewel.[23]

[21] From Çatapatha Brāhmaṇa 3. 3. 4. 18 on to Kathāsaritsāgara 17. 137 ff. See my Vedic Concordance, under ahalyāyāi. For lechery of the gods see Vāsavadattā (Gray's translation, p. 130, with note); Daçakumāracarita i, p. 44; Böhtlingk, Indische Sprüche, nr. 2170.

[22] savaṅço 'pi dhanurdaṇḍo nirguṇaḥ kiṁ kariṣyati; see Böhtlingk, Indische Sprüche, nr. 5369.

[23] Cf. Böhtlingk, ibid., 1618.

This he illustrates by the well-known (lokakhyātā) story of Prabhākara (527): In Vīrapura lived a virtuous Brahman, named Divākara, who had a son named Prabhākara, addicted to every vice: alchemy,[24] gambling, quarreling, and vagabondage. His father excoriated his evil ways, and bade him master the Çāstras, drink the sap of poetry, acquire the proper accomplishments, practice virtue, and thus raise high the family. Prabhākara answered all that with jeers and jibes: 'the Çāstra does not quench thirst; nor poetry still hunger'; and so on. The father sadly deplored his ownership of such a son, but in the end, out of parental affection, presented him with a çloka memorialis, recommending association with a grateful king; marriage of a noble wife; and choice of a disinterested friend[25] (442). The father died. A friend informed Prabhākara, just as he was gambling, of his father's death. So engrossed did he remain in his pursuit, that he bade the friend attend to the funeral. After a time Prabhākara, remembering his çloka, started to travel. On the road he heard of a certain village chief (Ṭhakkura), Siṅha by name, ungrateful, empty-headed, and stuck-up; to him he resorted for patronage. While in his service, he was married by him to a low-born, coarse, and ignorant slave-girl; he also struck up friendship with a rapacious merchant, named Lobhanandi (450).

It so happened that the Ṭhakkura was cited to the presence of the king, and Prabhākara accompanied him thither. Prabhākara recited a çloka in the hearing of the king, whose import was that birds of a feather should flock together.[26] The king was so much pleased that he

[24] dhātuṁ dhamati.

[25] Cf. Böhtlingk, Indische Sprüche, nrs. 691, 1859.

[26] Böhtlingk, Indische Sprüche, nr. 4933; cf. 5290, 5643.

rewarded Prabhākara with the gift of a city. Moreover, at the latter's request, the Ṭhakkura was entrusted with the sovereignty of a province. Prabhākara also disposed the king so favorably towards Lobhanandi, that he, who had been poor, became very rich (455). Now the Ṭhakkura had a pet peacock whom he loved better than a child. It came to pass that Prabhākara's low-born wife was taken with a pregnant woman's whim[27] (dohada) for the peacock's flesh. Prabhākara, instead of giving her the flesh of this peacock, gave her some other, and hid away the Ṭhakkura's pet.[28] As soon as the peacock was missed, the drum was sounded, and a reward of 800 dīnārs promised him who would tell of its whereabouts. Then his wife, deciding to get rid of him, and, at the same time, to obtain the reward, touched the drum.[29] She went before the Ṭhakkura, told him of her whim for peacock's flesh, pretending at the same time that she had tried to keep Prabhākara from killing the king's pet. Out of excessive love for her, he had killed the peacock, and given her his flesh. The Ṭhakkura sent his soldiers after Prabhākara, but he escaped to Lobhanandi's house, intending to test his friendship. He told him also that he had slain the Ṭhakkura's peacock. Then Lobhanandi betrayed him; he was fettered, and brought before the Ṭhakkura. He appealed to him pathetically to pardon this one fault of his, but was bidden inexorably to produce the peacock,

[27] See additional note 25, on p. 204.

[28] A similar story in Ralston, Tibetan Tales, p. 151 ff. In Jātaka 159; Chavannes, Cinq Cent Contes Chinois, nr. 20, the flesh of a peacock is eaten for its curative quality. In the sequel of the present story Prabhākara hides away a king's son, in order to test the king's generosity. This also is the theme of a story in Vikrama Carita (Indische Studien xv. 321; Lescallier, Le Trône Enchanté, p. 110). In Jātaka 86 a king is tested by doing him an injury; in Jātaka 218 a boy is hidden away.

[29] See additional note 3, on p. 185.

or meet death. Prabhākara, after reciting his father's çloka, produced the peacock, and then went away, reflecting sadly on the results of evil association with an unworthy lord, wife, and friend (484).

He wandered about until he arrived at the city of Sundara, where he happened upon Guṇasundara, the son of the king of that city, practicing military tactics on the field for military exercise (khalūrikā) outside the city. They struck up acquaintance: Prabhākara, finding him a gracious and noble prince, took service with him, in the hope of purging himself of the contact with his former evil lord (495). Then he married a noble, faithful and discreet wife, Çrī by name; also, he gained the friendship of Vasanta, a rich and generous merchant. At the death of his father, Guṇasundara, succeeding, chose Prabhākara for his minister. It happened that the two went on an expedition, riding two noble horses of inverted training.[30] When they, not knowing the peculiarity of the horses, attempted to check them, they ran off at a fierce gallop, landing them in a great forest, far away from their retinue. As they were galloping along, Prabhākara plucked three myrobalans from a tree. With these, one by one, he restored the king, who had been overcome by thirst and hunger. In time, they were found by the king's retinue, and were brought back to the city in triumf and great rejoicing (520).

Now the five-year old son of Guṇasundara was in the habit of visiting Prabhākara's house, to play there. He wore a child's necklace. In order to test the king's quality, Prabhākara, one day, hid the boy out of sight. At the end of a long and vain search, the king was not only deeply grieved, but also much perplexed, because he knew

[30] See additional note 26, on p. 204.

that the boy had gone to the house of the minister. All the court, excepting Prabhākara, assembled mournfully about the king on his throne. Then Prabhākara's wife asked him why he did not, on that day, go to the palace. He replied, that he did not dare to do so, because he had himself slain the boy in a fit of madness. He furthermore pretended that she had told him in the past, that the boy had cast the evil eye [31] on her on account of some pre-natal hostility (531). She went to the merchant Vasanta, for advice. He reassured her, and promised her that he would protect his friend with his life and his wealth. In the presence of the king he accused himself of the murder. While the king was in a state of doubt, Prabhākara's wife appeared before him, exonerated Vasanta, and assumed the guilt, pretending that the boy had been slain to satisfy a pregnancy whim of hers. Then Prabhākara, greatly perturbed, presented himself in person, and claimed that he had slain the boy in a fit of mental aberration, while living in fear of a misfortune which threatened him (542). The king, still perplexed, finally concluded that he could not punish Prabhākara, because he had saved his life in extreme need by giving him the three myrobalans. But for that, there would now be no king, nor kingdom; no son, and no royal train. When Prabhākara had thus tested the king, he produced the boy, sound and smiling, to the supreme happiness of the king. Then Prabhākara narrated his life's story, that hinged on the çloka given him by his father. The king forgave, and they continued in the relation of mutually confiding

[31] In Mahābh. 8. 87. 171 the heroes Karṇa and Çalya cannot endure the look of their enemies. In Vīracarita xvi (Indische Studien, xiv. 127) Sanaka curses Udaçocā, so that he whom she shall look at in her wedding hour shall die. Evil eye (jettatura), also in Day, Folk-Tales of Bengal, p. 108; Parker, Village Folk-Tales of Ceylon, i. 11, 173, 177.

king and minister. Prabhākara lived happily in the possession of a noble lord, a good wife, and a faithful friend (420-555).

Story of King Hariçcandra's courageous endurance[32]

The text turns to the exposition and praise of the last of the four worldly virtues (lāukikā guṇāḥ), namely sattva, or 'courageous endurance,' ending with the following illustration: King Hariçcandra, of Ikṣvāku descent, ruled in Ayodhyā. One night he heard a bard recite a çloka in praise of sattva;[33] this the king, much impressed with its meaning, memorized. In the morning a disturbance arose, because a boar was rampant in the Çakrāvatāra forest, tearing down trees and creepers, and endangering the peace of the ascetics living therein. The king rode into the forest, was told by his two companions, Kapiñjala and Kuntala, where the boar was, and, in due course, brought him down (585). The king, curious to know how much injury he had done to his unstable target, sent Kapiñjala to see. Kapiñjala, on his return, bade the king go and see for himself. The king found the victim covered with blood 'like a burning forest-fire,' so that he suspected him to be of divine origin. Kapiñjala, who knew the truth, tried to keep the king from closely investigating, but the king persisted, and found the victim

[32] This story is a skilful fictional rifacimento of an epic narrative, told in Mārkaṇḍeya Purāṇa 7. It is dramatized in Kṣemendra's, or Kṣemīçvara's play Caṇḍakāuçika, edited by Jayanmohana Çarman (Calcutta 1867), translated by L. Fritze, under the title 'Kāuçika's Zorn,' Leipzig, Reclam's Universalbibliothek, No. 1726 (cf. Pischel, Göttingische Gelehrte Anzeigen, 1883, p. 1217). Echoes of the same story may be found in Chavannes, Cinq Cent Contes et Apologues Chinois, nrs. 6 and 13, and in Stokes, Indian Fairy Tales, pp. 224 ff. On the character of the Epic story see Muir, Original Sanskrit Texts i², pp. 379 ff.

[33] Cf. Böhtlingk, Indische Sprüche, nrs. 6147-9.

to be a pregnant doe. Being greatly distressed at his mortal sin of having slain an embryo, he decided to go to the hermitage, in order to obtain there absolution for his sin. As he entered with his two friends, he was received kindly, but, when he asked whether there was any expiation possible for the crime of killing the embryo of a doe, the chief Sage of the hermitage answered evasively that, 'while Hariçcandra was king, no injury could happen to their hermitage' (603).

At that point a tumult arose, out of which was heard the voice of the Sage's daughter, Vañcanā. She wailed: 'O mother, if this doe of mine shall die, then I will starve myself to death!' And her mother in turn wailed: 'If you will starve yourself, then I will do likewise; bereft of you, life is of no use to me.' The Sage had the two women brought into his presence, and, with wily intent, asked Vañcanā why she was crying. In this manner he elicited from her the statement that she was crying over the loss of the doe, her play-fellow, raised by her from childhood. The Sage, now acting as if he did not know that the king was the offender, depicted in lurid colors, the misfortune that would befall his house thru the death of his daughter and his wife, as well as the loss of his spiritual sanctity. He then pretended to wonder whence such an unexpected calamity could have arisen during the rule of a king of the royal line of Ikṣvāku. The king, greatly dejected, exposed his guilt by asking what he should do: he could punish others, but not himself. The Sage hid his face in his garment of bark, excoriated the king with sharp invective, which he kept up even after the king offered to enter the fire, abandon the country, or take the vow (628). The Sage remained inexorable, but finally, at the suggestion of his pupil Añgāramukha, acting as his accomplice, prescribed that the king should make over to him his kingdom and all his possessions. The king consenting, the agreement was ratified in the presence of another pupil of the Sage, Kāuṭilya[34] by name, who had come from Benares (641). Even then Vañcanā pretended that she would enter the fire together with the doe, until the king bought her off with the promise of a lakh of gold. The king returned with train to his city of Ayodhyā (648).

Now the king's wise and trusty minister, Vasubhūti, hearing the whole story from Kuntala, guaged both the king's folly in making his promises, as well as the Sage's wile. He therefore told the king that he must not give up his kingdom, and make himself homeless. But the latter insisted on keeping his pact, and asked Vasubhūti to procure the lakh needful for the assuagement of Vañcanā. He did so. When the Sage arrived with Añgāramukha, the money was handed him. The Sage asked, 'What is that?' The king told him that it was the money for Vañcanā. The Sage refused to be paid from the king's treasury, because that meant paying him with his own money, since the king had previously given him all his possessions (669). The king, next, bade Vasubhūti procure from merchants a loan of the amount needed, but they, by the magic power of the Sage, had become hostile, and refused, on the ground that the Sage henceforth was their king. Even when he appealed to them in person, they persisted in refusing (678). A lengthy controversy arose between the king and Vasubhūti on the one side, and the Sage and Añgāramukha on the other side, in the course of which the latter two abused the king, charging him with breaking faith, and ruining his and his family's reputation. The king finally sent for the jewels of his Queen, Sutārā by name. She herself appeared on the

[34] The meaning of this name is 'Trickster.'

spot, and offered her jewelry, but the Sage refused, on the ground that her property also belonged to the king, and therefore to himself, so that it was not available to expunge the debt to Vañcanā. Kuntala then took a hand in these recriminations, accusing the two Brahmans of being Rākṣasas (ogres) in disguise. The Sage thereupon cursed him, so that he became a jackal, infesting cemeteries (707).

The king sought to soothe the Sage, but the Sage spurned him with his foot. Then Rohitāçva, the little son of the king, begged the Sage not to strike his father, but to take himself in payment. The Sage, moved to tears, whispered to Añgāramukha that his tear-choked throat was unable to make answer. But Añgāramukha advised him not to release the king. Hariçcandra then asked for a month's delay, within which he might obtain the money. The Sage asked whether he would beg the money; the king replied that a scion of the Ikṣvāku house might give alms, but could not beg for them. He explained further that he would sell himself in order to pay up (716). Then the king was acclaimed for his noble resolution by bystanding ascetics. Sutārā proposed to follow him into exile, clinging to her decision in the teeth of his and the Sage's remonstrances (724). In the end the Sage consented to the departure of Hariçcandra and Sutārā, on the condition that they leave behind all their possessions and jewels. Then Vasubhūti, outraged by the Sage's rapacity, called him a Brahmarākṣasa,[35] and was promptly punished by being turned into a parrot. The king, with wife and son, started on his journey, followed by the tearful people of his city, whom he finally dismissed with a voice softened by love (738).

[35] That is to say, in this connection, a Brahman ogre.

They traveled on the high-road, until Sutārā was worn out with fatigue. The king consoled her by pointing out that they were near Vārāṇasī (Benares), and bade her rest under a campaka tree on the shore of the Gaṅgā. While she was sitting there in sad thought, crying, with her head covered, Rohitāçva began to whimper for food. The king forgetfully cried out: 'Sirrah, give the child sweetmeats!' When no one responded, the child again cried. His mother grieved over the sad lot of a descendant of the imperial house of Bharata, while the king realized that he had fallen low indeed, when he no longer could give his child some breakfast. He entertained him, by pointing out the birds disporting themselves on the Gaṅgā, but, after a little, the boy again wailed: 'Daddy, I am very hungry!' It happened that an old woman came journeying along, carrying her provisions for the journey on her head. As she asked the way to the city, she observed that the family, notwithstanding their sorry plight, bore the marks of royalty. When Rohitāçva again begged his mother for food, the old woman offered some of hers. But the boy, keen set as he was, yet being the son of a courageously enduring man (sāttvikasya sutatvataḥ), refused. The king told her that he did not accept doles given in pity. Whereupon she went her way (762).

The king bade the queen rise, if she were over her fatigue, but she tried to discourage the journey, because Vārāṇasī belonged to an enemy. The king averred that he must somehow get the money for the Sage; Sutārā offered herself to be sold as a slave. The king replied that they must be sold altogether, if any were sold. Touchingly Rohitāçva begged his mother not to sell him, but to let him stay with her: he would do without sweetmeats. She consoled him by promising that he would become an emperor (cakravartin). They arrived at Benares, and went to the market-place. The king put grass on his head,[36] as a sign that he was there in the character of a slave. Again Rohitāçva was distressed; his father, to cheer him, promised him an elefant (778). After more sad reflections, the king proposed to Sutārā, that she and the child return to the house of her father, but the faithful wife refused to disgrace him: rather would she die, or become the slave of an enemy (786). A Brahman[37] came along, looking around for hired help. Attracted by Hariçcandra's form and presence, he asked him why he was demeaning himself as a menial. The king remained silent. The Brahman then surveyed Sutārā and Rohitaçvā; struck by their distinction, he blamed the Çāstras for their inaccurate characterization of the different classes of men. The king corrected him: the Çāstras speak truly; their state is due to fate (karma, dāiva). In the end the Brahman bought Sutārā at a price fixed by himself, five thousand gold pieces, with the stipulation that twice that sum should be her ransom. Rohitāçva persistently clung to his mother, so that the Brahman had to knock him down twice (804). But in the end he took pity, and, at Hariçcandra's suggestion, bought the boy also for a thousand. Then he went to his home with Sutārā and Rohitāçva (808).

At this juncture the Sage and his damned soul, or advocatus diaboli, Añgāramukha, appeared on the scene, to collect the debt due the Sage. The king offered what he had obtained from the sale of his wife and child, but the Sage angrily rejected it as not being enough. Añgāramukha suggested that he should go to King Candraçe-

[36] In the Caṇḍakāuçika 50. 2, when King Hariçcandra wishes to sell himself as a slave, the stage direction is çirasi tṛṇaṁ kṛtvā; see additional note 11, on p. 191.

[37] His name is given later on as Vajrahṛdaya, 'Stone-Heart.'

khara of Vārāṇasī, and ask for the money. Hariçcandra refused to beg money from an enemy: he would rather work as a Caṇḍāla, and pay from his earnings. Opportunely an old Niṣāda, Kāladaṇḍa by name, dressed in a loin-cloth, a staff in his hand, came along, and hired him as a watchman in a cemetery of which he had charge. He was to rifle the corpses of their garments, and save the half-burned faggots of the funeral-pyres. His pay was to be half-shares. The king agreed, stipulating that his share was to be paid to the Sage. The latter, hearing this arrangement, broke out in praise of the king's courage and faith. The king and Kāladaṇḍa went to their cemetery (828).

Now a pestilence suddenly broke out in that city of Vārāṇasī, which took off people by the thousand. The king called his minister Satyavasu in consultation. On the way to the king, he was addressed by a certain man, Kalahaṅsa, carrying a parrot in a cage. On inquiry, Kalahaṅsa said that he was bringing the parrot to king Candraçekhara, because the parrot was versed in all the Çāstras.[38] When the two were in the presence of the king, he complained of the pestilence, inexplicable, because both himself and his people were leading exemplary lives. He bade the minister find out its cause. Just then arrived a bawd (kuṭṭinī) [39] who had lost her 'daughter' by the pestilence. Beating her breast, she arraigned the king's character, as being the cause of the pestilence, and the death of her charming daughter, Anaṅgasundarī. The king, outraged by her cruel and false accusation, consulted the minister, who suggested the intervention of a mighty sorcerer that had come from Ujjayinī. The magi-

[38] See my paper, 'On Talking Birds in Hindu Fiction,' Festgruss an Ernst Windisch, pp. 349 ff.; and above, p. 77.

[39] See for this stock figure of fiction, the author in Proc. Amer. Philos. Soc. vol. lii, p. 631.

cian, cited, explained that the pestilence was due to the sport of a Rākṣasī (ogress) (845). At the request of the bawd he at once restored Anañgasundarī to life. The king still doubted the power of the sorcerer, until the latter boasted that he could bring Vāsuki from Pātāla;[40] Indra from heaven; or Lañkā (Ceylon) from the ocean. He then was given the materials for a great magic rite, by means of which he compelled the supposed Rākṣasī to fall down within his magic circle, where she lay still, the people shrinking away from her, as mice from a cat (855).

King Candraçekhara expressed admiration for the skill of the magician, who then pointed out that it was now the king's turn to perform his part by punishing the Rākṣasī. The king ordered the minister to call the executioner[41] (meaning Kāladaṇḍa). Instead, the minister called Kalahañsa, and, when he put down his cage, Candraçekhara asked what was in it. The minister answered: 'an omniscient parrot-king,' and bade the parrot sing the king's praise, which he did (862). The magician reminded the king of the punishment due to the Rākṣasī; just then Kāladaṇḍa (the executioner) arrived, followed by Hariçcandra. The parrot joyfully acclaimed Hariçcandra as king, but he angrily denied the allegation, and told the parrot not to talk nonsense. Then the minister told the executioner to uncover the Rākṣasī's face; he bade Hariçcandra do so. When the latter looked at her, he saw that she was his wife, queen Sutārā. Convinced as he was that she could not be a Rākṣasī,[42] he again

[40] The king of the serpents from his subterranean home.

[41] Here called çvapaca, 'dog-cook'; see the note on p. 59.

[42] Rākṣasīs often assume the form of beautiful women; consequently beautiful women are accused, justly or unjustly, of being Rākṣasīs; see Kathās. 32. 157; Kathākoça, pp. 106, 116, 153; Daçakumāracarita, ii, p. 38; Stokes, Indian Fairy Tales, pp. 5 ff. Cf. Tawney's note in his Translation of Kathāsaritsāgara, vol. ii, p. 631.

recognized the cruel hand of fate. Since he would neither acknowledge her guilt, nor divulge his true station in the justice hall of his enemy, he decided to await the decree of destiny. King Candraçekhara then spoke admiringly to his minister of Sutārā's beauty, whereupon the parrot hailed Sutārā as queen and daughter of Uçīnara. Candraçekhara thought him foolish or drunk, but the parrot insisted that he was right. Candraçekhara quizzed both Hariçcandra and Sutārā, but both continued to assert that they were what their stations showed them to be. After a consultation between the king and his minister, Hariçcandra was ordered to bring on an ass which Sutārā was made to ride.[43] Then the parrot, outraged, undertook to pass thru an ordeal to prove that Sutārā was a queen, and not a Rākṣasī. He was subjected to a fire-ordeal, from which he emerged unscathed. The assembled audience acclaimed Sutārā as a Satī (noble wife), and not a Rākṣasī; the magician was dismissed as an impostor; the parrot put back in his cage. After Sutārā had been released from the ass, Hariçcandra, by the order of the Caṇḍāla, returned to the cemetery, wondering at the part that the parrot had played in the unfolding of his destiny (902).

Hariçcandra entered the frightful cemetery, infested by foul animals, demons, and sorcerers, evil-smelling with the stench of corpses. There he heard wails, which sounded as tho they came from some woman who had lost her husband. He answered, asking the reason of her lament. She pointed to a noble man hanging head down upon a branch of a banyan tree. When he asked the man the cause of his evil plight, he turned out to be Mahāsena, son of Candraçekhara, carried off, together with his be-

[43] See additional note 9, on p. 188.

loved wife, by a Vidyādharī, who desired to institute a great sacrifice (mahāhoma) with the flesh of his body [44] (920). Just then the Vidyādharī had gone to bathe in the Gañgā. Hariçcandra, eager to die while performing a service to another, prevailed upon Mahāsena to escape with his wife, Hariçcandra acting as his substitute in the Vidyādharī's sacrifice. Joyfully he tied himself, face down, to the branch of the banyan tree (934). On her return the Vidyādharī asked a retainer to ascertain whether the sacrificial man bore auspicious marks. The retainer found that he bore the marks of an emperor (cakravartin). She then appealed to Hariçcandra to show courage, in order that the science 'All-conquering' (viçvavaçīkāravidyā),[45] accruing from this sacrifice, be kind and liberal to her. She began to cut off his flesh, but the sound of a jackal caused a disturbance. She asked her retainers to stop the noise, because it might arouse some ascetic. This actually happened, whereupon the Vidyādharī was greatly distressed. Hariçcandra suggested that she should finish by cutting off his head. But she replied that such a procedure would violate the order of the sacrifice. An ascetic then appeared, raging over the desecration of the hermitage, whereupon the Vidyādharī vanished with her retinue (954).

The ascetic, rummaging about, came upon Hariçcandra, hanging from the tree, his flesh cut from his body. From certain signs he was led to ask him whether he was Hariçcandra, and, when he said yes, he asked whether he had paid the debt owing the Sage. Hariçcandra replied that the payment would be complete in a few days. The ascetic turned out to be Kāutilya, the Sage's witness to

[44] See additional note 27, on p. 205.

[45] For these personified 'Sciences' see the author in Proc. Amer. Philos. Soc., vol. lvi, pp. 4 ff.

his contract with Hariçcandra. Kāuṭilya blamed him for lending himself to a sacrifice while in debt. Hariçcandra hung his head in shame. Then Kāuṭilya went home, after having cured him with herbs, lest he might die, and default on his debt. The king remained downcast, because he had neither paid his debt, nor aided the Vidyādharī in finishing her magic. While engaged in these reflections, he was ordered by his master, the Niṣāda, to take the garment off a corpse, which was then coming to the cemetery. The king learned from a lamenting woman that the corpse was that of her son, and found it not in his heart to snatch the garment off her boy. For this he was chided by the Niṣāda, who told him that there was no shame in doing this, since it was the custom of their caste (974). The woman continued her lament, until Hariçcandra gathered that she was Sutārā, and that the dead boy was his son Rohitāçva. Both father and mother grieved greatly. Sutārā explained that Rohitāçva had been sent into the forest to gather fagots and flowers, had been bitten by a snake, and had perished there for want of treatment (990). Tho he now knew that the corpse was that of his own and only son, and understood the agony of Sutārā over the loss of her only child, he asked her for the boy's garment, in order to fulfil his duty to his employer, the Niṣāda (1001).

Then a shower of flowers rained upon him from heaven, and his heroism was acclaimed to the beat of drums. All at once he found himself in Ayodhyā, upon his throne, with Rohitāçva playing in his lap, his minister Vasubhūti and his faithful Kuntala by his side, both in reverential attitude. And Sutārā was chatting with a friend, both having come to see a play (1007). In front of him was his assembly, citizens were engaged in festivities. As he gazed in bewilderment, wondering whether he was dreaming or mad, two gods, Candracūḍa and Maṇiprabha, told him that he was indeed a lucky mortal, whose courage was being acclaimed by Vāstoṣpati (Indra) himself before the heaven-dwelling gods (1014). That his noble soul had regained for him his kingdom; that Vasubhūti, in the body of the parrot, had proved the purity of Sutārā by passing thru the ordeal of fire; and that Kuntala, in the body of the jackal, had by his shriek, foiled the Vidyādharī's sacrifice, and thus saved him. That, moreover, the entire episode of his life, beginning with the boar adventure, had been a drama of illusion (kūṭanāṭakam). They then asked him to choose a gift, but all the king desired was, that his noble courage should continue with him. The two gods returned to heaven, and Hariçcandra continued to rule prosperously and piously (556-1033).

Frame Story: Conversion of Vajranābha and Kubera, and death of Vajranābha

The text returns to the frame story at the beginning of this sarga. The infidel Kubera was converted by the Sage Lokacandra's elaborate exposition of the four 'worldly virtues.' Kubera, furthermore, inquired after those virtues which reach beyond the world (lokottara). Lokacandra explained that the same worldly virtues, applied to the highest aims, constitute the virtues that reach beyond life (lokottarā guṇāḥ). At the end of the Sage's sermon on this theme, Kubera asked him to be his Guru (1048), and to instruct him on the four following points: choice of divinity; manner of worship; essential right (tattva); and the fruit accruing therefrom. The Guru told him that the Jina was the highest divinity, and expounded the manner of his worship; the nine essential rights, and their fruit (1069).

Prince Vajranābha, in the company of Kubera, returned to the city. His father, King Vajravīrya, made over to him his kingdom, and took the vow. Vajranābha, while ruling piously and righteously, was taken, in his turn, with misgivings as to the stability of the world and its allurements. He also decided to seek salvation. Notwithstanding the protest of his son Cakrāyudha, he appointed him his successor, and turned mendicant. He wandered to Sukacchavijaya. There the soul of the serpent (2.1048) had been reborn as a wild Bhilla[46] by name of Kurañgaka, who infested the mountain of Jvalana. Vajranābha went there and placed himself in kāyotsarga posture, fearless in the midst of the howls of elefants, jackals, Rākṣasas, and so on (100). Kurañgaka, out of prenatal hatred, hit Vajranābha with an arrow. Vajranābha, tho struck fatally, remained free from evil thought, remarking that he had been killed by the soul of the Bhilla in a former birth. He was reborn as the god Lalitāñga.[47] Kurañgaka, when he died, went to the Saptamāvani hell[48] (1034-1108).

---

[46] Sixth pre-birth of the future Meghamālin.—Bhilla is the designation of wild forest dwellers.

[47] Seventh pre-birth of the future Pārçva.

[48] Seventh pre-birth of the future Meghamālin.

Sarga the Fourth

Frame story: Story of the Emperor Suvarṇabāhu (with Çakuntalā motifs[1]*), and his death*

King Vajrabāhu of Surapura had a lovely and virtuous wife, named Sudarçanā. The soul of Vajranābha (of the previous sarga), in due time, fell from heaven, and entered the womb of Sudarçanā. The queen had the 'fourteen great dreams,'[2] which herald the birth of a Cakravartin (emperor). In due course she gave birth to a boy whom the king named Suvarṇabāhu[3] (15). He grew up so accomplished as to permit the king, who had become averse to the world, to take the vow, and to leave his kingdom in charge of his son. One day Suvarṇabāhu mounted an inversely trained horse,[4] which galloped off when checked by the rein. The horse did not stop until they came to a lake. After bathing in its clear waters, the king saw in front of him an ascetic's grove full of antelopes. His right eye twitched,[5] which encouraged him to enter the grove in joyous anticipation (32). There he saw a maiden, surrounded by companions, engaged in sprinkling creepers. The king thought her more beautiful than Rambhā[6]; she seemed the quintessence of the

[1] The story of Çakuntalā (Mahābh. 1. 69 ff.) is, occasionally, the prototype of love affairs between heroes and hermitage maidens. The present adventure is direct imitation. See also the story of Kadalīgarbhā, Kathās. 32. 99 ff., and the story of Ruru, Kathās. 14. 76 ff.

[2] See additional note 10, on p. 189.

[3] Eighth pre-birth of the future Pārçva.

[4] See additional note 26, on p. 204.

[5] A good omen. Very frequent motif; see, e. g. Samarādityasaṁkṣepa 5. 186, 289; 7. 374, 438.

[6] The loveliest of the Apsaras, or heavenly nymphs.

charms of Nāgas, Vidyādharas, and immortal women. While engaged in this thought, the maiden and a companion entered a bower of flowers. There she began to sprinkle a bakula-tree with her mouth, to the delight of its blossoms.[7] Ravished by her charms, the king reflected that she could not be an ordinary hermitage servitor, but must be of royal descent (39). Now a bee flew into the face of the maiden. She asked her companion to protect her, but received the reply, that this was King Suvarṇabāhu's business. Then the king showed himself, and asked who dared to injure her, while the son of Vajrabāhu was protector of the earth. The maidens remained silent. When the king again asked whether anything was disturbing their pious practices, the friend found courage to say, that during Suvarṇabāhu's rulership no one could do so; that a bee merely had disturbed her friend (47). Then she asked him who he was. Unwilling to declare himself, he pretended to belong to the king's retinue, commissioned by the king to protect the hermitage from intrusion. But the maiden knew him to be the king himself (52).

The king then asked who her mistress was. With a sigh she replied that her name was Padmā, the daughter of Ratnāvalī, the wife of the Vidyādhara king of Ratnapura. At his death his sons had quarreled,[8] the kingdom had been distracted; therefore Ratnāvalī had taken her young daughter to that hermitage, whose abbot was Ratnāvalī's brother Gālava (55). A soothsayer had

[7] Just as the açoka tree blossoms when touched by the foot of a young and lovely woman, so does the bakula tree blossom when sprinkled by the mouth of lovely femininity. The kadamba blossoms with the roar of the thunder. And day and night lotuses open their calyxes to the rays of sun and moon.

[8] See p. 16.

profesied that Padmā would be the wife of the Cakravartin Suvarṇabāhu,[9] carried there by a run-away horse. The king, recognizing the hand of destiny, asked to see the Sage. The maiden (whose name turned out to be Nandā) told him that the Sage had gone to pay his respects to another Muni, but would return on that day. Then an old nun told Nandā to go with Padmā to greet the Sage. Nandā reported to the Sage the king's arrival, whereupon he extoled the profet who had predicted it. Together with the ladies he went to do honor to the king, who received him with distinction. The Sage told him of the profesy, and the pair were wedded by the Gandharva rite of marriage (69).

Padmā's stepbrother, Padmottara, a Vidyādhara king, arrived, paid his respects to Suvarṇabāhu, and bade him follow him to the mountain of Vāitāḍhya, there to assume lordship over the Vidyādharas. The king consented. With Padmā he mounted the heaven-going chariot of the Vidyādhara. Padmā mourned her separation from her mother, the hermitage maidens, the gazelles, and the flowers she had been tending (80). Pointing out her glorious destiny, Ratnāvalī consoled her, bidding her live as an exemplar of wifely devotion. They arrived at the mountain of Vāitāḍhya, where Suvarṇabāhu was consecrated king of the Vidyādharas. After staying there for some time he returned to his own city (96). He acquired the fourteen great jewels,[10] celebrated the great festival (mahotsava) of eighteen days, and dispatched the wheel of sovereignty from his armory into the easterly direc-

[9] Predestined marriages, a cliché of Hindu fiction, recur in this text, 5 168; 8. 168.

[10] In Buddhist texts (Mahāvastu, p. 108 of Senart's edition); Mahāsudassana Sutta (Sacred Books of the East, xi. 251 ff.) seven 'jewels' of the Cakravartin are mentioned. So also Kathās. 101. 23.

tion. He cast an arrow which fell down before the king of Magadha, as he was sitting in his assembly hall. The king angrily took it up, but, when he read on it the name of Suvarṇabāhu, he went with presents in his hands to conciliate him. Suvarṇabāhu also conquered successively Varadāma and Prabhāsa, respectively the gods of the southern and western directions; Sindhu; the divinity of Vāitāḍhya; and other kings and divinities, so as to control the whole earth (116). Kings and gods then consecrated him emperor by the great consecration (mahābhiṣeka), which lasted twelve years, being performed with water from holy bathing places (tīrthas). He acquired sixty-four thousand wives; thirty-two thousand kings became his vassals. He had countless elefants, chariots, cities, and villages. Thus he ruled long in all the glamour of a Cakravartin (120).

One day, as he was sitting upon the roof of his palace, he heard of the arrival of Jagannātha, the Tīrthaṁkara (Savior). Removing his imperial insignia, he humbly went to greet him. After receiving instruction from him, he became enlightened, and decided to devote himself to salvation. He took the vow with Jagannātha, became an accomplished disciple (gītārtha), and continued to perfect himself still farther (144). Once, when he stood with a Jain image in the forest of Kṣīragiri, he was attacked by a lion, inhabited by the soul of the Bhilla Kuraṅgaka,[11] who had been reincarnated in the lion's body after leaving hell (see 3.1095 ff.). He died forgivingly; was reborn as a god in the Mahāprabhavimāna heaven[12]; but the lion, at his own death, went to the fourth-hell[13] (1-161).

---

[11] Eighth pre-birth of the future Meghamālin.

[12] Ninth and last pre-birth of the future Pārçva.

[13] Ninth pre-birth of the future Meghamālin.

Sarga the Fifth

Frame story: Early life of the Arhat Pārçvanātha

The soul of the lion (see 4.146), after passing thru wretched animal existences, was reincarnated as Kaṭha,[1] the son of a Brahman, named Rora. Both his parents died as soon as he was born, so that he had to be brought up by charity. As a grown man, he also carried on a miserable existence, wandering from house to house, shy and given to fear. One day, observing some rich men, resplendent in their finery, he became disgusted with life. Concluding that the rich owed their opulence to their penances in some previous existence, he decided to follow their example, turned ascetic, and subsisted on the roots of plants (8).

The soul of Suvarṇabāhu, on the other hand, was reincarnated in the womb of Vāmādevī, queen of the mighty Ikṣvāku king Açvasena of Vārāṇasī (Benares). The soul descended on the fourth day of the dark half of the month Cāitra, under the constellation Viçākhā. Fourteen great dreams of the queen,[2] here explained elaborately in a kind of key, or 'traumschlüssel,' announced to her the arrival of a glorious and virtuous son (37). At the end of an undisturbed period of pregnancy, the queen was delivered on the tenth day of the black half of the month Pāuṣa, under the constellation Viçākhā (43). All nature rejoiced at the event. The eight 'region maidens' (dikkumārī) of the lower world came on to acclaim the mother of the world, who had furnished the torch that

[1] Tenth and last pre-birth of the Kamatha soul, the future Meghamālin.

[2] See additional note 10, on p. 189.

would illumine the world, and prepared the festival of the birth of a Jina (55). The eight region maidens of the upper world showered flowers upon him. Other sets of eight divine maidens[3] each came from a different quarter to wait upon mother and son (68). Four region maidens from the island of Rucaka cut his navel-string,[4] buried it in a pit which they filled with jewels, and planted dūrvā-grass over it. Variously they continued to minister to mother and child, showering blessings upon them (77). A great tumult arose in heaven; the seats of the gods shook. Indra came from heaven; sang a hymn in praise of the mother; bestowed gifts upon mother and child. Hari, the thirty-three Vāsavas, the ten Vāimānikas, the thirty-two Vyantara lords, and other divinities[5] garlanded and bathed the child (96). Suras danced and sang about him, and performed other festal acts. Çakra, after performing sorcery for his good luck, praised him as the future Savior of the three worlds (112). Indra placed ambrosia into the thumb of the baby to suck,[6] and appointed five Apsaras as his nurses[7] (116). Other Vāsavas, coming from mount Meru, performed an eight day soma sacrifice to the eternal Arhats. Queen

[3] The names of these varieties of maidens are cataloged pedantically in sts. 51 ff.

[4] According to Kathākoça, p. 80, the day on which the navel-string is cut is auspicious.

[5] See for these classifications, Burgess, Indian Antiquary, xxx. 28; Hertel, Pariçiṣṭaparvan, pp. 14 ff.; Stevenson, Heart of Jainism, p. 181.

[6] In Mahābh. 3. 126. 31 Yuvanāçva begets a son out of his thigh. Indra gives the boy his first finger to suck; hence his name Māndhātar (= mām dhātar, 'self-sucker'). A different pun on this name, in Ralson, Tibetan Tales, p. 1; see the note there.

[7] In the Tibetan Tales a noble child is regularly handed over to eight nurses, two to carry him, two to suckle him, two to cleanse him, and two to play with him; see pp. 52, 273, 279. See also the descriptions in Jātakas 538 and 547.

Vāmā rejoiced in her son. The king, apprised of the happy event, had prisoners released in his honor. The people were jubilant. When the time for name giving had come, the queen remembered that she had seen in a troubled night a serpent moving by her side (pārçvataḥ). This she had told the king, who interpreted the serpent as the power of the boy; therefore he named him Pārçva [8] (126). He was petted by his nurses, the Apsaras, and sucked the ambrosia which Indra had put into his thumbs, whenever he was hungry. Young gods, in the shape of beasts and birds, sported for his delight (129).

He grew up with every youthful bodily perfection, because he possessed the twenty-two auspicious characteristics, so that all the accomplishments came to him of themselves. On reaching manhood his manly charms delighted numerous maidens (144). On a certain occasion a man, admitted to the audience hall of the king, reported that in Kuçasthala there had ruled a king Naravarman, who had taken the vow at the end of a glorious career, after having made over his kingdom to his son Prasenajit (155). The latter had an altogether perfect daughter, Prabhāvatī. She had once heard in the park a song in praise of Pārçva's perfections, since then had been beside herself with longing for him, and had been encouraged by her retinue in the hope that she would obtain him as her own (171). Prabhāvatī's parents had understood and approved of her feelings; Prasenajit, with a view to Pārçva, had decided to institute a svayaṁvara [9] (178).

[8] On name-giving by dream see note on p. 190. The name Pārçva thus means, 'Side.' In Vīracarita xxiii (Indische Studien xiv, 137) a pregnant woman sees a serpent and, therefore, begets a serpent.

[9] Ceremony by which a maiden of high caste chooses her own husband. She throws a garland over the man of her choice. The events just described echo the story of Nala and Damayantī.

But Yavana, king of Kaliñga, had been angered at the thought that Prabhāvatī should be given in marriage to any one but himself. He had therefore beleaguered Kuçasthala with a great host. The speaker himself, Puruṣottama, father of the minister Sāgaradatta, had been sent by Prasenajit to report these events to Açvasena, so that the latter might act accordingly (186).

On the strength of this report, Açvasena, being wroth, made preparations to go to the assistance of Prasenajit in Kuçasthala. When Pārçva heard of this, he promptly came out of his play-room; acknowledged his father's ability to prevail in war; but offered instead to gain the end in view by instructing Yavana (193). His father consented. Pārçva started with Puruṣottama and a great equipment. On the way Mātali, Indra's charioteer, at Indra's bidding, offered him Indra's car and his own services as charioteer. On arriving in Kuçasthala Pārçva dwelt in a seven-storied palace,[10] erected for him by the gods in the middle of a park. He sent an ambassador to announce to Yavana his peaceful mission, advising him to abandon the siege. But Yavana refused angrily; would not hear of either Pārçva or Açvasena; and threatened the ambassador with death at the hand of his soldiers (215). An old minister of his, however, warned them not to destroy the kingdom by attacking the ambassador of the holy Lord Pārçva. After they had desisted, he soothed the ambassador's wounded feelings by promising to do honor to Pārçva (221). The minister then urged Yavana to conciliate Pārçva: a contest with him would be like that of a spark with the sun; of a lion with a hare; of Garuḍa (Tārkṣya) with a crow; of the elefant with

[10] See note 8, on p. 46.

Kunthu.[11] He pointed out, moreover, that Indra's car with Mātali as charioteer was at Pārçva's disposal (227). Yavana saw the folly of his ways, tied an axe to his throat,[12] went submissively to the audience hall of Pārçva, and was received and dismissed forgivingly (239). When Prasenajit heard this he brought Prabhāvatī to be his happy bride. Pārçva said that he had come to act as his protector, and not to marry a maiden. Whereat Prabhāvatī was sorely grieved. Prasenajit proposed to join him on his return to Benares, and to interview his father. To this Pārçva consented; they returned to Benares and were received in state (1-254).

---

[11] Apparently a legendary allusion either to the 17th Jaina Arhat (Kalpasūtra 185 ff.); or to a Jaina Emperor (Cakrin) of that name. The Arhat Kunthu (Kunthunātha) is mentioned frequently in the Jain Aṅgas, as well as in ancillary writings; see Weber, Handschriftenverzeichnisse, vol. ii, Index, p. 1289; Indische Studien, xvi. p. 278, note 1; Stevenson, Heart of Jainism, pp. 56, 313.

[12] See additional note 11, on p. 191.

Sarga the Sixth

Frame story: Marriage and later life of the Arhat Pārçvanātha

King Açvasena rejoiced at the sight of Pārçva and Prabhāvatī, greeted Prasenajit, and inquired after his mission. Prasenajit, pointing out Prabhāvatī's love, asked that she be chosen as Pārçva's wife.[1] Açvasena replied that he shared his wish, but that Pārçva had grown averse to life and royal glory, and longed for nirvāṇa, so that he did not know what Pārçva might do. They both went to Pārçva, and stated their desire. Pārçva answered that eternal, and not perishable possessions were his desire; that, therefore, he wished to uproot the tree of existence. Açvasena agreed that such desire, of itself, spelled salvation, but asked that he should first fulfil his father's heart's desire, by founding a family (14). Pārçva consenting, festive preparations were made. Prabhāvatī was adorned in all the splendor of a royal bride (29). Pārçva, arrayed brilliantly, riding a white elefant, arrived at the marriage pavillion (34). The marriage took place; wedding gifts were bestowed; the people were entertained with sumptuous festivities; the bridal couple went to their house and passed their days in marital bliss (49).

Once, when the Lord was standing at a window of his palace, he noticed a great concourse of people. On inquiry, he found that they had come to do honor to the ascetic Kaṭha (see 5.1 ff.). Out of curiosity the Lord also went

[1] In Samarādityasaṁkṣepa 1. 5 Prabhāvatī is said to be Pārçva's mūrti, 'embodiment.'

to see, and found Kaṭha performing the severe five-fire penance (pañcāgnitapas [2]). And he saw that Kaṭha had thrown a great serpent into a fire-pan, which stood upon the fagots of his fire. He asked the reason for this pitiless practice, inconsistent with Kaṭha's own austerities. Kaṭha replied that kings understood only elefants and horses; that religion was understood by Sages alone (59. Pārçva ordered the fire put out; the agonized serpent came out; and the king made his people do honor (namaskāra) to him. Absorbing the essence of this worship, the serpent was reborn as Dharaṇa, the wealthy king of the Nāgas [3] (63). Kaṭha, on the other hand, as the result of his false practices, was reborn as an Asura (demon), by name of Meghamālin (68).

One day in spring Pārçva entered a palace in his park, and saw there, painted on a wall, the picture of Nemi, the Arhat, engaged in ascetic practice. Reflecting that Nemi had taken the vow in early life, he decided that he himself also would abandon the saṁsāra. The Sārasvatas and other divinities descended from the Heaven of Brahma, and encouraged him to save the world (77). At night, while lying on his bed in meditation, he decided to undertake the task of enlightening the world (83). In the morning, after informing his parents of his decision, he began to distribute alms, preparatory to his consecration (dīkṣā). He gave away enormous riches. The Vāsavas from heaven, and princes of the earth prepared his consecration. He shone like the wish-tree of heaven (kalpadru). He mounted a wonderful palankin, and, to the

[2] Consists of sitting between four fires, the sun as fifth burning down upon the head.

[3] See above, p. 19. For serpents, saved from danger, see Kathākoça, p. 87, and Tawney's note there. In each case, as in the sequel of the present story (see p. 118) they show gratitude.

songs and music of bards, acclaimed by the people of the city, went to a hermitage to enjoy the glories of renunciation (102). There the very plants and trees rejoiced over his presence. At the foot of an açoka-tree he renounced power and wealth, plucked out his hair,[4] and, at the age of thirty, obtained the knowledge due to mental perfection. Indra gathered five fistfuls of his plucked hair in his own robe, and threw them into the milk-ocean (110). Three hundred princes took the vow with him. Finally, after the gods, Asuras, and kings had left him, he remained behind in kāyotsarga posture (113).

On the next day he went to a place called Kopakaṭa, to obtain food in the house of a householder named Dhanya. He was received joyously, and given what he needed, to the applause of gods and men (120). Next he wandered, until he came into the forest of Kādambarī, at the foot of the Kaligiri mountain, and remained with a Jain image on the shore of lake Kuṇḍa. An elefant, named Mahīdhara, coming there to drink, remembered the events of his former life, in which he had been a householder, named Hemala. In the company of a friend, named Supratiṣṭha, he had taken the vow of Çrāvaka; had been mocked for his small body; had been angered thereby; had craved a large body, and therefore, had been reborn as a mountain-like elefant. Desiring now, tho an animal, to do honor to the Lord, he went into the lake and plucked lotuses which he placed at his feet (133). The gods arrived, worshiped the Lord with fragrant substances, and

Obligatory and universal practice of the Jaina Arhats and Yatis (monks); see Kalpasūtra in the lives of the Arhats; Kathākoça, pp. 85, 194; Jacobi, Ausgewählte Erzählungen in Māhārāṣṭrī, p. 38, l. 33; Daçakumāracarita i, p. 47. As Pārçva was first among the Jains to practice this form of austerity, he is known as Luñcitakeça 'Plucked-Head.' In Samarādityasaṁkṣepa 5. 576, gatakeça, 'hairless' is the designation of a Jaina monk. In explanation see, e. g., Stevenson, Heart of Jainism, p. 32.

joyously performed a mimic representation. The hermits of that region spoke of this occurrence to King Karakaṇḍu,[5] in Campā, who thereupon came to greet the Lord. The gods set up an image of the Lord which the king adored; he built for it an extensive cāitya. The image had the power to grant desires, and to remove untoward influences (139). The lake Kuṇḍa became a purifying tīrtha, assuming the name Kalikuṇḍa, because the mountain Kali was in its vicinity.[6] The elefant died piously in due time at that tīrtha, and was reborn as a wealthy miracle-performing Vyantara. Pārçvanātha then went to Çivapurī, and placed himself in kāyotsarga posture in the forest of Kāuçāmba. The serpent king Dharaṇa (see v. 63), remembering his former kindness, arrived there in great state to do him honor, and performed a mimic representation. During three days he held an umbrella over the Lord's head to protect him from the sun. From that time on the city there was called Ahichattrā ('Mushroom,' lit., Serpent's umbrella'). He then went to Rājapura, where King Īçvara came to do him honor. At the sight of the Lord the king remembered the events of a former birth, and narrated them to his minister (1-49):

Episode of the Brahman, Datta, who was afflicted with leprosy

In former days there lived in Çrīvasantapura a Brahman, Datta by name, skilled in omens and horoscopes. Having become afflicted with leprosy, he was despised by his family, and went to the Gañgā to die. As he was

[5] First of the four historic Pratyekabuddhas. For their history and literary belongings see Charpentier, Paccekabuddhageschichten, pp. 35 ff.

[6] kaleḥ kuṇḍasyāsannabhāvitvāt; see p. 22.

about to enter the water, a Vidyādhara Sage warned him that there was no profit in cutting the branch, but that he must cut the karma root of the tree of misfortune: 'Make the great elixir of the Jina take away every sickness!' When Datta asked what was that elixir, the Rishi replied: 'The five-fold vows, accompanied by perfection, and overthrow of mental blindness.' Datta was converted. One day he went into a cāitya and asked a Sage there, whether or not a person with his affliction was fit to worship the gods. The Sage replied that even ascetics worshiped the gods with bodies fouled by dirt. He then told him that he would be reborn as a cock. When Datta was distressed at this prospective misery, he consoled him by the promise that, after having fulfilled his karma, he would see a Sage in Rājagṛha, would remember his former birth, would then die from fasting, and ultimately become Īçvara, king in Rājapura. 'All this happened as predicted, and now, O Minister, I who came in this royal procession to do honor to Pārçvanātha, have remembered my former birth' (150-165).

Frame story: Life of Pārçvanātha, continued. Meghamālin's attack and conversion

Having worshiped Pārçva, Īcvara had a cāitya built on the spot where the Saint had been in kāyotsarga posture. In it he placed an image of the Saint. The cāitya then obtained the name Kukkuṭeçvara,[7] the city there being called Kukkuṭeçvara. The Lord then wandered again, surveying the earth, to find the place where dwelled the enemy Illusion. The Asura Meghamālin (formerly Kaṭha: see v. 68), prompted by his prenatal

[7] 'Cock-Īçvara, symbolizing the prenatal history of the king.

hostility, attacked Pārçva[8] with tigers, elefants, and scorpions, but, when the Lord showed no fright, they slunk off, as tho ashamed. Then the Asura tried to submerge him in the waters produced by a fearful thunderstorm, but the Lord did not budge from his place and from his pious meditations (90). The serpent king Dharaṇa found out, by avadhi insight,[9] that Kaṭha was attacking the Lord, went there with his divine wives, and placed lotuses at the feet of the Lord. By means of his seven hoods he fashioned an umbrella over his head;[10] the Lord stood there like a royal hansa bird, submerged in a deep trance (194). The wives of Dharaṇa honored him with songs and the music of instruments. But the Lord retained his equanimity in the face of both Dharaṇa's devotion and Kamaṭha's[11] attacks. Dharaṇa then excoriated Meghamālin's hatred of the Lord, pointing out that he had done him no injury, but, on the contrary, had saved him from the sin of burning him (Dharaṇa) on the occasion of his unholy practice (see p. 114). Meghamālin then repented, resorted to the Lord, and went home, determined to devote himself to piety (213).

Frame story: Life of Pārçvanātha, continued: Sermon on the fourfold dharma

Thereupon Pārçva went to his native city of Kāçi,[12] where he reached the state of Kevalin with all its supernatural powers. The thrones of the gods shook; they ac-

[8] Here called Çrīvāmeya, 'the holy son of Vāmā' (his mother).

[9] See for this term Tawney's Translation of Kathākoça, p. 241 note.

[10] Dharaṇa figures, alternately with Pārçvayakṣa, as the male attendant spirit of Pārçva. Jain sculptures show Pārçva regularly with seven cobras covering his head; see above, pp. 18 ff. A serpent king protects with his hoods Padumakumāra in Jātaka 472; cf. The Orientalist, vol. i, p. 146.

[11] The name Kamaṭha goes back to the first pre-birth of Meghamālin.

[12] Or Vārāṇasi, 'Benares.'

claimed him, showered marks of favor upon him, and built for him a magnificent resting place (242). Açvasena, his wife Vāmā, and Pārçva's wife, Prabhāvatī, went out to do him honor. Açvasena sang a hymn in his honor, after which he and his train encamped (257). Pārçva then preached on the banks of the Gañgā and Yamunā, pointing his sermon towards the fourfold dharma consisting of charity (dāna), virtue (çīla), asceticism (tapas), and character (bhāva).[13] Turning to the definition of charity, he established three kinds: giving of knowledge (jñānadāna); bestowing security from fear or danger (abhayadāna), and furnishing support to religion (dharmopaṣṭambhadāna). These he illustrated by stories, beginning with jñānadāna (166-279):

How Dhanamitra acquired respect for knowledge

King Jayanta of Rājapura had, by his wife Kamalāvatī, two sons, Vijaya and Candrasena, both virtuous. But, owing to sins in a former birth, they were unforgiving and intolerant towards one another. One day Jayanta received a letter from Kurudeva, a vassal king, stating that Sevāla, king of Sīmāla, was attacking his villages and disturbing the country. Jayanta appointed the older prince, Vijaya, to lead his troops against Sevāla, whereupon the younger, Candrasena, turned angrily from the palace. The king and his ministers remonstrated with him, pointing out that it would be improper to appoint him over the head of his older brother, but he remained sulky. Vijaya set forth, and, after trying to bring Sevāla to reason, was challenged by him. The

[13] The same four-fold division of the dharma is employed freely as the pivot of stories; see Hertel, Das Pañcatantra, p. 108. Cf. also Samarādityasaṁkṣepa 3. 156, 157; 7. 24, and Stevenson, Heart of Jainism, p. 229.

armies came to grips; Vijaya was defeated, and brought back by the ministers. Then Jayanta, about to go out to battle himself, was implored by Candrasena to intrust the command to him, which the king did. Candrasena conquered Sevāla, and was therefore appointed heir-apparent to the throne in place of Vijaya (312). Shamed by his disgrace, Vijaya wandered to a deserted city,[14] where he passed the night in a temple. In the morning he saw there a Sage who instructed him in the Law. In consequence thereof he took the vow, and received elaborate instructions on many points of religion. These led to the 'pentad of noble great vows' (sanmahāvrata-pañcakam), which is to be dealt with in the manner in which Rohiṇī managed her pañcaka-measure of rice. Vijaya then asked to be told the parable of Rohiṇī (280-388):

Parable showing how Rohiṇī managed her pañcaka of rice[15]

A merchant, Datta, desired to find out which of his four daughters-in-law was most fit to superintend his household. He gave them each a pañcaka of rice, and told them to manage it in such wise, that they could any time return the measure. The first daughter-in-law thought he was crazy, and threw the rice outside. The second thought it was sacrificial leavings, and ate it. The third kept the rice carefully. But the fourth, Rohiṇī,[16] sowed it, and made it multiply. After five years he asked for the rice to be returned. The first three daughters-in-law were assigned inferior duties,[17] but Rohiṇī was appointed mistress of the household (389-399).

[14] See note 15, on p. 51.

[15] For this parable of the talents cf. Kathākoça, p. 80.

[16] The name Rohiṇī seems to be chosen symbolically: it means 'Grower.'

[17] See Lexical Notes, under, ujjhikā, p. 228.

How Dhanamitra gained respect for knowledge, continued

'Just as the youngest wife obtained increase of her rice, and superiority over all her rivals, so, O prince, must the pentad of vows, by fitting conduct, be brought to increase!' Vijaya remained with the Guru, and engaged in study. After further instruction, the Guru installed him in his own position as teacher, went to the mountain of Sammeta, and there entered nirvāṇa. Vijaya obtained high distinction as a teacher, but grew tired of his profession, which merely dried up his throat. The elders encouraged him, but he insisted that ascetic practice, even without learning, constituted a Paṇḍit. He died unconfessed, and went to the Sāudharma heaven; fell thence; and was reborn in Padmapura as Dhanaçarman, the son of a merchant named Dhana (413). His father had him instructed, but, because he had sinfully despised knowledge in a previous birth, nothing stuck to him. The father, in distress, tried many devices to correct this, but nothing succeeded. One day he went with his son to a Sage to ask why his son was stupid. The Sage explained his son's plight, as due to contempt of knowledge in a previous birth. When Dhanaçarman heard this, he remembered his former existence, and, on the advice of the Sage, started to get learning by every effort. Again he died; was reborn as a god in Sāudharma; fell from that estate; and returned to earth as Dhanamitra. Once more he could retain no knowledge. However, as result of an unworldly life, he recollected his former existence, whereupon his aversion to knowledge fell away from him. He took the mendicant's vow. By constantly laboring to impart knowledge he himself obtained the knowledge of a Kevalin; used himself as an example to show the evil consequent upon contempt of knowledge; and thus led many people to perfection (400-438).

Story of the pardoned thief Vasanta[18]

Pārçva then turns to the exposition of the second of the charities, namely, the gift of security from fear or danger (abhayadāna: see v. 273), illustrating by story: King Druma of Vasantapura had five hundred wives, at their head the lovely Priyaṁkarā. It happened that a young thief was caught with his loot, and brought before the king. When the king quizzed him, he told that he was Vasantasena, son of the merchant Vasudatta in Vindhyapura. Spoiled in bringing up, he had become addicted to gambling, had committed many indiscretions, and had finally been driven from home by his father (458). He had then become a vagabond beggar, sleeping in empty temples, addicted to vice and gambling, and had finally found his way to that city. Seeing people enjoy themselves, he had been seized by a craving for pleasure, had committed theft, and been taken by the king's bailiffs: 'Do thou now, O king, decree the customary doom!' (463).

Tho moved by pity, the king condemned him to be impaled. Then queen Priyaṁkarā begged the king to lend her poor Vasanta[19] for one day, in order that she might satisfy his curiosity as to the pleasures of the saṁsāra. The king consented. She took him with her to her house;

[18] This story reappears in an inferior and briefer version in Samarādityasaṁkṣepa 9. 578 ff. It is analogous to Shakespeare's Prolog to Taming of the Shrew. The notion of royal power granted for a limited number of days appears in the present text 7. 426; Dhammapada Commentary 10. 9; 12. 4. Related with this theme is the idea of 'beggar on horse-back'; see Jātakas 241, 306.

[19] Vasantaka with intentional diminutive suffix; see p. 238.

had him bathed, clothed, and adorned most elaborately. She herself stood by his side, serving him with a great variety of dainty food (480). At the end of this feast he was placed upon a couch, and entertained with wonderful stories. Next, he was put upon a mettlesome horse, and led by a great retinue past the palace, to be exhibited before the king who stood at a window. In the evening he was housed in a dwelling outside the city, where he was entertained by the songs and blandishments of slave girls. In the morning he was put back into his former clothes; like a fallen flag, he was returned to the king who made him over to the executioner (492).

But now the second queen asked to entertain him for a day, and, in the same way, one after another, every queen of the court treated him with ever increasing luxury, rivaling with each other in these performances, so that he lived like a Dogundaga [20] god. And yet his soul was not satisfied (495). Now the last of the five hundred queens, Çīlamatī [21] by name, a sort of Cinderella wife, who was ordinarily too modest to importune the king for his favors, asked him to let her determine what was to be done to the thief. She then entertained him not at all sumptuously, but conferred upon him the gift of abhaya, freedom from fear, or safety. The thief, who had been dejected thruout his luxurious experiences with the other queens, now rejoiced more than tho he had obtained the suzerainty over the three worlds. In the morning the king observed that he was wearing a wholly different look from that of the preceding days. When asked the reason the thief said: 'When the word impalement had entered my ear like poison, all the world was empty for me. Food

[20] For this term see p. 226.

[21] 'Queen Virtuous.'

seemed offal; water, poison; the palace, the house of Yama (Pluto); the bed, like arrows; sandal, the ground-up body of my brother; my horse, an ass; my chair of state, an old winnowing-shovel; my jewels, chains; my necklace, a wreath of pots; my turban, a crown of thorns. My attendants seemed like lunatics; the soldiers, like executioners; music, like the confused beating of drums; and the poets seemed engaged in senseless shrieking. But to-day the world seems full to me, because the blessed Çīlamatī has conferred upon me the gift of abhaya' (520). The king thus became aware of Çīlamatī's superior character, showed her affection and made her chief queen. Vasanta also henceforth, by the king's favor, lived happily and prosperously; in due time he took the vow, died, and went to heaven (439-532).

Story of the four merchants' sons, and of Sundara [22]

Pārçva then turns to the exposition of dharmopaṣṭambhadāna, 'furnishing support to religion' (v. 273), by gifts to mendicants of food, shelter, medicine, clothes, and utensils, illustrating by story: During the rule of King Jayanara there lived in Jayapura four rich merchants' sons who were friends: Candra, Bhānu, Bhīma, and Kṛṣṇa. They lived in luxury on their parents, until they reached manhood. Then Candra bethought himself that the time had come to support himself; his friends fell in with his state of mind. They communicated with their parents, who warned them of the dangers of travel by sea and in strange lands. In the face of these warnings, and notwithstanding unfavorable omens, they started upon an expedition (563). A violent storm wrecked their ship, but Candra saved himself upon a plank.[23] Deeply de-

[22] The same story, with changed names in Kathākoça, pp. 70 ff.

[23] See note 13, on p. 49.

jected, because he had brought disaster upon his friends, he hanged himself upon a tree (568). A Sage cut him down, and told him that, if he really was tired of life, he had better make away with himself in the near-by holy bathing place (tīrtha) of Kāmuka. On the way there he heard a voice three times, saying, 'Act not in haste.' This, he discovered, came from another Sage, who bade him not to act like a woman; that only the living behold happiness. This he illustrated by the following story (533-575):

Story of the minister who found happiness after his wife's death [24]

Bhānu, minister of King Candrasena of Çrīmañgalapura, lived in great mutual affection with his wife Sarasvatī. One morning Sarasvatī rose dejectedly from bed, and, on pressure, explained that she had had a dream in which Bhānu had conversed with another woman. This came to the ear of the king who decided to make a test of Sarasvatī's devotion. He sent off Bhānu to Jayapura, and managed that a false report of Bhānu's death should reach Sarasvatī. She promptly died of a broken heart (586). The king, remorseful about his jest, fell at Bhānu's feet, and asked for a favor. When Bhānu granted it, the king told him that his wife had died in consequence of his practical joke, but that he, Bhānu, should not follow her to death. Bhānu granted the request, on the condition that the king should not ask him to marry again. Bhānu, on returning home, carried on a cult with his wife's bones, ever wailing and craving death,

[24] Hertel, Das Pañcatantra, pp. 140 ff.; reports this story as nr. 7 in the Gujarātī Pañcākhyānavārttikā, and as also occurring in Hemavijaya's Kathāratnākara.

but keeping himself alive, on account of his promise to the king (597). Finally, he decided to cast her bones into the Gañgā during his lifetime. There the daughter of the king of Benares, also Sarasvatī by name, heard him wail, asked his story, and, on hearing it, fell into a faint. Restored by her companions, she told the king, who had been cited to the spot, that she had remembered her former existence, in which Bhānu had been her husband. The king married her to Bhānu, and they lived together in happiness (605). Later on the king took the vow, leaving Bhānu to rule in his stead. Suddenly Sarasvatī sickened of an incurable fever. Bhānu, in despair, went to the seventh story of the palace [25] to cast himself down. A Cāraṇa Sage, wandering over the heavens, stopped him, and advised him to resort to the dharma and the Jina. Bhānu blissfully consented; went with the Sage to Sarasvatī's bedside; she was cured, and also converted. They lived in royal splendor, until they took the vow, making over the kingdom to their son (576-619).

Story of the four merchants' sons, continued

The Sage who was instructing Candra then continued: 'Now I am Bhānu; desist, O Candra, from suicide thru ignorance!' Candra asked how he was to get over his grief for the loss of his wealth and friends. Bhānu recommended the (fivefold) obeisance to the Lord, warned him against the desire of having things too much his own way (atilāulya), illustrating by two parables (619-629):

[25] See note 8, on p. 46.

Parable of the golden peacock feather [26]

A certain person, by the favor of a Yakṣa, is permitted to pick up a golden feather every day as it falls from the plumage of a golden peacock. Not content with this slow process of accumulation, he foolishly captures the peacock, only to find him like any other peacock. On coming home, his feathers are ordinary feathers, whereat he is sorely grieved (630-634).

Parable of the monkey-pair who became human [27]

A fond pair of monkeys arrive at the holy bathing-place Prapāta, on the side of which they climb a tree. The tree being very shaky, they tumble into the water, and come out a lovely pair of human beings. The male, surprised and delighted, proposes to his mate to try another fall, on the chance that they should become immortal gods. The wise female warns him against excessive greed, but he tries the fall, turning again into a monkey. She goes off with a Vidyādhara (635-640).

Story of the four merchants' sons, continued

The Muni then bade Candra remain content, whereupon Candra went to Puṣpapura, where he prospered greatly. One by one his three friends turned up; they

[26] A secondary, rather illogical version of this story in Jātaka 136. The idea of birds yielding gold is as old as Mahābh. 2. 62. Cf. Benfey, Das Pañcatantra, i. 378.

[27] Cf. Pārçva 7. 452 ff.; Pariçiṣṭaparvan 2. 407 ff.; Kathākoça, p. 50; Kathāprakāça, in Gurupūjākāumudī, p. 122; Prabandhacintāmaṇi, p. 283; Pañcākhyānavārttikā nr. 37, reproduced by Hertel, Das Pañcatantra, p. 150. Leumann, in Hertel's Translation of Pariçiṣṭaparvan, p. 234, cites Kalpabhāṣya Pedhiyā 283, and Jinabhadragaṇin's Viçeṣāvaçyaka Bhāṣya i. 862. Cf. also Samarādityasaṁkṣepa 2. 173 ff.

also prospered under his instruction. Candra and Bhānu were by nature upright and kind; the other two rather tricky. In time they were possessed with a longing to return home. They crossed the sea, and traveled by caravan. Meeting at a village a Sage who had fasted a month, they appointed a menial, named Sundara, to see to his feeding. Sundara was greatly rejoiced at the chance to perform a deed so holy:[28] the benefit of this act accrued to all, but especially to Sundara himself (660). In due time the four were reborn as divinities among the Jyotiṣkumāra gods. Candra and Bhānu fell from that estate, and became sons of rich merchants, named Çrīvardhana and Manorama; Bhīma and Kṛṣṇa also fell, and were born as Sundarī and Rukmiṇī, daughters of a rich merchant.[29] The two men married the two women and lived with them in great affection. The soul of Sundara was reborn as Viçvasena, king in Viçvapura (666). The two merchants undertook a trade expedition to Viçvapura, and there waited upon Viçvasena. On account of their prenatal love for one another, he received them kindly. Together they went to pay their respects to a Sage, who instructed them by a sermon, leading up to the exposition of samatā or sāmya ('equipoise,' or 'equanimity'), illustrated by the following story (641-690):

[28] Cf. my paper, 'The Character and Adventures of Mūladeva,' Proc. Amer. Philosoph. Soc., vol. lii, p. 643, bottom. Especially in Jain and Buddhist literature, such an act is performed frankly for the reward that is sure to follow; see Prabandhacintāmaṇi, p. 24; Kathākoça, pp. 53, 60, 64, 79, 181; Pārçva 7. 29; Jātakas 307, 415; Dhammapada Commentary 17. 3; 24. 12. Cf. the legend in Stevenson, Heart of Jainism, p. 219. Kathās. 27. 95 illustrates the same feeling in Brahmanical fiction; cf. the story of Puṇyabala, Benfey, Pañcatantra, ii. 537. Contrariwise forgetfulness, after promise, to break the fast of an ascetic (pāraṇā) is regarded as a great sin: see Çatruṁjaya Māhātmyam (Indian Antiquary xxx. 297); Pradyumnasūri's Samarādityasaṁkṣepa 1. 109 ff.

[29] They are born as women in allusion to their defective character, above.

Story of the girl who died because she had four wooers [30]

Nandā, lovely daughter of the merchant Candana in Çrīpura, was promised in marriage by four of her relatives to four different men. When they came severally to marry her, they got into a quarrel, whereupon Nandā, in order to remove its cause, entered the fire. One wooer entered the fire with her; the second, disgusted with life, wandered to a distance; the third took her bones, and started for a holy bathing place to dispose of them there; the fourth built a mound [31] over what was left of her. Then he went to the city to beg alms, which he deposited there, watching over the mound by day and night (705). The wooer who had gone abroad managed to acquire the magic art called 'Resuscitation' (saṁjīvinī), returned with it, and joyously restored Nandā to life. Now a dispute arose, as to which of the four wooers was entitled to Nandā. A wise man decided, that he who had taken her bones to the holy bathing place was her son; that he who had restored her to life was her father; that he who died with her was her brother; but, that he who had fed her was her husband (712). The text then strains to draw the parallel: just as support by food is the essential need in marriage, so equipoise is essential for salvation (691-717).

[30] This is the second story of Vetālapañcaviṅçati; Kathās. 76; Baitāl Pachīsī (Oesterley, pp. 39, 183); Lakṣmīvallabha in his Commentary to Uttarādhyayana Sūtra (translated by Charpentier, Paccekabuddhageschichten, p. 125). Hertel, Das Pañcatantra, p. 108, note 7, reports the story also from the Dharmakalpadruma. A very interesting variant, in Jülg, Mongolische Märchen, p. 235; cf. Benfey, Das Pañcatantra, p. 490; Kleinere Schriften, vol. ii, p. 233. The story has also passed into folk-lore; see Parker, Village Folk-Tales of Ceylon, vol. i, p. 378, and the note at the end.

[31] sthaṇḍilaka. In Kathākoça, p. 105, a sthaṇḍila is made in the place of burial.

Story of the four merchants' sons, concluded

After listening to further instruction from the Sage, King Viçvasena (formerly Sundara) asked why he felt so great a love for the two merchants. The Sage narrated the events of the four merchants' sons' lives, as well as that of Sundara himself. In the end they all took the vow, became gods, and will, in due time, obtain the station of Siddhas, or 'Enlightened' (718-732).

Frame story: Pārçvanātha continues his sermon on dharma

Having concluded his exposition of the threefold dāna, Pārçva turns to the second branch of the dharma, namely çīla, or 'virtue' (see 6.272), which he subdivides and classifies, especially with regard to its application to ascetics (yati) on the one hand (ten vratas), and to householders (gṛhin) on the other (twelve vratas) [32] (767). He then turns to that highest virtue which even the gods find difficult to observe, namely bramharūpa, or avoidance of illicit attachment to those who belong to others. This he illustrates by the following story (732-772):

Story of Madanarekhā and her son Nami. David and Uriah [33]

In the city of Sudarçana, in the land of Avanti, ruled a king Maṇiratha; he had a younger brother Yugabāhu. Yugabāhu had a wife, Madanarekhā, beautiful and vir-

[32] Cf. Stevenson, Heart of Jainism, pp. 205 ff.

[33] A fine Prākrit version of this story, in Jacobi's Ausgewählte Erzählungen, pp. 41 ff.; also Kathākoça, pp. 18 ff. A variant of part of the same theme in Kathākoça, pp. 14 ff. According to Leumann, in a note to Taw-

tuous. Maṇiratha became infatuated with Madanarekhā's beauty, sent her flowers, betel, and so on, but she took them as signs of kindness on the part of an elder brother. Then he sent a female messenger to ask her to be, as his wife, queen of the realm. She rejected his addresses, warned him that hankering after strange women led to hell, and bade him relinquish his wicked lust (787). The prurient king, realizing that, as long as his brother was alive, Madanarekhā would not consent, looked for a chance to kill him.[34] (791). One night Madanarekhā dreamt of the moon,[35] and was told by her husband that she would beget a brilliant son. It was in the spring of the seasons that Yugabāhu went one day with Madanarekhā, in pregnant condition, to a park to witness the sports of the townspeople. At night he retired to an arbor of kadalī-trees, protected by a small guard (807).

Then Maṇiratha, sword in hand, asked the guard where his brother was, pretending that he wished to protect him in the wood. Maṇiratha entered the arbor, and, when Yugabāhu rose up excitedly, told him to come to the city, because it was not advisable to remain there. Thereupon Maṇiratha smote him on the shoulder, so that he fell in a faint to the ground. Madanarekhā cried out in horror: 'Alas, an unknightly deed'; Yugabāhu's guard came running to the spot. The king pretended that he had carelessly let his sword fall out of his hand (815), but the guards, understanding the whole proceedings, took the king away to the palace by force. The facts were told to Yugabāhu's son, Candrayaças, who, in great distress,

ney's Translation of Kathākoça, p. 236, a version of this story is contained in the commentary on Avaçyaka-Niryukti 17. 45. For its literary connections see Charpentier, Paccekabuddhageschichten, pp. 84 ff.

[34] See additional note 28, on p. 206.

[35] See additional note 10, on p. 189.

hurried with physicians to attend to his father's wounds Madanarekhā perceived the symptoms of death, went close to Yugabāhu's ear, and in a soft voice instructed her moribund husband. With impressive speech she bade him die in peace and forgiveness, and to resort to the religion of the Jina. The fire of Yugabāhu's anger was quenched by the nectar of Madanarekhā's words; he died, thinking pure thoughts, and became a god in the world of Brahma (855).

Madanarekhā, afraid that the king, in his unbridled passion, would seize her and slay her child, wandered away into the forest, where she lived upon fruits and water. In the middle of the night she gave birth to a son, endowed with auspicious marks. In the morning she placed in the hand of her babe a seal marked with the name of Yugabāhu, wrapped him up in a jeweled shawl, left him there in an arbor of plantains, and then went to a lake to wash her clothes. While she was bathing there, she was tossed up in the air by a water-elefant.[36] As she was falling from the sky, she was intercepted by a Vidyādhara youth, who was on his way to the island of Nandīçvara. Bewildered by her beauty he took her to the Vāitāḍhya mountain. She cried pitifully, told him what had happened, and begged him to rescue her child, who was in danger of being killed by wild beasts, or perishing from hunger. The Vidyādhara agreed, on condition that she should accept him as her husband (872). He explained that he was Maṇiprabha, the son of Maṇicūḍa, a Vidyādhara king in the city of Ratnāvaha. His father had taken the vow, had gone as a hermit to the island of Nandīçvara, and had placed him on the throne. Moreover, her son had been discovered in the forest by Padmaratha, king of

[36] jalabha: for this interesting new word see p. 225 bottom.

Mithilā, who had been run away with by his horse.[37] He had taken the boy, and given him to his wife Puṣpamālā, who was cherishing him as her son. All that he had learned from the Science called Prajñapti ('Prescience').[38] Now she should kindly adorn his throne (879).

The queen, anxious to preserve her vows to her dead husband,[39] sparred for time. She asked the Vidyādhara to allow her to make a pilgrimage to Nandīçvara, after which she would comply with his desire. Together they worshiped there the images of the eternal Arhats, Ṛṣabha, Candrānana, Vāriṣeṇa, and Vardhamāna. They then paid reverence to the Sage Maṇicūda,[40] who instructed them in religion to such purpose, that Maṇiprabha declared himself thenceforth the brother and servant of Madanarekhā. Madanarekhā asked the hermit for tidings of her son. He related that, 'long ago there were two princes who died and became gods. One of them fell and became king Padmaratha; the other became your son. Padmaratha, when run away with by his horse, found your son, and gave him to his wife Puṣpamālā, on account of his love for him in his former existence. He is living happily in Mithilā' (897).

While the hermit was telling this there arrived a god in great state. He first circumambulated Madanarekhā to the right three times,[41] and bowed down before her;

[37] See additional note 26, on p. 204.

[38] See the author in Proc. Amer. Philos. Soc. vol. lvi. pp. 4 ff.

[39] As satī, or devoted wife.

[40] Maṇiprabha's father.

[41] This ethnic practice, Latin dextratio, Celtic deaiul, famous in Hindu ritual, is also a standard mode of showing honor in fiction; see this text, 6. 997; Kathās. 14. 30; 15. 137; 43. 214; 63. 83; 100. 54; 106. 84; 107. 126; Daçakumāracarita i, p. 37; ii, p. 1; Jātakas 193, 251, 276, 457; Kathākoça, pp. 23, 27; Jacobi, Ausgewählte Erzählungen aus dem Māhārāṣṭrī, pp. 14,

after that he did reverence to the hermit and sat in front of him. Maṇiprabha considered his behavior out of place, but the Sage explained that the god was the soul of Yugabāhu become god in the fifth Kalpa; that Madanarekhā had made Yugabāhu's peace with everyone when he was at the point of death; that, therefore, Madanarekhā stood in the relation of religious instructor to this god. The god then asked Madanarekhā what he might do to please her, and she asked him to take her to Mithilā, that she might behold the face of her son; after that she would devote herself to religious works (914). The god took her to Mithilā, where they met a holy woman in a neighboring nunnery, who preached to them the true religion. When the god offered to take Madanarekhā to the palace to see her son, she answered that there was no profit in natural affection, the cause of saṁsāra, and that she would take refuge with the feet of the holy women living there. The god then returned to heaven. Madanarekhā took the vow, received the name of Suvratā, and commenced a course of austere asceticism (921).

By the power of her son all princes were made subject to Padmaratha, who, therefore, bestowed upon him the name Nami.[42] When he had grown up, Padmaratha married him to 1008 wives; he himself, after destroying his karma by severe penance, went to bliss. After that, Nami, having subdued all kings, ruled the realm. Now in the very night in which Maṇiratha killed his own brother Yugabāhu, he was bitten by a serpent and went to the fourth hell. He was succeeded by Candrayaças,

l. 18 (tippayāhiṇam = tripradakṣiṇam); 45, l. 15; Pariçiṣṭaparvan 2. 44. See Tawney's notes to his Translation of Kathāsaritsāgara, vol. i, pp. 98, 573; vol. ii, pp. 365, note, 629.

[42] There is untranslatable pun here: 'subjected' is nata, from the root nam; Nami is construed as 'subjector.'

Yugabāhu's son. It happened that one of king Nami's elefants tore out his hitch-post and started for the Vindhya forest. He was caught and tamed by king Candrayaças. Nami, hearing of this, sent an envoy to Candrayaças, demanding his property, but his request was rejected haughtily. Thereupon he laid siege to Sudarçana, Candrayaças' capital city (936).

The nun Suvratā, mother of both kings, came upon the field, and was received with distinction by Nami. After pointing out the futility of war in general, she divulged to him that he was battling against his own brother, and that she herself was his mother. Suvratā next went to Candrayaças and told him the same history. Both brothers hastened to meet one another in mutual love; Candrayaças resigned his kingdom to his younger brother, and Nami's royal splendor blazed like the sun (958).

It happened that king Nami contracted a fever that lasted six months. When all expedients of the doctors had failed, the queens themselves began to pound sandalwood [43] for his benefit. The tinkling of their bracelets annoyed the king, so that, by his order, the queens took off their bracelets one after another, but each left one bracelet on her wrist for luck. The king then, no longer hearing the sound, inquired whether the queens had stopped pounding sandal. The ministers explained that they were still pounding, but that no sound came from a single bracelet. From this the king saw a light, namely, that the solitary state is bliss.[44] When he had recovered from his fever, he placed his son on the throne, and took the vow. Indra, wishing to tempt Nami, stood before him

[43] Sandal is proverbially cooling.

[44] Nami is one of the four traditional Pratyekabuddhas; see the note on p. 116.

in the guise of a Brahman, and said: 'King, show compassion to living creatures. This city, without you, laments for its ruler.' The hermit answered: 'Mankind receive the fruit of their own individual actions; so I attend to my own business.' The Brahman next said: 'The city of Mithilā is in flames.' The hermit answered: 'In the burning of the city of Mithilā nothing of mine burns.' The Brahman said: 'Set up a rampart round the city.' The hermit said: 'Round the city of self-control I have set up the rampart of soul peace, and mounted on it the engine of prudence.' Indra tried still other lures, but, when the Sage remained firm in his resolve, he praised and circumambulated him thrice to the right,[45] and flew up to heaven. The Sage attained to bliss, and his mother Madanarekhā reached the state of purity (773-998).

Story of the Cakravartin Sanatkumāra.[46]

Pārçva then turns to the exposition of the third item of the dharma, namely tapas, 'asceticism,' illustrating by the story of the Emperor Sanatkumāra: In the land of Bharata, in the district of the Kurus, in the city of Hastināgapura, ruled king Açvasena, together with his beloved queen Sahadevī. A prince, Sanatkumāra, endowed with all good characteristics, was born to them, after he had been announced to his mother by the four-

[45] See note 41, on p. 133.

[46] A Prākrit version, in Jacobi, Ausgewählte Erzählungen in Māhārāṣṭrī, pp. 20 ff.; a Sanskrit version in Kathākoça, pp. 31 ff.; and in Lakṣmīvallabha's commentary on the Uttarādhyayana-Sūtra, pp. 522 ff. This story is told by itself, as 'Sanatcumāra Cadha,' digested in Taylor's Catalogue Raisonné, vol. iii, p. 248 ff. Cf. Stevenson, Heart of Jainism, p. 159. A different story of Sanatkumāra's Cakravartinship is told in Samarādityasaṁkṣepa 5. 28 f.

teen great dreams.[47] He was brought up in the company of a boy named Mahendrasiṅha, with whom he played in the sand.[48] After he had grown to manhood, the prince, one spring day, mounted a noble horse, named Abdhikallola,[49] which flew up in the air. The king went out to search for his son, but did not find him. Then Mahendrasiṅha told the king to desist from the search, and himself started to look for his friend. After roaming in a great forest during a year, he heard one day the sound of cranes, and, going forward, perceived Sanatkumāra recreating in the company of ladies on the shore of a lake. At the same time a bard was singing a verse in glowing praise of the prince. Mahendrasiṅha went to meet him, and there was great joy on both sides. Sanatkumāra asked his friend how he had come there; inquired after his parents; and, finally, Mahendrasiṅha asked to be told the prince's adventures (1039).

Prince Sanatkumāra said that he did not think it becoming in him to narrate his own exploits. So he called his Vidyādharī wife Bakulamatī, and, alleging that he was overcome by sleep, requested her to enlighten his friend. She told how the horse, which had carried off Sanatkumāra, had entered a great forest, had galloped unchecked, until, on the third day, it fell down exhausted with hunger and thirst. The prince wandered about in search of water, until he fell senseless under a saptachada tree. A Yakṣa sprinkled him with water from lake Mānasa, and, at his request, took him to that lake to bathe and drink. While siting on the shore there, he was seen

[47] See additional note 10, on p. 189.

[48] pāṅsukrīḍitaḥ: our 'making mud pies together,' standard expression for boy friends; see the author in Proc. Amer. Philos. Soc. lii, p. 616, note 3.

[49] In the Prākrit version, p. 20, l. 20, the name of this horse is Jalahikallola.

by another Yakṣa, named Asitākṣa, who had been his enemy in a former birth. Mahendrasiṅha asked what was the cause of the enmity between the prince and the Yaksa. Bakulamatī narrated (1056):

Previous births of Sanatkumāra and the Yaksa Asita[50]

King Vikramayaças of Kāñcanapura had five hundred lovely wives. In the same city lived a merchant, Nāgadatta, who had one exceedingly beautiful wife, Viṣṇuçrī. One day, the king saw her, succumbed to her fascinations, and took possession of her as a member of his harem. Nāgadatta wandered about in despair, calling her with endearing names, while the king, deeming himself lucky, passed his days in degraded satisfaction. But the queens, tortured by jealousy, slew Viṣṇuçrī by sorcery, and now the king was exceedingly grieved. He would not permit his ministers to perform funeral rites over her body, so they cast her body into a park outside the city. The king continued to abstain from eating and drinking, until they took him, on the third day, to the park, and showed him the cadaver of Viṣṇuçrī, overrun by worms, dripping with putrefaction, eyes picked by crows, infested by birds of prey, and smelling foully. The king became averse to the world, and took vows with a teacher, Sudharma. Having performed severe asceticism, he was reborn in the third Kalpa, fell thence, and was born again in Ratnapura as Jinadharma, the son of a merchant. In the meantime Nāgadatta had died from grief, passed thru many animal existences, and finally was born in Siṅhapura, as the Brahman Agniçarman. As wandering, three-staved[51]

[50] See p. 13, and the additional note 28, on p. 206.

[51] tridaṇḍin, 'carrying a bunch of three staffs'; see Tawney, Kathākoça, p. 33, note; Hertel, Pariçiṣṭaparvan, p. 189.

ascetic, he reached the city of Ratnapura. There he was invited by king Naravāhana to break his fast. It happened at this very time that the merchant Jinadharma came there, and was seen by Agniçarman. Remembering his enmity in a former life, he said to the king: 'Sire, if I may be allowed to eat a hot pudding off the back of this merchant, I will break my fast, but not otherwise.' After some remonstrance the king consented, out of regard for the ascetic. When the meal was finished the dish was wrenched from the merchant's back, together with blood, sinews, fat, and flesh. The victim bore patiently the fruit of his actions in a former life, turned ascetic, and was reborn as the god Indra in the Sāudharma heaven. The three-staved ascetic also died, and was reborn as Airāvaṇa, Indra's elefant. Both fell from their stations, Airāvaṇa was reborn as the impious Yakṣa Asitākṣa; Indra as the prince Sanatkumāra. This is the cause of their enmity (1091).

Story of the Cakravartin Sanatkumāra, concluded

Then a terrific conflict arose between the Yakṣa and Sanatkumāra, in which the Yakṣa not only employed weapons, but also the elements and demons. But, after many indecisive bouts, Sanatkumāra finally felled the Yakṣa with a blow of his fist. Tho smashed into a hundred pieces, the Yakṣa, being immortal, did not die, but fled. Gods and Vidyādharas in heaven shouted the victory cry, and rained a shower of flowers upon the hero (1104).

Afterwards Sanatkumāra proceeded to the forest Nandana, saw there the eight daughters of the Vidyādhara King Bhānuvega, and was conducted by them to their city of Priyaṁgamā. The prince was received by Bhānuvega, who told him that a Sage had predicted that the conqueror of Asitākṣa would become the husband of his eight daughters. Sanatkumāra married the eight. Later on he freed a captive princess, Sunandā from the thrall of a Vidyādhara, named Vajravega, and married both her, as well as Sandhyāvalī, the sister of that Vidyādhara. After that he engaged in a great conflict with the Vidyādhara king Açanivega, slew him, and wrested from him his royal fortune. He married yet a hundred more Vidyādhara maidens, and thus accumulated 110 wives (1168). After that he went to his native city of Hastināgapura, and ruled there as Cakrin, or emperor (1175).

At that time a god, named Saṁgama, came from the heaven of Īçāna to the court of Indra in the Sāudharma heaven. Saṁgama's lustre outshone the gods there, as the sun outshines the moon and the stars. The gods asked Indra, whether there existed any other god as lustrous as he, and Indra answered, that Sanatkumāra in Hastināgapura outshone even the gods. The two gods, Vijaya and Vāijayanta, went to the presence of Sanatkumāra,[52] while he was engaged in anointing himself, and found that his beauty exceeded even Indra's description. Sanatkumāra bade them wait, went to make an elaborate toilet, and then exhibited himself once more in all his still greater royal splendor. But then they appeared dejected and said: 'Alas, that all this perfection of beauty, brilliance, and youth of men should be seen one moment, and then vanish!' They went away. The emperor, in astonishment, looked at his bedizened two arms, and found that they had grown dim; looked upon his breast, hung with necklaces, and saw that it had become unbeautiful.

[52] Cf. for this part of the story, Leumann, Die Avaçyaka-Erzählungen, pp. 34-36, in the Abhandlungen für die Kunde des Morgenlandes, vol. x, nr. 2. For Western parallels see J. J. Meyer, Hindu Tales, p. 88, note.

He exclaimed: 'Alas, in the world all is perishable: beauty, youth, and brilliance; no one craves a pudding mixed with poison.' He placed his imperial diadem upon his son, took the vow with the Guru Vinayaṁdhara, and wandered forth into homelessness. His people followed him on his way for six months, but he did not look upon them even with a lion's glance[53] (1213).

It came to pass that, after a fast of two days and a half, he was given porridge with goat's buttermilk, after which he fasted again for two days and a half. Owing to this regimen he was afflicted by seven diseases: scab, fever, cough, asthma, nausea,[54] opthalmia, and pain in the body, which he bore for seven hundred years, while performing the severest austerities. Owing to this, he obtained the power to cure diseases, but, even thus, he did not apply any remedy to his own body. Again he was praised by Indra in Sāudharma, and the same two gods (Vijaya and Vāijayanta), having assumed the guise of two Çabara physicians,[55] went before him, and offered to remove his diseases. Then he rubbed his finger with his spittle, and made it bright as gold,[56] and said: 'Ah, if you are true doctors, then do ye quickly cure the disease whose name is Saṁsāra.' They replied, that the deep-seated disease Saṁsāra they could not cure; that he him-

[53] siṅhāvalokana, 'the lion's backward look.'

[54] annāruci: Kathākoça, p. 36, reads annāruci; the Prākrit version bhattachando. The last two seem to mean the opposite, namely, 'morbid appetite.' But Prākrit bhattachanda may be Skt. bhakta + achanda, and aruci is the medical term for 'lack of appetite.' It seems, therefore, that Pārçvanātha has the right word, and that Kathākoça is to be corrected accordingly.

[55] Wandering village doctors; they occur also in Samarādityasaṁkṣepa 6. 402.

[56] To show that he might cure himself, if so disposed, see additional note 6, on p. 187.

self was the mighty physician. Then they went their way. But the Saint Sanatkumāra, having fulfilled his life, went to the Kalpa of bliss called (after him) the Sanatkumāra Kalpa (999-1231).

Story of the two princes Puṇḍarīka and Kaṇḍarīka[57]

Pārçva then turns to the exposition of the fourth division of the dharma, namely bhāva, or 'character' (see 6.272). This is extoled as the soul of the dharma, the friend of its heart, the doorkeeper to bliss, etc., followed by many other ecstatic similes. Its importance is illustrated, as follows (1237): In the city of Çrīpuṇḍarīkiṇī ruled King Mahāpadma, whose lovely and virtuous wife Padmāvatī bore him two sons, Puṇḍarīka and Kaṇḍarīka, both of them proficient in war and learning (çastra-çāstra-viçāradāu). King Mahāpadma was converted by the sermon of a Guru, who had come to the park Nalinīvana in company with many Sthaviras, or Elders. He made over his kingdom to Puṇḍarīka (1254). In time, the same Sthaviras returned, whereupon Puṇḍarīka, along with his brother and retinue, went out to pay their respects. Puṇḍarīka, in his turn, was converted, proposed to take the dīkṣā,[58] and to pass his sovereignty on to Kaṇḍarīka (1266). Kaṇḍarīka, however, himself also seized by the spirit of the occasion, insisted upon becoming monk. After some argumentation Puṇḍarīka permitted him to take the vow, and arranged a great festival

[57] A Puṇḍarīka-Kaṇḍarīka-(Kuṇḍarīka)-kathā is mentioned in Weber, Handschriftenverzeichnisse, vol. ii, pp. 950 and 1103. But see the different story connected with the same two names in Kathākoça, pp. 13 ff. The present legend seems to be familiarly known to the Jains; see Stevenson, Heart of Jainism, p. 159.

[58] Consecration for an ascetic life.

of departure (mahān niṣkramaṇotsavaḥ).[59] For a long time Kaṇḍarīka lived in pious bliss (1284). But one spring-time, when all nature became sensuous, and the people celebrated the season of love, the Muni, overwhelmed by his youth, fell from grace. In consequence thereof, he was abandoned by his pious associates, and despised by his Guru (1305). After a time Kaṇḍarīka returned to a park outside the city, and bade the keepers call his brother, King Puṇḍarīka. Upon his arrival Kaṇḍarīka showed his changed state, whereat his brother warned him against the consequences of his fall, pointing out the worthlessness of everything, except the law of the Jina. But Kaṇḍarīka, deaf to remonstrance, asked his brother for the kingdom. Puṇḍarīka gladly agreed; they exchanged their insignia—the royal insignia for the marks of the Sādhu (1319). Kaṇḍarīka then entered the palace, accompanied by citizens, ministers, etc., wearing black looks on their faces; despised by them, because he had gone out like a lion, and returned like a jackal. Greedily he, that was accustomed to the spare food of the forest, ate to repletion of the rich food set before him. He was attacked by cholera, colic, and pain. His attendants would not minister to his needs, because he had fallen from grace. While planning to kill in the morning his ministers and physicians, who contemned him, he died in evil thought (rāudradhyāna), and was born as a hell-dweller in the Saptamāvani hell (1330).

Puṇḍarīka, considering himself lucky in having reached the Law that is hard to attain, went to a Guru to be initiated in the asceticism that would destroy his karma. In his presence he renounced the eighteen items of sin, such as injuring life, falsehood, etc., and gave up

[59] Cf. Buddhist mahānikkhamaṇa.

the things of pleasure and desire. He died after his soul had been purged of its filth by the water of bhāva, and became a superior god in the heavenly palace, called Sarvārthasiddha (sarvārthasiddhākhye vimāne) (1232-1342).

Frame story: Life of Pārçvanātha, continued

At the end of this sermon on the fourfold dharma many were converted, or even reached perfection. Among them was Pārçva's father, King Açvasena (verse 257), who took the vow, after having made over his kingdom to his son Hastisena. Then also Vāmādevī (Vāmā, his mother), and Prabhāvatī (his wife), took the vow. Ten distinguished men, Āryadatta [60] and others, took the vow, and became heads of assemblies (gaṇabhṛt). Lord Pārçva poured divine perfume, procured by Çakra, upon their heads. The gods also showed them honor, and Pārçva, after having further instructed them, went to a temple (devachanda) in the north, to enjoy there the bliss of tranquility (1343-1360).

---

[60] Cf. above, p. 18. The list here of Pārçva's Gaṇabhṛts is: Āryadatta, Āryaghoṣa, Vasiṣṭha, Brahmanāmaka, Soma, Çrīdhara, Vārisena, Bhadrayaças, Jaya, and Vijaya.

Sarga the Seventh

Frame story: Life of Pārçvanātha, continued

At this juncture the Jain leader (gaṇabhṛt) Āryadatta (6. 1352), a follower of Pārçva, undertook to preach, in order to strengthen devotion to the Jina: Wise people become ascetics (yati); those destined to be reborn become (pious) householders (gṛhin). If the latter show honor (pūjā) to the Arhats, the tree of their existence becomes fruitful. The pūjā is threefold, consisting either of flowers, unhusked grain (akṣata), or hymns of praise (stotra). The 'flower honor' (puṣpapūjā) is illustrated by the following story (7):

The adventures of Princes Amarasena and Varasena[1]

In the city of Ṛṣabha ruled King Kuça. In his domain lived the merchant Abhayaṁkara with his wife Kuçalamatī. They employed two laborers, of good disposition; one to do house-work, the other to tend cattle. Once these laborers contrasted complainingly their destiny with that of their master: 'We poor wretches, shut out from all human interests, pass fruitlessly thru existence, like a

[1] This story, with variations, in Kathākoça, p. 125 ff.; and in the Gujarātī Pañcākhyānavārttika, nr. 34 (see Hertel, Das Pañcatantra, p. 147, who cites other Kathās, containing the same story). 'The Adventures of Rup and Bussant,' in Swynnerton's Romantic Tales from the Panjāb, pp. 410 ff., shares some features with the present story. Thus, the manner in which the two princes are driven from home by a hateful step-mother; their entrance upon a life of adventure; and their separation from one another. In other respects the stories diverge. Yet more remote is, 'The two Brothers,' Steel and Temple, Wide-Awake Stories, pp. 138 ff. See also Rouse's Translation of the Jātakas, vol. iv, p. 117 note.

snuhi-tree [2] (14). The merchant became aware of their thought, took them to the temple of the Jina, and instructed them to honor the Jina with flowers. They did not react upon his advice; so he brought them before a Muni who also recommended them to exercise this form of piety. The herdsman possessed 25 kapardakas. With these he bought flowers with which to honor the Jina; but the other, the house servant, had no money. He was advised to practice asceticism (tapas) and, accordingly, decided to give his own food to any mendicant that happened along. A sage came to beg for food; to him he gave all he had. The merchant, delighted at his devotion, gave him other food, and showed both of them great kindness (33).

The two servants, after death, were reborn respectively as Amarasena and Varasena, in the womb of Vijayādevī, wife of a Kaliñga king, Sūrasena.[3] A relative of Sūrasena had dispossessed him of his kingdom, but he, later on, found favor with the king of Gajapura, who presented him with four villages, in one of which, Sukara, he resided. The two boys grew up, beautiful and accomplished, but a co-wife, Jayā by name, conceived hatred for them. Once Sūrasena went to serve the king. On his return Jayā feigned anger, and entered the 'anger house' (kopagṛha, 'swearing room') [4] (42). She accused the two boys of having made improper advances to her, which she had barely warded off.[5] 'Act now in accordance with the customs of a noble family (kulocitam)!' Sūrasena, uxorious and gullible, in wrath, ordered

[2] Euphorbia Antiquorum; its juice is an emetic. The tree is despised, like the nimba in Pārçvanātha 1. 316.

[3] Probably Çūrasena.

[4] Mentioned also by Swynnerton, l. c., p. 412.

[5] See the additional note 19, on p. 199.

a Mātañga,[6] named Caṇḍa, to go outside the village, where the two boys were sporting with their horses, to cut off their heads, and show them to him. The Mātañga, wondering why the king was in such rage at his two virtuous boys, went to them, and told them. They, in turn, told him to do as their father commanded: they must have committed some heinous crime, else their father would not have given so severe an order. Caṇḍa induced them to take flight, after first assuaging their fear for his own safety. He took their two horses to show the king, and had two skulls of clay fashioned and painted over. These also he showed to the king, who ordered him to place them in a hole outside the village.[7] The evil co-wife was triumfant (59).

The two princes wandered to a lone and dread forest, described grafically (77). There they discussed their father's rage, concluding that it was due to their stepmother's machinations. Amarasena falling asleep, Varasena overheard[8] the conversation of a parrot couple. The male said: 'These two youths are worthy of good fortune, but there is nothing at hand to help them with.' The female replied: 'On the mountain of Sukūṭa, in a deep ravine, grow two mango-trees whose seed has been sprinkled by the Vidyādharas with their 'Science' (vidyā). We heard them say, these trees have each a magic

[6] A low caste man.

[7] This is a motif of rather wide application: order to slay disobeyed by pitying executioner. It recurs in Pārçvanātha in the story of Vanarāja, 7. 501 ff., again in connection with a boy; see the parallels there mentioned. See also Kathās. 3. 40 ff.; 5. 41; Vikrama Carita (Indische Studien xv. 229, 236, 237; Lescallier, Le Trône Enchanté, pp. 66 ff.); ZMDG. lxi. 53; Frere, Old Deccan Days, pp. 6 ff.; 662ff.; Bhojaprabandha, Part i; Parker, Village Folk-Tales of Ceylon, i. 161. Cf. Benfey, Das Pañcatantra, vol. i, p. 593.

[8] See the additional note 2, on p. 185.

property: he who eats the fruit of one of them is made king on the seventh day after; he who has the fruit of the other in his stomach, from his mouth fall every morning 500 dīnars into his rinsing water.[9] Now you took with you a fruit of each of these trees, so this is your chance to do good.' The male agreed, the birds flew off, and left the two fruits behind (99).

Varasena gave the royalty fruit to Amarasena, keeping the gold-producing one for himself. With the gold which he duly found in his rinsing water he procured clothes, food, and other luxuries. On the seventh day they arrived at Kāñcanapura, whose king had just died without successor. Amarasena lay asleep under a tree outside the city, was duly selected as king by the five-oracle process (pañcadivyādhivāsana),[10] and was led in state to the city, where he henceforth ruled as king (115). Varasena, unwilling to intrude upon his brother in his high station, gave himself over to pleasure, living in the house of a courtezan, Magadhā by name. His brother searched for him diligently, but vainly, and finally forgot him in the stress of his regal cares (128).

Varasena lived in such extravagant splendor, as to arouse the cupidity of Magadhā's bawd, or 'mother.'[11] Having induced Magadhā to coax out of him the secret of his wealth, she gave him a cūta fruit as an emetic,[12] in order to obtain the gold-producing mango. Since, however, in her stomach it had no magic power, she ejected

[9] Cf. Jülg, Kalmükische Märchen, p. 11, for the manner in which gold-spitting is acquired, and the trick by which Varasena, in the sequel, is robbed of this delectable property. Also Çukasaptati 7. See additional note 22, on p. 202.

[10] See the additional note 20, on p. 199.

[11] See for this stock figure of fiction, the author in Proc. Amer. Philos. Soc., vol. lii, p. 631.

[12] This feature of the story occurs also Kathās. 108. 77 ff.; and in the Pañcākhyānavārttika, cited in the note on p. 145.

Varasena from her house. His magic possession gone, he wandered outside the city to a cemetery (146). In the middle of the night four thieves came there. He overheard them quarrel about the division of their loot: a pair of shoes, a staff, and an old garment; and learned that every morning 500 jewels fall from the garment; that the staff beats off swords; and that the shoes carry one to any place that one thinks of.[13] Offering to arbitrate their quarrel, he sent one thief to each of the four directions, while pretending to reflect on the case. As soon as they were gone, he put on the shoes, flew off with the other two magic articles, went back to the city, and lived in great state on the proceeds of the jewels, like a Dogundaga [14] god (163). The bawd, hearing of this from a servant maid, again waxed greedy. Having dressed up Magadhā in a white garment,[15] she told Varasena that she had expelled him from her house because of her excessive attachment to Magadhā. But why, on coming to the city, did he not return to his own house? Magadhā, from the day of his expulsion on, had been angry, and had not spoken to her; tho he was alive, Magadhā had mourned him; she had lived only thru him; and so on. Varasena saw thru the slut's guile, yet decided to return. In due time, in answer to her greedy importunities, he told her about the shoes; that he was in the habit of fetching his wealth by putting them on and flying with them. After a while, feigning sickness, she made him carry her by means of the magic shoes to a temple of Kāma, on an island in mid-

[13] Stock motif, from the story of Putraka, Kathās. 3. 45 ff., to Pañcadaṇḍachattraprabandha 1 (p. 17), to Chavannes, Cinq Cent Contes Chinois, vol. iii, p. 259 (hat of invisibility; shoes for walking on water; stick that strikes dead).

[14] See p. 226.

[15] Mourning costume.

ocean, where, she pretended, she could divest herself of her evil. On arriving there she told him to precede her in worshiping Kāma. When he entered the temple, leaving the shoes behind, she stepped into them, and flew away, leaving Varasena to his sad reflections (186).

As Varasena wandered about there, a Vidyādhara arrived in the air, inquired the cause of his trouble, and imbued him with courage. He bade him stay there a fortnight, worship the divinity of the temple, and enjoy himself in the park which had been planted by the gods; after that period he would conduct him home. The Vidyādhara forbade him to go near two trees [16] which were standing in front of a cāitya; after that he provided him with provisions, and went away. Yet it happened one day that Varasena smelled of the blossom of one of these two trees, whereupon he was immediately transformed into an old ass.[17] On his return the Vidyādhara, by making him smell of the blossoms of the other tree, restored him to his original form (204). After five days the Vidyādhara took him back to Kāñcanapura, with a blossom from each of the two trees in his possession. Again the bawd appeared before him, this time with her knees bandaged. She pretended that a Vidyādhara had snatched the shoes, while Varasena was performing his devotion in the temple of Kāma, and that she had thus injured herself while following him. On arriving at her house, Varasena tricked her into the belief that he had a drug which re-

[16] For taboo, or forbidden things see Kathās. 26. 72; Vāsavadattā (Gray's Translation), p. 136; Steel and Temple, Wide-Awake Stories, p. 415; Parker, Village Folk-Tales of Ceylon, vol. i, p. 121.

[17] Animal transformation: see Kathās. 71. 273; Prabandhacintāmaṇi, p. 174; Kathākoça, pp. 50, 130, note, 135, 137. See Tawney, Translation of Kathāsaritsāgara, vol. ii, p. 168, note 2, and Index, under, Animal Transformation.

stored youth. She fell into the trap: first he secured his cloth and staff; then, by giving her the ass-making flower to smell, turned her into a she-ass.[18] The courtezans over whom the bawd presided, raised a disturbance before King Amarasena, who laughed when he heard their story. He sent policemen, ministers, and vassals to apprehend Varasena, but he beat them off with his magic staff. Thereupon he went himself, out of curiosity to see what was up. As soon as Amarasena saw his brother he embraced him, and ultimately made him crown-prince (yuvarājan) (242). At the request of the king, Varasena gave the bawd the second flower to smell, thus restoring her to her natural form. In due time the brothers were reunited with their father; their stepmother was forgiven, because her act had been instrumental in procuring the boys' kingdom; the trusty Caṇḍa was rewarded. A Muni explained their happy fate. Amarasena's gift to the Sādhu, in his previous birth, but more especially Varasena's offering of flowers, out of his pittance of 25 kapardakas, had had the effect of procuring their brilliant success. The Muni promised them happiness in subsequent births, and ultimate salvation. They lived happily and piously, and finally reached the world of Brahma (7-264).

The faithful parrot couple, and the son who fell in love with his own mother [19]

The discourse turns to the second form of pūjā, namely, with unhusked grain, which is illustrated by story: In the city of Çrīpura, in the neighborhood of a

[18] Ass-making flower occurs also in Rāuhiṇeya Carita, and in Kingscote, Tales of the Sun, p. 106. Cf. the additional note 9, on p. 188.

[19] Essentially the same story, in Kathākoça, pp. 42 ff.

Jaina temple, dwelled upon a great mango tree a devoted pair of parrots. The female was seized by a pregnancy whim [20] for a head of rice which grew in a field belonging to King Çrīkānta. When the male pointed out the danger to his own head thru pilfering from the king's field, she chided him for being a coward. Thereupon, in shame, he brought her a head of rice day by day, until the king, noticing the depredation, was told by the watch that the parrot was the culprit. The king told the watch to trap him; the male was caught while the female looked on, and brought before the king. The latter was about to slay the male with his sword, when the female intervened; offered herself in his stead; explained her delicate condition; and pointed out that her mate did not count his life worth a blade of grass by the side of her wish (290). The king, in banter, told the male that he, tho famed for wisdom in the world,[21] was yet enough of a fool to jeopardize his life for the whim of a woman. The female retorted, that a man will abandon father, mother, wealth, etc., but not his wife, 'just as you, O king, did abandon your own life for the sake of queen Çrīdevī: how can you then blame the parrot?' The king, surprised at her acquaintance with his history, bade her narrate, to wit (295):

Çrīdevī, one of the king's wives had consulted a certain nun (parivrājikā) as to means by which she might become the king's favorite. The nun gave her a philtre to put into the king's drinking water, and taught her a mantra which promptly impelled the king to cite her, in great state, to his presence, hereafter to be treated as chief queen. But, not yet satisfied with this proof of the

[20] See the additional note 25, on p. 204.

[21] See my paper, 'On Talking Birds in Hindu Fiction,' in Festgruss an Ernst Windisch, pp. 354 ff.

king's love, she desired to be convinced that he would die in the event of her own death. The nun gave her a 'root' (mūlikā) which produced a death-like trance when put into the nose, promised at the same time to revive her by means of a second mūlikā [22] (317). The queen did as bidden. The king, in despair, after his doctors and wizards had failed to revive her, ascended the pyre with her, as she was about to be cremated (327). The nun then turned up and revived the queen. The king, delighted, offered her a great reward, which she refused, asking only for the privilege of begging in his city. He had a sumptuous pavillion built for her, and, when she died in evil thought (ārtadhyāna), she was born again as that very she-parrot which was begging the king for the life of her offending mate. At that very moment she had remembered the events of her former birth (339).

The king then granted the life of the male parrot, as well as provision for their sustenance. They returned to their tree, where the female, her pregnancy whim satisfied, laid a pair of eggs. Just then a co-wife who lived on the same tree also laid an egg. It happened that the co-wife went out for grain, whereupon the first she-parrot, jealous of her, stole her egg. When the cowife on returning exhibited her distress by rolling on the ground like a carp (çapharī), the first wife grew penitent, returned the egg, and thus gained merit. The parrots and their offspring then lived happily (357). A wandering ascetic (cāraṇaçramaṇa) happened along, and praised the Jinen-

[22] Devices of this sort are discussed by the author in Proceedings of American Philosophical Society, vol. lii, p. 627, note 22. See also ZMDG. lxi. 45; Hertel, Das Pañcatantra, p. 109, note 4; Kathās, 12. 42 (cf. Tawney, vol. i, p. 572); Daçakumāracarita, ii, p. 26; Pañcadaṇḍachattraprabandha, 4 (pp. 42, 44, where the magic pill is called guṭikā); Samarādityasaṁkṣepa 6. 114 (again, guṭikā).

dra in the Jina temple with an elaborate hymn (366). The ascetic pointed out that the merit of honoring (pūjā) the Jina with unhusked grain (akṣata) produced imperishable (akṣata) glory. When the parrot pair heard this, they decided to act accordingly. Thru the merit of that act they and their offspring attained to the abode of the gods (375).

After enjoying heavenly bliss the souls of the parrot pair fell, and were reborn as king Hemaprabha of Hemapura and his wife Jayasundarī. The soul of the co-wife parrot was reborn as Rati, the king's other favorite among hundreds. The king was taken with fever which could not be cured,[23] even by resorting to the gods (397). A Rākṣasa, Kelīkila by name, told the king by night that he might be cured thru the sacrifice of one of his wives. The king told his ministers, who pointed out the impropriety of such unkingly conduct. None the less the king decided to tell his wives, whereupon Rati begged him to allow her to sacrifice herself. As she leapt into the fire, the Rākṣasa, delighted with her courage, caught her in his arms, and removed her to a distance (412). He then offered her a gift, which she accepted, asking that her husband should long remain sound. After granting this, he threw her into a golden lotus, whereupon the multitude acclaimed her, because she had given life to her husband (417). The king, out of gratitude, offered her a gift, but she pointed out that his life was the most desirable gift of all. When he insisted, she reserved the gift for a future occasion (421).[24]

[23] This is accompanied by a controversial description of fever and its cure.

[24] This turn is common in fiction: see my paper on Mūladeva, Proceedings of the American Philosophical Society, vol. lii, p. 638 (note 47); Kathākoça, p. 48; Prabhandhacintāmaṇi, p. 129; Jātakas 6, 461, 528.

It came to pass that Rati asked the house divinity for a son, promising in return to offer to her as a bali-offering Jayasundarī's son. Thereupon, when each queen begot a promising boy, Rati considered how she might fulfil her promise to the house divinity. She remembered the gift she had in reserve with the king, and asked him for control of the kingdom during five days [25] (427). The king granted her wish. Then she had Jayasundarī's boy taken away from her, put into a chest which was placed on the head of a slave girl, and deposited in the grove of the temple of the divinity. There the Vidyādhara king of Kāñcanapūḥ saw the boy, substituted a dead child in his place, and placed him before his wife, pretending that she had born him during sleep. She, being sterile, asked him why he was mocking her. He then told the truth, but induced her, that was childless, to accept the boy as her son, whereupon they raised and educated him (438). Rati, triumfant, then had the substituted dead child returned to Jayasundarī, who henceforth passed her days in grief (441).

The Vidyādhara couple named their adopted boy Madanāñkura, and had him instructed in the magic arts (vidyā) of their race. Madanāñkura, while roaming in the heavens, once perceived his mother, Jayasundarī, standing sadly at a window of the palace. Falling in love with her, he put her upon his chariot. She, in turn, was taken with love for him. The people and the king observed the rape of the queen, and the king was grieved.

The young parrot pair, children of the faithful parrots, that had gone with them to heaven (verse 375), knew by superior insight that their brother [26] (Madanāñkura) had

[25] See note on p. 122.

[26] In a later birth.

carried off his own mother. Assuming the guise of a pair of monkeys, they jumped upon a branch of the tree under which Madanāñkura sat with his mother. The male monkey suggested to the female that they should bathe in the holy bathing place of Kāmuka, which has the property of turning animals into the glorious state of men.[26a] The female refused to enter into the arrangement, because the human being under them, who had eloped with his own mother, was too depraved even to have his name mentioned. From this Madanāñkura gathered that he was Jayasundarī's son, and, simultaneously, Jayasundarī gathered that she was his mother (459). They verified their relation by consulting a Muni, who, in turn, referred them to a Kevalin in Hemapura.[27] Madanāñkura asked his foster parents for his true life's history, but was referred by them to the same Kevalin in Hemapura (473). They went to his presence, were joined there by King Hemaprabha, and were told the entire story, beginning with Rati's prayer to the house divinity for a son (482). He explained that Jayasundarī's separation for sixteen years from her son was the retribution for her having, in her former existence, put to grief her co-wife parrot for sixteen seconds, at the time when she had stolen her egg. Rati begged Jayasundarī's pardon for the wrong she had done her (493). The king asked the Sage what good deed in a former existence had elevated him to his present high station, and was told that his offering of unhusked rice to the Jina was responsible for his luck. In time the king and his family obtained salvation (265-500).

[26a] See the parable on p. 127.

[27] A similar story is told roughly in Day, Folk-Tales of Bengal, pp. 105 ff.

Story of Vanarāja, the waif who became king [28]

Āryadatta's exposition turns now to the third variety of worship, namely, by song of praise (arcā). This is illustrated by story: In the city of Kṣitipratiṣṭhita, under the rule of king Susthita, lived a young man of good family, but orfaned, poor, and evil-minded. He begged from house to house in the city, but on account of his shabby appearance, got nothing, and finally left the city in disgust (513). In a wood he met a Sage, who preached to him the Law. Impressed by the sermon, he showed reverence to the Sage, asked for help in his sore plight, and was advised by him to address a certain song of praise to the Jina. He did so, adding a prayer that he might attain to the exalted station of king Susthita. In due time he died, and was reborn as the child of a servant woman in the house of Soma, the king's Purohita (542).

This event was reported to the Purohita, as he was sitting in the durbar next to the king. On hearing it he was surprised, his head shook, and his nails split ominously. The king, noticing this, asked him to explain. The Purohita told him that a slave-girl in his house had brought forth a son, destined to usurp his, the king's, royal power (547). The king rose from the throne and dismissed the assembly. He reflected that fate might indeed bring about this seemingly impossible consummation; that the boy might usurp his kingdom over the head of his own son; therefore he decided to cut out the disease, while it was still curable. He ordered a cruel retainer, Caṇḍa, to slay the infant son of the servant woman. At

[28] A close parallel to this story in Kathākoça, p. 168 ff. See also Chavannes, Cinq Cent Contes, nr. 45; and Hertel in ZDMG. lxv. 447 ff., 454 ff. The story seems to have an historical kernel; see Prabandhacintāmaṇi, pp. 32 ff.; Stevenson, Heart of Jainism, p. 82.

dusk, when the woman happened to be out, he got hold of the boy, and carried him under a mango tree near an old dry well in the forest. But when he bared the child, its face brilliantly illumined the forest, so that Caṇḍa, in surprise and joy, decided to ignore the king's cruel mandate to kill the godlike child, that seemed marked for great fortune.[29] He left the child under the tree, told the king that he had executed his command, and was rewarded munificently (566).

In the morning a gardener discovered the child in the forest, which had flowered out miraculously in the splendor of new vegetation. Being himself childless, he decided that the forest divinity, pleased with him, had presented him with this wonderful child. He brought it to his wife, who received it with delight, spread the report that she had born it, and arranged a birth festival. They gave the boy the name of Vanarāja ('Forest King'). When the boy was five years old, the gardener's wife went, one spring day, to pay her respects to the king with a garland of various flowers, and the boy, out of curiosity, went with her (591). The Purohita of the king, sitting by, again was affected by the same omens: his head shook, and his nails split. This he interpreted as before, and verified by certain auspicious marks on the body of the boy, which he expounded at length in accordance with the rules of palmistry (sāmudrika çāstra)[30] (630). The king called Caṇḍa, and told him: 'Be not afraid! Tell the truth, was the boy killed by you, or not?' Caṇḍa told him the truth. In the evening he ordered a follower of his, Bhīmasena, to kill the boy. Bhīma, seizing the boy who was playing outside the gardener's house, took him

[29] See note 7, on p. 147.

[30] A full treatise of the subject is comprised in çlokas 596-630.

away from the city. The boy asked Bhīma: 'Father, where are you taking me to?' Bhīma's heart softened, and he said: 'I shall take you where you shall have a good time.'[31] Thereupon he took him to a wild forest, where stood a temple with an image of a Yakṣa, Sundara by name, left the boy in his charge, and went off. The boy said to the image: 'Give me sweetmeats (modaka), I am hungry,' and touched the belly of the Yakṣa. The Yakṣa, tho of stone, gave him sweetmeats[32] (642). Then a merchant arrived, Keçava by name, who lay worrying by night, because his bulls had been lost. The Yakṣa told him in a dream not to worry: his bulls would return in the morning. Furthermore he bade him, seeing that he was childless, to accept Vanarāja as a son. To this the merchant agreed. In the morning his cattle came back; he returned home to the city of Suçarma; made over the boy to his wife; and educated him until he was sixteen years of age. It happened that the merchant traveled to the city of the king (who desired Vanarāja's death), and appeared before him. Bidden to sit down, he did so, but when Vanarāja saw the king, he remained standing erect (653). The Purohita, beholding the boy, divine in appearance, again split a nail, and repeated his prediction that the king would lose his kingdom thru him. The king, unable to understand how the boy had managed to survive, since he had commissioned a trusty servant to kill him, wondered if he were an Asura, Vyantara, or Vidyādhara. He asked the merchant whether he really was his son, and when he affirmed the relation, got him to leave the boy with him for some time. Reluctantly he did so, consoled by Vanarāja himself (666). The king,

[31] sundara, pun on the name Sundara in the sequel.

[32] Cf. 3. 131: 'Even stone idols, to whom devotion is paid with intent mind, straightway show delight.'

externally kind, appointed Vanarāja provincial commander. His adopted father, Keçava, sent him great wealth (672). It happened that the king sent his own son, Prince Narasiṅha, to suppress a rebellious vassal, but Narasiṅha was defeated. Then he sent Vanarāja, who was victorious, and became famous in the world. Since the king had hoped that Vanarāja might perish, he became surly and sent camel drivers (āuṣṭrika) with a letter to Narasiṅha, commanding him to poison Vanarāja (vanarājasya dātavyaṁ viṣam). The camel drivers stopped overnight in the temple of the Yakṣa Sundara, who changed the message so as to read: 'Kamalā is to be given to Vanarāja (kamalā vānarājasya dātavyā).[33] Thereupon Narasiṅha gave his sister, the Princess Kamalā, with great ceremony, as wife to Vanarāja. The latter, along with his bride and Narasiṅha, returned to the city. The king, tho rejoicing at the defeat of the rebellious vassal, was grieved over Vanarāja's marriage, and his unshakable prosperity. Tho again baffled, he once more plotted his destruction (709).

He called two Mātaṅgas of his, and told them secretly to slay any one who might come by night to worship the divinity at the door of the palace. He then told Vanarāja that he had promised to worship that divinity at the time Vanarāja had gone forth against the rebellious vassal,

[33] In the parallel, Kathākoça, p. 172, the alteration is, much better, from viṣam to viṣā. Possibly the Pārçva version is a blend of two forms in one of which the alteration is from kamalam in the sense of 'drug' to Kamalā. As the trick stands here, it is rather foolish. Cf. Indian Antiquary x. 190; xi. 84. The presence or absence in a word of the small anusvāra dot changes Prākrit adhīyau 'he shall study,' to aṁdhīyau, 'he must be blinded,' in the tragic story of Kuṇāla as told in Pariçiṣṭaparvan 9. 14 ff.; cf. Divyāvadāna, pp. 417 ff. Further instances of the Uriah letter in Parker, Village Folk-Tales of Ceylon, vol. i, pp. 193, 195, 275, 276, 389; vol. iii, pp. 73, 76, 291, 294.

and commissioned him to do so in his behalf. Vanarāja accepted the order, but, when he went to execute it, was intercepted by Narasiṅha, who undertook the mission in his stead. Narasiṅha was thus killed by the sharp swords of the ambuscading Niṣādas[34] (719). When the king found out the miscarriage of his horrible plot, he wailed bitterly, but, realizing the inevitable fatality of this chain of events, asked Vanarāja's pardon, made over his kingdom to him, and went into the forest (731). Vanarāja lived happily with his beloved Kamalā. A Muni, Nandana by name, arrived in the Nandana park. Vanarāja went out to greet him, and asked him how he came by so unusually successful a career. The Muni told him that his praises[35] of the Jina in a former birth were responsible for his happiness. Vanarāja then remembered his former birth, and devoted himself henceforth fervidly to Jaina duties (501-747).

Parable of the selfish religious, and the unselfish Pulindra[36]

The text rounds out its disquisition on pūjā with the claim that worship must be disinterested, otherwise it is futile, illustrating by the following parable: A certain religious, Mugdhaka by name, came from a distance to worship and make expensive and showy offerings to an

[34] See additional note 8, on p. 188.

[35] This is the third way of honoring the Jina, as preached above, çloka 4.

[36] Benfey, Das Pañcatantra, vol. i, p. 389: 'In a South-Indian legend the sacrificer takes out his eyes and puts them into the eye-sockets of a statue (Mackenzie Collection ii. 5). This is a phase of the Çibi motif (see p. 192) which often involves loss of the eyes by way of self-sacrifice or contempt of life; see Subhā, Therī-gāthā, nr. 71; Jātaka 499; Jātakamālā nr. 2; Cariyāpiṭaka 1. 8; Avadāna-çataka nr. 34; Avadāna-kalpalatā nr. 91; Chavannes, Cinq Cent Contes, nr. 197; Divyāvadāna pp. 407-417; Pariçiṣṭaparvan 9. 14-54; Kathās. 28. 18-24.

image of Çiva, inhabited by a Vyantara. Constantly he prayed: 'Since thou, O Lord, art pleased, may my fortunes ever prosper; to thee alone, do I resort. Show favor, supreme Lord!' Thus importuned, the god became worried (sacinta). Then the religious observed that his offering had been removed. He made another, and stood in hiding to see what would happen to it. A rough Pulindra (! pulindraka),[37] with bow and arrow in his left hand, with flowers in his right, and his mouth full of water, came there in a hurry, pushed aside with his foot the previous offering, squirted water out of his mouth, threw down a heap of flowers, and reverenced the idol. Thereupon the pleased god started to hold conversation with the Pulindra. The religious, observing this, grew angry. After the Pulindra was gone, he abused the god: 'Just as he is a Pulindra, so you are a Kaṭapūtana;[38] you converse with a low-born individual, but you do not show yourself to me, even in a dream!' (761). The god told him to wait; he would show him the difference between himself and the Pulindra. Next day, when the religious came there, he saw that the god was blind of one eye. The religious deplored this greatly, and hinted that the god's association with low-born people (meaning the Pulindra) had got him into this evil plight. While he was thus condoling, the Pulindra came along, took in the situation, gouged out his own eye with an arrow, and gave it to the idol. The god offered the Pulindra whatever he might desire, but he wanted nothing, and went as he came. The god pointed the moral: the divine powers do not take delight in external worship (bāhya-

[37] See pp. 223 and 230.

[38] A kind of preta, or ghost. According to Manu 12. 71, the ghost of a renegade Kṣatriya.

pūjā), but in devotion showing itself in courageous action (sāttvika bhakti) (748-768).

Parable of the man who wished to rid himself of his vixen wife [39]

The discourse turns to the theme of unreasonable desires, showing by parable that they defeat their own end: A gentleman, Soma, in Devapura, handsome, accomplished, and virtuous, had a wife Rudrā, of opposite qualities, yet devoted to her husband. They quarreled so as to resemble a face with an earring in one ear. The husband, reflecting that he could not get rid of her any more than a tree of its creeper, decided to make certain that he would at least be rid of her in another existence. Having heard of a holy bathing place (tīrtha), named Kāmuka, on the mountain of Parṇa, he went there to die, leaving all he had behind. He jumped from the mountain with the wish that Rudrā should not be his wife in another birth. But his wife, who had found out his intention, went there also and committed suicide in the same way, while wishing that she should have the same husband in another birth. The divinity of the tīrtha opined that worship is rewarded by the gods, only when unencumbered by wishes. Epecially in asking the Jinendra for dharma (religion) or mokṣa (salvation) one should not harbor hope for personal advantage: it will bear small fruit (769-781).

[39] For vixens see Pañcatantra 4. 6; Kathās. 74. 156; Çukasaptati 46; Jātaka 13. Cf. Benfey, Das Pañcatantra, vol. i, pp. 519 ff.

Allegory of the four friends on the treasure island of human existence

Āryadatta has now completed his sermon on the virtues of pūjā, as guide of householders into a happy state; he now issues a final warning that the blessing of holy religion is difficult to attain, and that men, when they have reached the treasure island of human existence,[40] should not waste their capital there as did the merchant Mūḍha in the following allegory:

In the city of Çrīvasantapura lived four merchants, friends of one another: Cāru, Yogya, Hitajña, and Mūḍha. They went on an expedition to a jewel island across the sea, Ratnākara ('Jewel-mine') by name. Cāru, staid and cool, a skilled appraiser, accumulated a complete assortment of jewels in their five different colors (788). Yogya also, being instructed by Cāru, did some business, and got to know something of the art of appraising jewels. And, tho he was rather flighty, being given to pleasure and dalliance, he managed to accumulate some treasure. Hitajña did not himself know how to judge jewels, swallowing whole whatever any one told him. He also gladly listened to Cāru, but nothing remained in his mind, because he was foolish, and given to running about to plays and other amusements. So he was cheated by rogues, and collected glass and other worthless stuff (794). Mūḍha, finally, knew nothing himself, did not ask Cāru, did not hear what he said, or attach importance to it. A fool, who thought himself clever, he accumulated only conch-shells and other rubbish, and lost much wealth. Cheated by rogues, and not relying upon his friends, he

[40] According to a familiar belief of the Jains, the state of man is the most favorable stepping-stone to nirvāna, more so than the state of god.

foolishly passed his time (796). Cāru, having filled a vessel full of jewels, wished to depart, and called upon his friends to return, if they had gained their ends. Yogya was unwilling to leave the island, acknowledged regretfully that he had neglected to attend sufficiently to business, and begged Cāru to see to it that he also should accumulate a real fortune; then he would go with him. Hitajña showed the glass and other trifles which he had accumulated to Cāru. Cāru reproved him, and taught him how to appraise jewels. Thus he also managed to get some wealth, and followed Cāru (806). Mūḍha, when asked by Cāru, replied petulantly that he had no means with which to go. Cāru offered him capital wherewith to do business, so that he might be able to get away. But Mūḍha said that his home was where he was enjoying himself;[41] that he was immersed in all sorts of pleasures, and engrossed with spectacles, and that he would stay just where he was (873).

The allegory is explained: The city of Vasantapura represents the vulgar herd. The four friends are yati 'Ascetic,'; çrāddha, 'Faithful'; bhadraka,[42] 'Good'; and mithyādṛṣṭi, 'False-sight.' The jewel-isle is mortal existence; the crossing of the sea is the entrance of the soul into a womb; the arrival by ship on the island is the attainment to the position of mortal man, owing to good karma. Cāru, who filled his ship with the five different kinds of jewels, representing the planting in himself of submission to the five vows on the part of the ascetic (yati), the fifth being brahma.[43] Yogya's desire for wealth, which resulted in the acquisition of but little, represents

[41] Ubi bene ibi patria.

[42] Also in 2. 190.

[43] Comm.: brahmacaryam, or chastity.

devotion to the lighter vows (aṇuvrata) on the part of a house-holder (gṛhin) who has first devoted himself to a life of the senses.[44] Hitajña, whose folly induced him to collect glass and other baubles, by the goodness (bhadratvena) of his soul becomes altogether devoted to religion.[45] Mūḍha, who is deceived by rogues, so as to collect shells and other trash, represents the choice of irreligion on the part of one who sees falsely thru the prompting of unlawful impulses. That Cāru induced Yogya and Hitajña to go to their homes, represents their enlightenment by an ascetic who is on the eve of salvation (yater āsannamokṣasya); that they, thru respect for Cāru, regained their wealth, represents submission to the true religion on the part of the çrāddha and the bhadraka. That Mūḍha, tho instructed by Cāru, did not go to his home, represents the disregard of salvation on the part of the worthless, even when taught by the teacher (823). The three first (yati, çrāddha, and bhadraka) attain salvation; the fourth (mithyādṛṣṭi), like Mūḍha, remains in the ocean of saṁsāra. The wise man who remembers this essential instruction must strive, even tho it be late, to attain salvation (782-825).

Frame Story: Life of Pārçvanātha, continued

After the Gaṇabhṛt (Āryadatta) had finished his sermon, all the people paid reverence to Lord Pārçva, and then dispersed to their various homes. A black, four-armed Yakṣa, Pārçva by name, who was born at that tīrtha,[46] who carried as an umbrella the hood of a cobra, who had the face of an elefant, who had a tortoise for a

[44] Such a one is called çraddha, 'Faithful,' above.

[45] That is, his devotion to religion, after error, constitutes him a bhadraka.

[46] The connection does not make it clear which holy place is meant.

vehicle, who held an ichneumon and a serpent in his left two forearms, a citron and a serpent in his right two forearms, became a devotee at the side of the Lord.[47] Then a four-handed goddess, Padmāvatī by name, arose at that tīrtha, golden of complexion, of distinguished might, having a kurkuṭa-serpent as chariot, holding in her right two hands a lotus and a noose, in her left two hands a fruit and a hook. She also stood, as orderly of the Arhat (çāsanadevatā[48]), at the side of the Lord.[49] Then the Lord, followed by the assembly (saṁghā), went elsewhere, the wheel of the law upon a throne going in front, a drum sounding in the air. He was served by an umbrella and by chowries. He went on his journey upon golden lotuses, and, as he went, trees bent, thorns turned down; the seasons, the sense-objects (sound, smells, etc.), the winds, and the birds were propitious. By the might of his lordship diseases fled to a distance of 100 yojanas; and where he dwelt, from there vanished hostility and other afflictions. Superior to every one, the lotus of his feet ever attended by scores of gods, the Lord traversed the earth (826-836).

[47] The text has here, bhaktaḥ pārçvo' bhavad vibhoḥ, where pārçvo must be changed to pārçve; compare stanza 830.

[48] So here; elsewhere çāsanadevī or çāsanasundarī. Hemacandra, Abhidhānacintāmaṇi 44-46 has a list of these female orderlies which serve each Jina. They are pictured in full panoply in the iconografy of the Jinas; see p. 19. Padmāvatī, as conceived by the Digambaras, is reproduced on a plate in connection with Burgess' article, Indian Antiquary xxxii, pp. 459 ff., which is copied by Guerinot, Essai de Bibliographie Jaina, opposite to p. 281. See Pariçiṣṭaparvan 9. 93; 12. 214; Çatruṁjaya Māhātmyam sarga 2 (Burgess, Indian Antiquary, xxx. 246); Pañcadaṇḍachattraprabandha, p. 8; Kathākoça, p. 27.

[49] Pārçvayakṣa, or Dharaṇendra (see, p. 19) and Padmāvatī are the traditional attendant male and female spirits of the 23d Tīrthaṁkara; see Burgess, Appendix to Bühler, Indian Sect of the Jainas; Stevenson, The Heart of Jainism, p. 313.

Sarga the Eighth [1]

Story of the misogynist Sāgaradatta, who was redeemed by a clever woman

The Lord of the world, in the course of his progress, in time arrived at Puṇḍradeça. There, in the city of Tāmraliptī, lived a pious young merchant's son, Sāgaradatta by name. In a former existence he had been a priest, and had been poisoned by his lewd wife. Cast out while unconscious he had been revived by a shepherd's wife (gokulinī). He then became a wandering ascetic (parivrāj), and, after death, was reborn as Sāgaradatta. Owing to the memory of his former birth, he became a woman-hater. The kind shepherdess, who also died in piety, was reborn as the beautiful daughter of a merchant. Sāgara cast longing eyes upon her; his relatives, knowing his sentiments, chose her as his wife; but his eye only was pleased with her, not his mind. For he looked upon women afright, as tho they were swords (6).

Then the woman, undismayed, wrote him a çloka message: 'Why, o wise man, dost thou neglect a devoted lady? The full-moon day makes shine the moon; lightning, the ocean; woman, the householder.' Sāgara replied with a çloka: [2] 'Like a river, woman is by nature unstable, tends downward; she is ill-behaved, stupid, destroys both partners.' Again, concluding that his mind was poisoned by the memory of a woman's corruptness in a former birth, she sent him a second çloka: 'Surely, the

[1] The episodes in this sarga are in loose connection with the frame story containing the life of Pārçva. The sarga is probably a later addition.

[2] See Böhtlingk, Indische Sprüche, nr. 7209, and note 18, on p. 199.

fault of a single woman must not be visited on her race: is the full-moon night to be shunned because of the dark night before the new-moon?' Then Sāgara, attracted by her insight and cleverness, married her, and enjoyed happiness with her (13).

Sāgara started on an expedition, but seven times his ship was wrecked. On reaching home he became despondent, until he saw some one draw from a well seven times, but get no water until the eighth. He again started for Ceylon, was driven by a storm upon a treasure island, and gathered a mass of treasure. On the way home, he was thrown overboard one night by his ship's crew. He floated ashore on a plank[3] to the city of Pāṭalāpatha, where he was seen by his father-in-law, who was traveling on business. On arriving home he recovered, by the aid of the king, his wealth from the mutinous crew, who had also returned (23).

As part of his generous benefactions he decided to fashion a divine image of precious jewels, and asked the dharmatīrthikas[4] what divinity would procure salvation (mukti). A certain Āpta or Proficient told him to invest with divinity a precious jewel.[5] When he had gone thru the act eight times[6] he was to think of a certain goddess, who would tell him what he wished to know. He did this, whereupon a certain divinity placed before him a golden image of the Arhat. Returning to the Sādhus who had advised him, he showed them the image, and asked them who this god was, and how he was to be placed. They told him to consult Pārçvanātha in Puṇḍradeça. Pārçva

[3] See note on p. 49.

[4] Some sort of Jain Sages.

[5] sadratnam adhivāsya; see Edgerton, JAOS. xxxiii. 164, and additional note 20, on p. 199.

[6] This in allusion to his own seven failures, and success the eighth time.

instructed him on these matters; Sāgara placed the image, and delightedly worshiped it. But, when Sāgara the next day desired to take the vow with Pārçva, the Lord, together with his retinue, had moved to another place (1-33).

Story of the four pupils who, even tho sinning, attained perfection

Pārçva had four well-born pupils, named Çiva, Sundara, Soma, and Jaya. They asked Pārçva whether they would attain perfection (siddhi) in their present existences. Pārçva answered in the affirmative, whereupon, feeling secure, they devoted themselves to riotous living. But in time, when mokṣa (salvation) was at hand, they regretted their lapses, resorted to Pārçva, attained the knowledge of Kevalins, and became Siddhas (34-48).

Story of Bandhudatta[7]

At that time there lived in Nāgapurī a merchant, named Dhanapati, who had an excellent son, named Bandhudatta. He married Candralekhā, the daughter of Vasunanda. At the moment when the bride's bracelet was tied around her arm, she was bitten by a serpent, and died. In the same way six wives died as fast as he married them. He was, therefore, regarded as a 'poison-hand' (viṣahasta),[8] and could not obtain any other maiden. His father, seeing him despondent, sent him on an expedition to Ceylon, where he acquired great wealth (53). On his return he was shipwrecked, but, catching

[7] Several features of this story recur in Samarādityasaṁkṣepa 6. 62 ff.

[8] See additional note 17, on p. 198.

hold of a plank,[9] reached a treasure island. He managed gradually to climb the mountain of jewels, where he saw a jeweled cāitya containing an image of the Arhat Nemi. Certain Sādhus who lived there, hearing his story, converted him to the religion of the Jina (58). A Vidyādhara, Citrāñgada by name, himself a devout Jaina, was pleased with his piety, took him home, entertained him, and offered him the choice of two gifts: either the Science of flying thru the air, or a maiden in marriage. Bandhudatta remained silent, which the Vidyādhara interpreted to signify the maid. A niece of his, Mṛgāñkalekhā, told the Vidyādhara that she had a friend, Priyadarçanā, in Kāuçāmbī, about whom a Sage had predicted that she would beget a son, and then take the vow (64).

Then Bandhu was sent in charge of some Vidyādharas to Kāuçāmbī, where there was a temple of Pārçva. He lauded Pārçva with an elaborate hymn. While thus engaged, Jinadatta, the father of his prospective bride, came there to praise the Jina, was pleased with Bandhu's piety, took him home, and married him to Priyadarçanā. He lived there four years, at the end of which he started home with his wife in a pregnant condition (85). After passing thru a wild forest, his caravan, camping by a lake, was attacked by Bhillas,[10] belonging to a village chieftain, Caṇḍasena. They brought the loot with Priyadarçanā to Caṇḍasena. He saw her dejected, and learned from her that she was the daughter of Jinadatta. Astonished at this revelation, he bowed before her, and told her that she was his sister, because she was the daughter

[9] See note on p. 49.

[10] Encounters with Bhillas, Çabaras, Mlechas, Tājikas, Pulindas, Kirātas, Ābhīras, Niṣādas, wild hunters, and robbers, are as much stock motifs of Hindu fiction, as are encounters in forests with thieves and robbers in Western fiction.

of his benefactor, Jinadatta. The latter had once saved him from being executed as a thief (92). Then he asked her what he might do for her:[11] she told him to find Bandhudatta, from whom she had been separated in the mêlée of the attack. He went in search, but did not find him, whereupon he took oath that he would enter the fire, in case her husband was not restored to her within six months. Caṇḍasena then sent out all his Bhillas, but even so they did not find Bandhu. In great worry, Caṇḍasena concluded that Bandhu, in despair, had made away with himself (98). He decided to take Priyadarçanā back to Kāuçāmbī, after she had brought forth her child; after that he would enter the fire. While in this state of mind, a handmaiden announced that Priyadarçanā had born a son. Thereupon he vowed to his house divinity, Caṇḍasenā by name,[12] that he would offer up teṇ men[13] to her, in case Priyadarçanā and her son should remain in good health for a month. After 25 days had passed peacefully he sent out his men to capture ten men fit for sacrifice (103).

In the meantime Bandhudatta had wandered despairingly in the Hintāla forest. Unable longer to endure separation from Priyadarçanā, he was about to hang himself upon a saptachada tree, when he saw a separated haṅsa-bird couple reunited,[14] gathered hope from the sight, and decided to return to his own city. But worrying, because it seemed improper to return without his

[11] The trait of gratitude in otherwise depraved Bhillas or Çabaras is not uncommon; see, e. g. Samarādityasaṁkṣepa 6. 62 ff.; 7. 287 ff. In the first of these instances the hero's name is also Bandhudatta.

[12] Mentioned later in verse 168 in the short form Caṇḍā = Durgā.

[13] See note on p. 205. This feature in Samarādityasaṁkṣepa 6. 49 ff.

[14] The separation of a pair of haṅsas is typical of separated lovers; see Gray's translation of Vāsavadattā, p. 57, note 11; Samarādityasaṁkṣepa 5. 162, 185, 232, 273, 490 ff.

wife, he decided to go to an uncle of his, Dhanadatta by name, in Viçālā, to borrow from him the money wherewith to ransom Priyadarçanā from her captor, the Çabara chief. As he traveled, he came, tired, to the house of a Yakṣa, and there met another wayfarer. He found out that he was from Viçālā, so he inquired after the welfare of his uncle Dhanadatta. The traveler related that Dhanadatta's son and his wife had offended the king, and were confined in prison; that Dhanadatta had undertaken to ransom them; and, for that purpose, had set out for Nāgapurī, to get the money from him, namely Bandhudatta. In despair at this prank of fortune, Bandhudatta remained there, awaiting Dhanadatta, who was sure to come that way to Nāgapurī. After five days Dhanadatta with some friends came along and halted at the same shrine. Bandhu made sure it was his uncle, but did not reveal his own identity (123).

In the morning Bandhu went to bathe in a river, near which he discovered in a mine-pit a copper chest full of treasure. Then he made himself and his adventures known to Dhanadatta, and offered him the chest wherewith to ransom his family. Dhanadatta refused, bidding him first to ransom his wife, Priyadarçanā (128). In the mean time soldiers of the king arrived, and held up every one who had passed there on the suspicion of robbery. Dhanadatta and Bandhudatta, frightened, threw the chest down by the temple of the Yakṣa, were discovered in the act, and cross-examined about themselves and treasure. They alleged that they were merchants from Viçālā, on their way to Laṭa, and that the treasure was inherited. The king's minister, who was with the soldiers, himself opened the chest, and discovered the king's name upon jewels contained therein (135). He suspected that the chest was only part of the loot taken from the king; had them beaten; but could extract no more information. They were thrown into a hell-like pit, but nothing further came to light (138).

Now at the end of six months a certain rogue in the garb of an ascetic,[15] having been caught with money on his person, was brought before the minister. Because a mendicant should not have so much money, he was condemned to death as a thief, and taken outside by the soldiers. He then confessed that he had formerly stolen the king's treasure, of which the chest was a part, and all was duly found except that chest (144). The thief then tells his story. He is the son of a Brahman in the city of Puṇḍravardhana; his name is Çrīdhara. Once he saw some men apprehended as thieves, and cried out that those criminals ought to be executed. A Muni reprimanded him for his ignorance, telling him that those offenders were merely harvesting the fruits of a previous existence: 'You also will certainly gather the fruit of your previous faults.' When asked to explain, the Muni narrated (49-150):

Prenatal history of the thief in the guise of an ascetic [16]

In the city of Garjana, you lived as a pious Brahman, named Caṇḍradeva. There also lived a celebrated ascetic, Yogātman. Now a certain widow, Vīramatī by name, went off with a gardener, named Siṅhala; as fate would have it, Yogātman disappeared on the same day. When all the people of the town gossiped that Vīramatī had gone somewhere, you stated that she had certainly eloped with Yogātman; the people, therefore, became

[15] See additional note 12, on p. 191.

[16] This story recurs in Samarādityasaṁkṣepa 4. 201 ff.

scurrilous about that ascetic (159). Having committed this detestable (nikācitam [17]) deed, you died, and were reborn successively as goat, jackal, and whoreson, being now in your fourth birth. The Brahman (Yogātman) died of mouth disease [18] in all his existences, and was reborn into his same state. Therefore you still have a remnant of your karma to work off (151-156).

Story of Bandhudatta, continued

The thief continued his history: [19] Frightened by the Muni's exposition, he had resorted to asceticism under the instruction of a Guru. Out of regard for him the teacher had bestowed upon him the Sciences (vidyā) of going in the air, and of opening locks, with the proviso that these would prove ineffective, unless he preserved purity of life and avoided lies. But, in case he did lie from carelessness, he was to stand in water up to his navel, and, with his arms held upward, recite the vidyās 1008 times. The teacher then went to heaven, but the thief, dissolute person that he was, did everything otherwise. Next day some women in the forest inquired why he was an ascetic. He told them, because his wife had died; moreover he did not perform the expiation for this lie. Next, he performed theft by night,[20] and was seized by guards, whereupon the Science of going in the air

[17] See p. 230.

[18] Symbolizing the slander from which he had suffered.

[19] This feature of the thief's story, less well told, recurs in Samarādityasaṁkṣepa 4. 218 ff. The theme of Jātaka 474 is likewise the power of lies to suspend the action of a profitable magic charm. See also Paksi Pakaranam xx, in the analysis by Hertel, Das Pañcatantra, p. 351; and Samarādityasaṁkṣepa 6. 41 ff.

[20] By the aid of the lock-opening science or charm, verse 158.

failed to operate. Therefore, the thief concluded, 'do what is customary' (163).

The minister asked the thief why one jewel casket was missing,[21] and he answered that some traveler had found it by chance (dāivatas). The minister then mercifully discharged him, and called the two confined suspects.[22] After they had repeated their story, they were released. But, as they went their way, they fell into the hands of the Bhillas, whom Caṇḍasena had ordered to capture victims for his goddess Caṇḍā.[23] They were joined to others who had been caught for the same purpose, being kept in the temple of the goddess. The chieftain Caṇḍa arrived with Priyadarçanā and her boy. Considering that she would not be able to endure the sight of the horrible rite, he covered up her eyes with a garment (170). It happened that Bandhudatta was first to be brought on for the sacrifice. As he pronounced the parameṣṭhinamaskāra,[24] his wife recognized his voice, and uncovered her eyes. The chieftain released him, and asked his pardon (177). Bandhudatta begged off the other victims, the goddess thereafter being content with praise, flowers, and the like. He then introduced his wife to Dhanadatta who blessed her and praised her husband. Their boy was named Bāndhavānanda in allusion to Bandhu's name and the fact that he was a joy to his relatives. Dhanadatta with the money he needed (to ransom his family) returned home. Bandhudatta, escorted by the Bhilla chief, returned to Nāgapurī, was honored by the king, and the story of his adventures converted many to the religion of the Jina (157-191).

[21] Namely, that which Bandhudatta had found.

[22] Bandhudatta and Dhanadatta.

[23] Mentioned previously by fuller name as Caṇḍasenā; see verse 101.

[24] See note on p. 26.

Story of Bandhudatta's former lives[25]

Twelve years later in the autumn of the year, Pārçva came to Nāgapurī. Bandhudatta went out to do him honor, and asked what karma of his had caused the death of his first six wives; why his separation from Priyadarçanā; and why his captivity. The saint narrated (199):

In the Vindhya forest lived a fierce Çabara chieftain, Çikharasena, who had a wife, Çrīmatī. They entertained a Sādhu who had lost his way, in return for which he instructed them especially in ahiṅsā.[26] Once the chief and his wife were attacked by a lion. The chief was about to discharge his bow, when he was reminded by Çrīmatī of the Sādhu's instruction. He desisted; they were both devoured by the lion, being reborn in the Sāudharma heaven as gods who lived an enormous length of time (209). Çikharasena fell, was reborn in Cakrapurī in Videha as Mṛgāñka, son of the Bhilla king Kurumṛgāñka; his wife, as Vasantasenā, daughter of Kurumṛgāñka's brother-in-law King Subhūṣaṇa. Again they were united in marriage. Mṛgāñka's father turned ascetic, so that the son became king (213). His karma, left over from his Bhilla life, sprang up, to wit: A king, Vardhana in Jayapura, demanded Vasantasenā, his beloved wife, else he would wage war against him. They joined in battle, Vardhana was defeated, fled, but later on engaged Mṛgāñka and killed him. Owing to his rāudradhyāna (fierce thought), Mṛgāñka went to the sixth hell, joined on the funeral pyre by Vasantasenā (220). Rising thence, they were reborn on the island of Puṣkara, in the homes of two laborers, and again married. Owing to

[25] This episode recurs in Samarādityasaṁkṣepa 8. 255 ff.

[26] See above, p. 43.

good deeds they again attained to the world of Brahma, fell thence, and were reborn into their present state, namely, as the children of merchants. Their misfortunes in their present lives were due to karma left over from their lives as Bhillas (225).

Bandhudatta expressed his delight at having met the Lord Pārçva, and having been led by him from vice to virtue. He asked for further instruction, and heard many items of the true religion (saddharmaçāstra), illustrated finally by the following story (192-236):

Story of Çrīgupta, gambler, thief, and murderer, who was ultimately redeemed

A merchant, Mahīdhara, enjoyed the favor of Nala, the righteous king of Vāijayantī. The merchant had a son, Çrīgupta, addicted to every vice. On one occasion Mahīdhara poured out his heart before the king, but even he was unable to help. Mahīdhara, related that Çrīgupta had broken into the house of a merchant, Soma, and robbed him of his all. To compensate, he offered to give all his own property. The king consoled him, and, when he learned from the people of the city that Çrīgupta had stolen 25,000 gold pieces, he restored them from his own treasury (250). After chiding a negligent watchman, he upbraided Çrīgupta, and bade him return the loot. Çrīgupta denied all knowledge of the theft, whereupon the king proposed resort to an ordeal. Çrīgupta asked who was the complainant; the king assumed the rôle, and appointed the judges. Then Çrīgupta checked the action of the ordeal by means of a magic mantra, so that he remained untouched by the fire of the heated ploughshare. The king was desolated by his own apparent injustice as complainant, and declared that he himself must suffer the thief's punishment (259). At the urgent request of his ministers, as well as Çrīgupta's father, he finally agreed to subject Çrīgupta to a second ordeal, this time supervised by a manager of ordeals (divyamāntrika), named Kuçalin (266). In this ordeal Çrīgupta's hands were burned, whereupon he confessed. Out of regard for his father, Çrīgupta was allowed to go free, but was banished. He went to Gajapura, there met Kuçalin, slew him, but was caught, and hanged upon a tree. The weight of his body broke the branch, he fell to the ground, regained consciousness, and fled to a distance (274). Arriving at a jungle he heard the sermon of a Muni, and was converted (286).

While going to sleep upon the branch of a banyan tree he overheard the conversation of a pair of parrots.[27] The male told the female that he had learned from a certain Sage that there was a tīrtha at Çatruṁjaya to which all the blessed Sādhus, beginning with Çrīpuṇḍarīka [28] had resorted; by bathing there one might rise in the scale of existences. Çrīgupta asked the parrot to communicate to him the instruction which he had received from the Sage, which he did. Thereupon Çrīgupta turned ascetic, and the parrot went to the mountain of Çatruṁjaya (309).

In the mean time Çrīgupta's father had gone in search of his son. He found him a devout ascetic, and took him home with him. The king received him kindly. The parrot, who had in the mean time become a god in the Sanatkumāra Kalpa, visited him in a dream, and told him that he would die at the end of seven days. Çrīgupta devoted his last days to severe penance, died, went to heaven, and will gradually attain perfection (237-328).

[27] See additional note 2, on p. 185.

[28] See the story on p. 142.

Parable of the pitcher that fell from an old woman's head

Pārçva's sermon goes on to show that diligent study of the Çāstras imparts refined judgment, as shown by the following parable: Two pupils, studying on the bank of a river, saw an old woman with a pitcher of water on her head. The granny, delighted with their sight, asked them whether her son, who had gone to foreign parts, would return safely. At the thought of her son, old as she was, her limbs began to shake; the pitcher fell from her head, and was smashed upon the ground (333). At the sight of this mishap, one of the pupils had a stupid intuition, and said, that was a sign that her son was dead. The other pupil told the first not to talk nonsense, and bade the old woman go home, she would find that her son had returned. The granny found her son at home. Delighted, she went to the house of the pupils' teacher, and got him to ask the wise pupil how he had read from the seemingly sinister omen of the broken pitcher the happy arrival of her son (338). The pupil said that he had read it out of the union of the water with the earth. The teacher praised him, and predicted that he would become a teacher of noble men (329-342).

Story of Bandhudatta, concluded

After this instruction, Bandhudatta asked the Lord what would be the fate of himself and wife. Pārçva predicted that, after death, they would go to the Sahasrāra heaven; fall thence; become respectively emperor and empress in Videha; turn ascetics after having enjoyed the world; and then enter into perfection (siddhi). Thereupon Bandhu and his wife took the vow (347), and finally obtained mokṣa (salvation) (349-357).

Frame Story: Life of Pārçvanatha, concluded. His nirvāṇa

Lord Pārçva, knowing that nirvāṇa was at hand, went to the Sammeta mountain[29] (363). In the company of 33 Munis he practised a month's asceticism (368). He attained to various forms of spiritual refinement, to the point when his karma was destroyed (kṣīṇakarmā), died, and reached the summit of heaven (lokāgram āsadat). Çakra bathed the body in the fluid of the 'ocean of milk' (kṣīrāmbhodhijalāiḥ), and adorned it with divine ornaments (378). The gods placed his body upon a pyre of sandal and aloe wood, and threw fragrant substances upon it (383). Cloud youths (meghakumārakāḥ) quenched (vyadhyāpayan) the pyre (385). Over the bones of the Lord the gods erected a jeweled stūpa, and then dispersed to their several homes (358-393).

---

[29] Henceforth known as the mountain of Pārçvanātha (Pārçvanātha-çikhara); see Indian Antiquary ii. 354. According to Wilson, Asiatic Researches xvii, p. 276, there is a temple of Pārçvanātha on Mount Sameta Sīkhar or Parasnāth in Pachete, on the frontier of Rāmgarh, described in 'Description of the Temple of Pārçvanātha at Samet Sīkhar,' by Lieut-Col. William Franklin, in the Transactions of the Royal Asiatic Society, i. 507 ff. See also Colebrooke's Essays,[2] vol. ii, p. 191, note 3.

ADDITIONAL NOTES

These are, in general, longer comments whose presence in the body of the book would interrupt the connection, or distract the attention of the reader. They are for the most part either small treatises, or bibliografical summaries of the leading fiction motifs which are braided into the stories. The author, with a view to future encyclopedic treatment (see his Program in the Journal of the American Oriental Society, xxxvi. 54 ff.), has undertaken to furnish these motifs with that caption under which it seemed to him fit or likely that they may in future pass current among students of fiction. For these subjective conclusions he begs, where possible, the complacent, or even indulgent consent of other workers in this field. Settled conventions in this regard are a prime technical help in the systematical study of fiction, more important than personal preferences, however justified these might be when taken up singly by themselves; consider, e. g., such motif captions as 'Cave Call,' 'Tortoise-on-Stick,' or 'Count not your chickens before they are Hatched,' on pp. 58 ff. of the article cited above.

The numerous citations following, for the most part, explain themselves. The Daçakumāra Carita is cited in the edition in two volumes, by Bühler and Peterson, in the Bombay Sanskrit Series, volumes x and xlii. Pradyumnācārya's Samarādityasaṁkṣepa (ed. Jacobi, Ahmedabad 1906) is cited as Samarād. The source of the last-mentioned work, the Prākrit Samarāïccakahā, is not completely in my hands, and is, therefore, cited rarely.

Additional note 1, to p. 29: *Promise to return*

This motif of fiction may be designated conventionally as, 'Promise to return.' The return, on its face, it always to sure destruction or to an evil fate; yet turns out happily for the returner. In Kathāsaritsāgara 123. 170 ff. Keçaṭa comes upon a Rākṣasa who proposes to devour him. Keçaṭa swears that he will return, after having done a service he promised. He is allowed to go, and marries Rūpavatī. In the night, after lying awake despondently, he starts to return, but is followed by Rūpavatī, who has noticed his queer actions. The Rākṣasa acclaims him a noble man, but prepares to eat him. Rūpavatī says, 'Eat me, for if my husband is eaten, what will become of me?' The Rākṣasa says, 'You can live on alms, if any one refuses to give you alms, his head shall split into a hundred pieces.' Then she says, 'Give me my husband by way of alms.' The Rākṣasa will not give him: his head splits into a hundred pieces.—N. B. This story introduces two additional familiar motifs: 'Head bursting' (e. g., Bṛhaddevatā 4. 120; Pārçvanātha 2. 812; Jātakas 210, 358, 422); and 'Devil Tricked' ('Dummer Täufel'); e. g. Kathās. 28. 156 ff.; ZDMG. lxi. 20, with note on p. 69.

Vetālapañcaviṅçati: Çivadāsa, 9; Kathāsaritsāgara 84; Baitāl Pachīsī 9, Madanasenā is engaged to Samudradatta. Dharmadatta sees her, falls in love with her, and exacts from her a promise that she will come to him, untouched, on her bridal night. Her husband generously permits her to go to her ardent lover. On the way she is seized by a thief, who is also ravished by her beauty. She tells him of her tryst with Dharmadatta, and begs him to wait for her return, because she must keep her promise. When she comes to Dharmadatta, she tells what has happened. Rejoiced at her truthfulness, he lets her return to the thief, who in turn is moved by her faith, and allows her to return to her husband, with whom she lives happily ever after.—For parallels outside India see Tawney in his Translation of Kathāsaritsāgara, vol. ii, p. 281; Oesterley, Baitāl Pachīsī, p. 197 ff.

Hitopadeça in Braj Bhākhā (Hertel, Das Pañcatantra, p. 56, who cites a variant from Hemavijaya's Kathāratnākara): A cow strays from the herd, is attacked by a hungry lion, but begs him to spare her, until she has given suck to her calf. The lion allows her to go, but when she approaches her calf, the latter notices her grief, and refuses to suck. The cow tells of her promise; the calf accompanies the cow back to the lion, because its grief for its mother would, in any case, have killed it. The lion is rejoiced, and declares that the cow henceforth is his sister; the calf his nephew.

Jātaka 513, a king is seized by an ogre, while hunting. The ogre allows the king to go home on a promise to return next day to be eaten. His heroic son returns in his place, but is spared by the ogre.

Additional note 2, to p. 30: *Overhearing.*

One of the most fecund of Hindu story motifs is 'Overhearing,' either under natural human circumstances, or, oftener, in the sequel of magical interference in the fate of the hero of the story on the part of some sentient beings. In the latter case, especially, overhearing serves as *deus ex machina,* to save from death, sickness, or grave danger; to lift from poverty, or low station, to wealth and glory; and to instruct in wisdom or morality. The conversing parties are usually a pair; sometimes a large or indeterminate number; rarely a soliloquist. Birds are the favorite conversers; spirits and Rākṣasas ('dumme täufel') are common, but other animals and even men occur. The subject will figure as an important rubric in the future Encyclopedia of Hindu Fiction. By way of preliminary bibliography we may mention: Chāndogya-Upaniṣad 4. 1. 2; Mahābhārata 13. 42. 17 ff.; Pañcatantra 2. 2; 2. 5; 3. 10; Kathāsaritsāgara 5. 20 ff.; 11. 63 ff.; 17. 115 ff.; 20. 162; 26. 28; 28. 123; 29. 128 ff.; Vikrama Carita 11 and 14 (Indische Studien, xv, pp. 344, 359); Lescallier, Le Trône Enchanté, pp. 30 ff.; Jātakas 284, 314, 386, 445; Pārçvanātha Caritra 2. 518 ff., 839 ff.; 3. 382; 7. 87, 428 ff.; 8. 287 ff.; Pariçiṣṭaparvan 7. 290 ff.; Kathākoça, pp. 49 ff., 55 ff., 125 ff., 160 ff.; Prabandhacintāmaṇi, p. 174; Kathāprakāça (Eggeling, in Gurupūjākāumudī, pp. 121, 123); Suvābahuttarīkathā, nr. 71 (Hertel, in Festschrift f. Ernst Windisch, pp. 149 ff.); Hemavijaya's Kathāratnākara, nr. 29 (Hertel, Das Pañcatantra, p. 145); Pañcākhyānavārttika, nrs. 26 and 34 (Hertel, ibid. 145, 147); Jülg, Mongolische Märchen, pp. 11, 147 ff.; Kalmükische Märchen, pp. 27 ff., 53 ff.; Siamese Paksi Pakaranam nr. 24 (Hertel, ibid., p. 351); Pavie, Contes Populaires du Cambodge, pp. 110 ff.; Day, Folk-Tales of Bengal, pp. 40 ff., 105 ff., 132 ff.; Frere, Old Deccan Days, pp. 74 ff., 120 ff., 136 ff.; Steel and Temple, Wide-Awake Stories, pp. 138 ff.; Stokes, Indian Fairy Tales, p. 5; Neogi, Tales Sacred and Secular, p. 87; ZDMG. lxi. 26; Indian Antiquary, iv. 261; x. 366 ff.; xi. 342; xvii. 75.

Additional note 3, to p. 30: *Proclamation by drum.*

Proclamation or advertizing is regularly done by beat of drum. He who responds to the advertizement touches the drum, and is brought before the king for a hearing. Thus Pārçvanātha 3. 460,

Prabandhacintāmaṇi, p. 112; Kathākoça, pp. 29, 151, 164; Pañcatantra 5. 13; Çukasaptati 46; Suvābahuttarīkathā nr. 72 (Hertel, in Festschrift für Ernst Windisch, p. 151); Jātakas 27, 231, 233, 241, 243, 257, 432; Story of Udāyana (Jacobi, Ausgewählte Erzählungen, p. 29, l. 6); Pañcadaṇḍachattraprabandha 4 (p. 44); Samarād. 4. 145 ff.; Day, Folk-Tales of Bengal, pp. 25, 91, 213.

Additional note 4, to p. 30: *Princess and half the kingdom.*

The offer on the part of a king, of the princess' hand and half the kingdom, or half the kingdom by itself, is a cliché of the fairy tale; see, e. g., Kathāsaritsāgara 29. 164; 64, 85; Çukasaptati 46; Pañcadaṇḍachattraprabandha 4 (p. 44); ZDMG. 61. 21; Suvābahuttarīkathā (Festschrift für Ernst Windisch, p. 151); Ralston, Tibetan Tales, p. 43; Frere, Old Deccan Days, p. 37; Day, Folk-Tales of Bengal, pp. 25, 78; Parker, Village Folk-Tales of Ceylon, vol. i, p. 142; Neogi, Tales Sacred and Secular, pp. 61, 67, 125. See Benfey, Das Pañcatantra, i. 520, 522.

Additional note 5, to p. 31: *On a certain aspect of the overhearing motif.*

This curious statement must not be regarded as a general proverb, such as 'the earth hears.' or, 'walls have ears,' but as a brachylogic allusion to a definite occurrence. Kathākoça, p. 164, states in the same connection: 'My child, I will tell you in the day, after looking round, and not at night. Very cunning people wander about under the banyan-tree, like Vararuci.' This stanza is quoted in Sanskrit in nr. 26 of the Gujarātī Pañcākhyānavārttika (see Hertel, Das Pañcatantra, p. 144, note 2), to wit: divā nirīkṣya vaktavyaṁ rātrāu nāiva ca nāiva ca, saṁcaranti mahādhūrtā vaṭe vararucir yathā. According to Hertel this stanza stands also at the head of nr. 29 in Hemavijaya's Kathāratnākara. The stanza alludes to the well-known story, Kathās. 5. 14 ff., in which Vararuci solves the riddle why the dead fish laughed, and so saves the life of a Brahman, and himself gets out of a tight place. The same notion of hindering overhearing appears also in the Kāthaprakāça; see Eggeling in Gurupūjākāumudī, p. 121. This trait of fiction tends to become quasi-proverbial, but does not quite reach the status of a proverb.

Additional note 6, to p. 31: *Miraculous cures.*

Miraculous or skilful cures are common in fiction. Thus, e. g., secretions of ascetics cure diseases in our text, 6. 1226; Kathākoça, p. 36; Jacobi, Ausgewählte Erzählungen aus dem Māhārāṣṭrī, p. 27, l. 35 ff.; dust from ascetics' feet does the same thing, Daçakumāracarita, ii, p. 45; leprosy is cured by dung, Hertel, Das Pañcatantra, pp. 128, 279. Poison is cured by prayers, charms, or charmed water, Kathākoça, p. 102; Daçakumāracarita, i, pp. 11, 49; Jacobi, l. c., p. 83, verse 274[b]. Especially the jewel from a serpent's head cures poison in Campakaçreṣṭhikathānakam; see Hertel, ZDMG. lxv, pp. 436 note 1, 451. See also the tale of Jīvaka in Ralston, Tibetan Tales, pp. 58 ff. Cf. Benfey, Das Pañcatantra, vol. i, pp. 518, 534. For folklore, see Steel and Temple, Wide-Awake Stories, p. 417, bottom.

Additional note 7, to p. 32: *Haṅsa bird and crow.*

This fable of the haṅsa and the crow, as well as its integral traits, are most popular in Hindu fiction. The fable itself Hitopadeça, 3, 4; Jātaka 140; Hemavijaya, Kathāratnākara, 90; Pañcākhyānavārttika, nr. 20 (the last two quoted or cited by Hertel, Das Pañcatantra, p. 143); Rouse, The Talking Thrush, pp. 53, 203. Alluded to fragmentarily, Kathākoça, p. 165. The Siamese Paksi Pakaranam contains two fables directed against any kind of intercourse between swan and crow; see Hertel, Das Pañcatantra, pp. 348, 353. The lowness of the crow is contrasted with the distinction of the haṅsa in Kathākoça, pp. 186, 223; Samayāmātṛkā (Meyer's Translation), p. xvii; ZMDG. lxi. 51 note 4, 57; Böhtlingk's Indische Sprüche, 1137, 1613, 1616, 3500, 6211. Kathās. 112. 96 asks, 'How can a crow and a female swan ever unite?' See also the old fable of the race between the haṅsa and crow, Mahābh. 8. 41. 1 ff., and cf. Jātaka 160. For defecating crow see also Sprüche 5204; Parker, Folk-Tales, vol. i, p. 224.

In Pañcatantra 2. 3; Pūrṇabhadra 1. 12 association between haṅsa and owl results in destruction of the former. On the other hand the vile crow is contrasted with other birds than the haṅsa, especially the kokila: Kathās. 21. 80; Pārçvanātha 5. 174; Bambhadatta (Jacobi, Ausgewählte Erzählungen), p. 5, l. 20; Sprüche, 1612, 1922, 2928, 3248, 6124, 7292. Other animals that misbehave are the cock, Jātakas 284 and 370; and the monkey, Jātakas 174, 244, 278, 404, 412.

Additional note 8, to p. 34: *Biter bit.*

This is the popular fiction motif which may be designated, 'Biter bit.' 'Often the harm that one wishes to do to another, recoils on one's self, as a ball thrown against a wall,' Kathās. 20. 213. In the version of the present story in the Suvābahuttarīkathā, nr. 72, the plotting servitor (here a barber) is boiled in oil. In the story of Vanarāja, Pārçvanātha 7. 710 ff. (see p. 157), Narasiṅha, son of King Susthita who plots against Vanarāja, is killed instead of Vanarāja, and Susthita comes to grief. The son of the treasurer who sends Ghoṣaka to be killed by a potter, changes places with Ghoṣaka and is killed, Dhammapada Commentary 2. 1 (page 80 of Burlingame's Digest). In Kathās. 20. 195 ff. King Ādityaprabha plots to victimize the Brahman Phalabhūti, but, instead, his own son Candraprabha comes to grief. Excellent 'Biter bit' stories are told in Jülg, Kalmükische Märchen, pp. 43 ff., 55 ff.; Kathākoça, p. 130. The theme is implicated with that of the 'Uriah letter'; see note on p. 160. For other Oriental and Western parallels see Benfey, Pañcatantra i. 320; Tawney, Translation of the Kathāsaritsāgara, vol. i, p. 162 note; and Cosquin, Le conte de 'la chaudière brouillante et la feinte maladressée' dans l'Inde et hors de l'Inde, Revue des Traditions Populaires, January-April, 1910. For the same psychic motif in folklore see Steel and Temple, Wide-Awake Stories, p. 408. Cf. also Indian Antiquary, x. 190; xi. 84 ff.

Additional note 9, to p. 39: *Lecherous Ass.*

The popular conception that the ass is a lecherous animal is reflected especially in ritualistic texts and fiction. Weber, Indische Studien, x. 102, and Pischel, Vedische Studien, i. 82 ff., have gathered a considerable number of passages from both kinds of sources; cf. also Benfey, Pañcatantra, i. 432. In fable and fairy-tale the ass scarcely ever appears out of this rôle; see, e. g. Pañcatantra 4. 7; Hitopadeça 3. 3; Kathās. 63. 134; ZDMG. lxi. 20; Dhammapada Commentary 1. 9[c]. In Pārçvanātha 7. 225 a bawd (kuṭṭinī) is turned into a she-ass; similarly in Pañcadaṇḍachattraprabandha 3 (p. 39). In Vikrama Carita (Indische Studien xv. 252; Lescallier, Le Trône Enchanté, p. 4) Indra's doorkeeper atones for his unchastity in the same distressing way. But the more frequent use of this idea as an incidental or progressive motif in fiction is, as here, 'ride on the ass' on the part of the delinquent. Thus Pārçvanātha 3. 885; Vetālapañcavinçati (Çivadāsa) 21; Ralston, Tibetan Tales, p. 232; Samayāmātṛkā (Meyer's Translation), p. 79, note. The ideal procedure is, to place the delinquent face to tail, holding the tail of the ass in hand in place of bridle, and so to be paraded round the city. See Elliot's History of India (ed. Dowson), vi. 300, and cf. Weber's note to Pañcadaṇḍachattraprabandha, p. 75.

Additional note 10, to p. 44: *Dreams as auguries.*

The science of dreams is especially expert in foretelling the birth of a noble son, or of a son who is, quite unexpectedly, destined to become a king. Conspicuous are the fourteen great dreams that indicate, especially in Jain literature, the birth of a Tīrthaṁkara (Savior), or a Cakravartin (emperor); they are described with the utmost elaboration in Kalpasūtra 32 ff. Otherwise, e. g., Pārçvanātha 3. 10; 4. 13; 5. 31; 6. 1014; Jacobi, Ausgewählte Erzählungen, p. 4, l. 34; p. 20, l. 16; Nirayāvalīsuttam, ed. Warren, Aanteckingen, pp. 22 ff. (Amsterdam Academy, 1879). Sixteen great dreams are treated by Hardy, Manual of Buddhism, pp. 314 ff.; Wilson, Mackenzie Collection i. 148; Weber, Çatruṁjaya Māhātmyam, p. 37, note 2; J. Burgess, Indian Antiquary, xxx. pp. 293, 298. Cf. Bidpai's fables (Keith-Falconer) xxxi ff., 209 ff.

Drinking the moon, or being entered by the moon, or seeing the moon is an equally frequent augury of royalty. The Tīrthaṁkara Candraprabhu is born, after his pregnant mother has longed to drink the moon; see Stevenson, The Heart of Jainism, p. 53. Mūladeva dreams that the full-orbed moon has entered his belly,[1] a sign that he will become king. The sight of the moon in a dream secures to Madanarekhā (Madanarehā) an imperial son, in the story of Nami.[2] In Pariçiṣṭaparvan 8. 231, a pregnant woman desires to drink the moon, a sign that her son will become king.

[1] Jacobi, Ausgewählte Erzählungen, p. 62, l. 5.
[2] Jacobi, ibid., p. 41, l. 23 ff.; Kathākoça, p. 19; Pārçvanātha 6. 792.

In Kathākoça, p. 71 queen Çrīsundarī is foretold by dream of the moon that she will be the mother of king Kurucandra. See also Samarād. 5. 8.

Again, a dream lion is a sign of royalty. Thus the present passage; Samarād. 2. 8; and Pariçiṣṭaparvan 2. 52, where Dhāriṇī, after seeing a lion in a dream, conceives a son, Jambū, who is an incarnation of the god Vidyunmālin. The rebirths of Guṇasena and Agniçarman in Pradyumnasūri's Samarādityasaṁkṣepa 2. 8, 357; 3. 10; 4. 13; 5. 8; 7. 8; 8. 8 are regularly heralded by glorious dreams. And Kuntī gives birth successively to three sons, each ushered in by auspicious dreams in the Çatruṁjaya Māhātmyam (Burgess, Ind. Ant. xxxi. p. 299). Cf. also Kathākoça, p. 64. For other dreams that augur royalty see my article on Mūladeva, Proceedings of the American Philosophical Society, vol. lii, p. 646, note 63.

In other ways also dreams are associated with child birth and child happiness. Especially, children are named to match dreams. In Çālibhadra Carita 2. 51 Bhadrā, wife of the merchant Gobhadra, sees a ripening rice-field, and bears a son who is given the name of Çālibhadra ('Rice-luck'). In the present text, 5. 125, the Saint Pārçva owes his name to a dream. Apparently this mode of naming is particularly popular with the Jainas; see the accounts of the naming of the Arhats in Stevenson, The Heart of Jainism, pp. 51 ff. Similarly, Kathākoça, p. 125, queen Kumudinī sees a heap of jewels in her sleep, therefore names the son with whom she is pregnant Ratnaçikha ('Jewel-crest'). Kathākoça, 146, queen Madanasenā sees in a dream a lotus lake; when her son is born they give him the name Madanaçekhara. Kathākoça, 195, the girl Davadantī (Damayantī) is so named because, when her mother is pregnant with her, she sees in her dream an elefant (dantin) being burned in a forest fire (dava). See also Jātaka 547.

In Daçakumāracarita i. 6 a queen beholds towards morning an auspicious dream vision, hearing the words, 'Conceive by His Majesty the fruit of the creeper that fulfils wishes.' Thereupon she conceives a child, the blossom of her beloved's heart's desire. Kathās. 43. 143, King Karpūraka of Karpūrasaṁbhava is visited in a dream by Çiva, who says: 'Rise up, a daughter shall be born to you, who shall be superior to a son, whose husband (Naravāhanadatta) shall obtain the sovereignty of the Vidyādharas. In the tale of Domuha,[3] one of the four Pratyekabuddhas, Guṇamālā, king Domuha's queen, has seven sons, but no daughter. She vows an oblation to the Yakkha, called Mayaṇa. She obtains a daughter, announced by a dream, in which she receives a cluster of blossoms from the tree Parijāta. And she names her Mayaṇamañjarī, 'Love Blossom.'

For sixteen inauspicious dreams, see Jātaka 77.

Additional note 11, to p. 45: *Eating grass.*

Enemies must be spared, when they place themselves in the humble condition of non-carnivorous animals. For, carnivorous animals, that do not eat grass, are, by implication noxious, and may be slain; cf. Benfey, Pañcatantra ii. 316 (i. 599). On the principle of *noblesse oblige* human beings that present themselves by some sign in the character of grass-eaters are exempt from injury. See this text 3. 592; Prabandhacintāmaṇi, pp. 93, 300. Accordingly, in Pārçva 3. 377, king Hariçcandra puts grass on his head to show that he is willing to sell himself into slavery. In Prabandhacintāmaṇi 161, 279 grass and water are thrown, by way of challenge, into the house of a prospective disputant, to symbolize his ultimate submission. See Tawney on p. 210 of his Translation of Prabandhacintāmaṇi; Pischel, Proceedings of the Royal Prussian Academy, 1908, vol. xxiii, pp. 445 ff.—Note that in Pārçvanātha 5. 227, 229; Samarād. 2. 409, 412, a sword or axe is tied to the throat, as a more obvious sign of submission.

Additional note 12, to p. 47: *Wicked ascetics.*

Kāpālikas are worshipers of Çiva of the left hand (çākta), who carry skulls of men as ornaments, and eat and drink from them. They are always engaged in evil and cruel magic for their own aggrandizement, or their own lust, thus acting the rôle of the malignant wizard in Hindu fiction. The tales about them, or about wicked Yogins or mendicants are legion. As a rule they come to grief in the end. See, e. g. Kathās. 24. 82 ff.; 38. 47 ff.; 121. 6 ff.; Vetālapañcaviñçati 24; Çatruṁjaya Māhātmyam 10. 99 ff.; Pārçvanātha 8. 139; Samarād. 4. 183 ff.; 6. 467; 7. 201 ff.;

[3] See Jacobi, Ausgewählte Erzählungen, p. 39, l. 15 ff.

Lescallier, Le Trône Enchanté, pp. 177 ff.; Neogi, Tales Sacred and Secular, pp. 93 ff.; Parker, Village Folk-Tales of Ceylon, vol. i, pp. 347, 359, 367.

Additional note 13, to p. 51: *Çibi motif.*

The story of king Çibi (Çivi), or Uçīnara, in which he offers his own flesh in order to spare other life, from Mahābh. 3. 130, 197; 13. 32 and Jātaka 499 (Çivi-Jātaka), and Kathās. 7. 88 on, is not only itself reiterated in narrative and Buddhist sculpture, but becomes typical of noble self-sacrifice. Especially the Vikrama Carita makes its hero a sort of standard Çibi, whose āudārya ('native nobility') obliges him to sacrifice himself for others; see Weber, Indische Studien xv. 314, 333, 335, 347, 396, 410, 421, 424; Lescallier, Le Trône Enchanté, pp. 94, 164. Brahmanical, Buddhist (Hindu, Chinese, and Tibetan), and Jaina literature vie with each other in exploiting the idea. The subject is one of the standard motifs of fiction. Of more recent literature (since Benfey, Das Pañcatantra, vol. i. 388) we may mention Chavannes, Cinq Cent Contes, nr. 2; Rockhill, JAOS. xviii. 3, 5; and Hertel, Das Pañcatantra, pp. 14, 296, 375, bottom. In the present text see also 3. 42 ff.; 7. 749-769, and cf. the note on the last-named passage, p. 159.

Additional note 14, to p. 52: *Animated Statues and Dolls.*

Aside from the classical throne statues (siṅhāsana-puttalikā: Indische Studien xv. 185 ff.), animated statues occur frequently in fiction. Especially single idols become alive, as occasion demands. In Pārçva 7. 638 ff. a hungry boy says to the image of a Yakṣa, 'Give me modaka, I am hungry,' touching the belly of the Yakṣa, who, tho made of stone, gives him sweetmeats. Cf. the saying in 3. 331 of the same text, 'Even stone idols, to whom devotion is paid with intent mind, straightway show delight.' In Pārçva 7. 763 a foolish religious visits an idol of Çiva, and finds that it has gone blind of one eye. The religious is very sorry, expresses loathing for the dastardly deed, but himself does nothing. A Pulindra comes along, sees the same thing, gouges out his own eye, and places it in the socket of the idol's eye (Benfey, Pañcatantra i. 389, quotes a similar South-Indian story). In Jātaka 155 the Bodhisat and his father Gagga attempt to pass the night in a house haunted by a Yakkha who lives on a pillar. In Ralston,Tibetan Tales, p. 81, a gate-keeper of Vāiçālī dies, and is born again among the demons. He asks the inhabitants of Vāiçālī to confer upon him the position of a Yakṣa, and to hang a bell around his neck. Whenever any foe to the inhabitants of Vāiçālī appears, he will make the bell sound, until the foe is arrested, or has fled. In Prabandhacintāmaṇi, p. 312, an image of Gaṇeça on the banks of the Siprā is worshiped by a Brahman of Avanti. By way of recompense the image teaches the Brahman the grammar of Pāṇini. In Jülg's, Mongolische Märchen, p. 240, King Ardschi-Bordschi (Bhojarāja) has 71 wives, the noblest of whom he asks to consecrate herself for the throne. As she approaches the throne a wooden statue addresses her: 'Stop, the wife of the saintly King Vikramāditya never had an improper thought away from her husband; if you are such, receive consecration; if not, desist!' Cf. Benfey, Pañcatantra i. 248. In Pariçiṣṭaparvan, 3. 249, Lalitāñga is smuggled into the harem by the queen's order, in the disguise of a Yakṣa statue.

Very often statues are animated by beautiful women destined for love. In Vīracarita xiii (Ind. Stud. xiv. 119) a Brahman, Raviprabhu, sees in a Çiva temple four wooden statues, one of which is so beautiful that he looks at it uninterruptedly for eight days. The figure then steps out of the wood, and discloses herself as an Apsaras, conjured into a wooden statue, until a man should look at her unceasingly for eight days: that man should be her husband. Similarly, Kathās. 121. 145 ff., the heavenly nymph Kalāvatī is cursed into a temple statue, until that temple, which it has taken many years to complete, shall perish, and be leveled to the ground. Her lover, the gambler Ṭhiṇṭhākarāla, by a trick, gets the temple destroyed, and lives ever after happily with Kalāvatī. Cf. with this Vāsavadattā turned to stone by a hermit's curse in Subandhu's novel; see Gray's translation, p. 136, note 7 (folk-lore parallels). Once more, Kathās. 37. 8 ff., a Vidyādhara maiden Anurāgaparā, enters an image of Gāurī, carved on a stone pillar. A merchant's son, Niçcayadatta, comes there, first anoints his limbs, and then places unguent on the pillar in order to anoint his back, by rubbing it against the stone. The maiden in the pillar, enamoured of him, rubs his back for him; he seizes her hand, makes her come out of the pillar, and ultimately marries her.

Kathās. 123. 130 ff. Vikramāditya, in company with a Vetāla, enters a temple, and beholds there a dance before a Liñga, executed by singers and players. At the end of the spectacle the dancing nymphs disappear in the figures carved on pillars of the temple; in the same way the singers and players go into the figures of men, painted on the walls. The Vetāla says: 'Such is this heavenly enchantment produced by Viçvakarman, lasting forever, for this will always take place at both twilights.'

There are next, animated dolls, which are inhabited by more or less divine persons. In Vīracarita vii (Ind. Stud. xiv. 108) Çālavāhana hears the cry of a woman, who declares that she is Sāmrājyalakṣmī ('Royal Fortune'), wailing over the downfall of virtue in the world. She desires to live four days in the body of a beautiful woman. Çālavāhana vows that he will marry all maidens, in order that she may find refuge on his breast. The Brahmans fear that the castes will become confused, and implore Karṇakumārī (perhaps, Kanyakumārī = Bhavānī), who promises aid. Brahmā gives a doll made of dough to the Brahman Çamīka; she turns into a beautiful maiden. Çālavāhana wishes to wed her, but, as the veil is being drawn from the bride, she proves to be Karṇakumārī. Çālavāhana flees horrified, and penetrates thru Abhihrada into hell.

In Vīracarita xi (Ind. Stud. xiv. 116) Pārvatī makes for herself a doll girl, Candanaputrī, so beautiful, that she sees fit to hide her from the sight of her spouse. She hides her away in Malayagiri, where she goes daily to adorn her. Çiva becomes suspicious, dogs her steps, sees the doll, and, when alone with her, caresses her. When the goddess finds out the misdemeanor cf her creature, she curses her into a she-jackal, the curse to last until she has born a child to Çiva.

Less often than might be expected, animated statues or dolls appear in the rôle of automatons (Hebrew, Golems). In Ralston, Tibetan Tales, p. 361, a mechanician sends an artificial maiden to wait upon a guest. She washes his feet, and then stands still. Desiring to enjoy her, he seizes her by the hand, whereupon she collapses and turns into a heap of chips. In Jülg, Mongolische Märchen, pp. 235 ff., one of four shepherd boys fashions a woman out of wood; the second of them paints her yellow; the third gives her 'characteristic marks'; and the fourth breathes into her the breath of life, so that she becomes a charming, marriageable woman. The four boys quarrel as to who is the rightful owner, and the case is decided, as follows: 'He who made the figure is her father; he who gave her her color, her mother; he who gave her the characteristic marks, the Lama; he who breathed life into her, her husband.' This story is analogous to that of the dead bride (Pārçva 6. 691 ff.). See p. 129, and Hertel, Das Pañcatantra, p. 376.

There are finally a number of stories in which a statue or gold figure serves as a model of a beautiful woman which arouses the love of a man: Kathākoça, p. 149 ff.; Ralston, p. 191; Jātaka 328; Dhammapada Commentary 16. 5. At this point the theme passes into that of 'picture and dream maidens,' to be treated elsewhere.

Additional note 15, to p. 52: *Marriage with low-caste person.*

Marriage, or intercourse with a low-born person is condemned, criticized, or regretted, Mahābh. 13. 47. 1 ff.; Pārçvanātha 3. 350 ff., 449 ff.; Prabandhacintāmaṇi, p. 46; Daçakumāracarita, i, p. 67; Jātakas 152; 465; Bambhadatta in Jacobi, Ausgewählte Erzählungen, p. 5, l. 20 ff.; Parker, Village Folk-Tales of Ceylon, vol. iii, p. 309. It is like the mating of haṅsa or kokila with a crow, reprobated in all Hindu literature; see note 7, on p. 187, and cf. my paper, 'On talking birds' in Festgruss an Windisch, p. 355, note. Nevertheless, 'the heart-deer of some noble lover runs occasionally into the net of the hunter love,' even tho the beloved person is low-born, as is shown by the chain of stories beginning with Kathās. 112. 89 ff. Cf. the above-mentioned paper, 'On talking birds,' p. 358; Çatruṁjaya Māhātmyam (Indian Antiquary, xxx. 296). In the first story of Pañcadaṇḍachattraprabandha, no less a personage than Vikramāditya marries a clever low-born maiden. The story in the end justifies this by a verse: 'Garner high knowledge from low people; money from the impure; nectar from poison; a beautiful wife from a low family (cf. Manu 2. 238-239; Böhtlingk, Indische Sprüche, nr. 6227).

Additional note 16, to p. 57: *The sin of sacrificing a dough cock (piṣṭakurkuṭa)*

The extreme attitude of Jaina religion in forbidding ahiṅsā, or injury of living things, takes, in this instance, the view that it is criminal to injure even the image of a living thing, namely a piṣṭakurkuṭa, or piṣṭamaya kurkuṭa, 'a cock made of dough.' In Samarādityaṁkṣepa 4. 260 ff., Surendradatta, beloved son of King Amaradatta and Queen Yaçodharā, rules in Viçālā; he is married to the beautiful Nayanāvalī. Discovering 'the messenger of Dharma' (a grey hair: see JAOS. xxxvi. 57 ff.) in his head, he decides to take vows, and tells Nayanāvalī, who pretends to be so attached to him, that she would follow him into homelessness. But by night, while reflecting how hard it would be, after all, to leave behind Nayanāvalī, he discovers her in a bower, in the company of a hunchbacked night watchman, who is chiding her because she has come late. Surendradatta is about to cut down both, but is deterred by the low caste of the offender, and his purpose of turning ascetic.

He has an evil dream about which he consults his mother Yaçodharā. She advises him to make a sacrifice of living things from earth, water, or air to the family divinities, to avert the evil (çāntikarma, averruncatio). He is horrified at the suggestion, proposing instead to offer flesh and blood from his own body. As he is about to use his sword on himself, his mother stops him, bidding him sacrifice a cock who is just then crowing. But he persists in refusing to injure any other than himself.

He then consents to a proposal of his mother that he offer a cock made of dough (piṣṭakurkuṭa). The mother 'slays' the cock with his sword, in front of a family divinity, with the express prayer that the sacrifice avert the evil dream. She then orders the cook to prepare the cock's 'flesh'; the son eats of it, after his mother has pointed out that it is only make-belief flesh. He thus establishes for himself a fateful karma, which his mother shares with him.

Surendradatta makes over his kingdom to his son Guṇadhara, and proposes to go out into the life of an homeless ascetic. Nayanāvalī decides to poison him, so as not to have to join him. In order to elude the eyes of the poison-detecting cakora birds, she sets unpoisoned food before him, but gives him a poisonous magic pill with his rinsing-water. This he drinks down with the water and falls to the ground. A watchman perceives the situation, but, while he calls physicians, Nayanāvalī, in pretended grief, falls upon her husband and chokes him to death.

Surendradatta is reborn as a peacock on the mountain of Silindhra. While still young, he is caught by a hunter, who presents him to an officer living in Nandāpāṭaka. He grows up, living on worms, suffering from thirst, cold, and heat. In time, the officer presents him to king Guṇadhara, Surendradatta's own son. In the meanwhile his mother Yaçodharā, who has also died, of diarrhoea, is reborn as a fleet dog in the village of Dhānyapūraka. This dog is also presented to Guṇadhara, who conceives affection for both dog and peacock. One day the peacock climbs to the turret of the palace, and sees there his former wife Nayanāvalī in amorous intercourse with the hunchback. Remembering his former birth, he angrily pecks at her with claws and bill. She takes up an iron hammer belonging to the hunchback, and hits the peacock on the head, so that he rolls down stairs where the king is amusing himself by gambling. The king cries out, 'catch him, catch him!' The dog (Surendradatta's former mother) seizes the peacock by the throat. Somebody hits the dog on the head, who, spitting blood, lets go; both animals fall to the ground, nearly dead. Surendradatta, in his death throes, reflects on the dire karma which has consigned him to the life of a worm-eater, and to die eaten by a dog. Thus both animals perish.

Similarly, Surendradatta and Yaçodharā pass thru other animal existences, full of suffering and degradation. First, as antelope and serpent, in which the antelope catches the serpent by the tail, and the serpent bites the antelope in the foot. Next, as rohita fish and crocodile, in which the crocodile is killed in the act of swallowing the fish; the fish is caught and eaten by Guṇasena and Nayanāvalī, his former son and faithless wife. In the last animal existence they are reborn in the womb of a hen. At the moment of their birth a cat eats the mother; the two eggs fall upon an ash-heap, are covered up by a female sweep (tyajantī), and are hatched out as a cock and hen of fine plumage. They come into the possession of an officer, who presents them to Guṇadhara for his sport. The king goes to a pleasure grove, where he is attended by the officer with the two cocks. There the officer meets a Sage, listens to his sermon, but refuses to renounce the slaughter of animals. The Sage reproves him, assuring him that, unless he does so, he will endure the same fate as did this pair of cocks who had in a former birth 'killed' a cock made of dough (piṣṭakurkuṭa). As he summarizes the story of their tragic rebirths, the cocks are enlightened and give forth a joyous crowing. King Guṇadhara, sporting with his queen Jayāvalī in a tent, hears their noise, tells her that he will make a hit by sound, and slays the pair with an arrow. The cocks are then reborn as the boy Abhayaruci and the girl Abhayamati in the womb of Jayāvalī, and in due time all are converted and saved.

Additional note 17, to p. 62: *Poison-damsel.*

The idea that a woman, or, more rarely, a man, may thru personality, exercise a baneful influence is common. It has crystallized into the term viṣakanyā, 'poison-damsel'; or viṣa-hasta 'poison-handed'; or viṣāñganā 'poison-woman.' The notion is frequently put to use in fiction. In Pariçiṣṭaparvan 8. 327, king Nanda has a beautiful girl fed on poison, and in due time marries her to Parvata. When he seizes her hand, her poisonous sweat penetrates thru his skin, he dies, and Candragupta takes possession of the kingdom. Such a poison-damsel figures in a plot against Candragupta, Mudrārākṣasa (ed. Hillebrandt), p. 15, l. 11; p. 131, l. 6; p. 133, l. 1. In Kathās. 19. 42 the minister Yogakaraṇḍaka sends poison-damsels as dancing girls among the host of King Vatsa. For this trick Tawney, in a footnote on p. 149 of the first volume of his Translation, aptly compares the xith tale in Gesta Romanorum, where an Indian queen sends a poison-damsel to Alexander the Great, but Aristotle frustrates the stratagem. Benfey, Das Pañcatantra, vol. i, p. 598, reports from the Anvār-i-Suhailī a similar tale, in which a queen has the chin and neck of her rival, a slave girl, rubbed with poison, in order to kill her husband, who is, however, rescued by a faithful servant. This trick costs a lion his life in Jātaka 93, where he licks a doe smeared with poison for his destruction. In the 71st tale of the Suvābahuttarīkathā the minister Siddreh quenches king Dharmdat's desire for king Kāmsundar's daughter, by telling him that she is a poison-damsel: see Hertel in Festschrift an Ernst Windisch, p. 146.

The same idea is carried out figuratively. In Pārçvanātha 8. 51 Bandhudatta marries Candralekhā, but she dies at the wedding by serpent's bite; in the same way six wives die as soon as he marries them. He is, therefore, regarded as a 'poison-hand,' and can obtain no further maidens. Cf. the story of the woman who slew eleven husbands, Kathās. 66. 78 ff. In Çukasaptati 46. 47 a Brahman's wife is such a holy terror as to be named Karagarā 'Poison-Hand'; cf. Benfey, Pañcatantra, i. 521.

There exists in India a treatise for finding out whether a woman is a 'poison-damsel.' It is called Viṣakanyā-lakṣaṇa. It is part of a treatise on horoscopes; see Weber, Handschriften-Verzeichnisse, vol. i, p. 263 (nr. 879), note 2.

Additional note 18, to p. 62: *Pragmatic çloka.*

This motif may be designated as pragmatic, or, perhaps, drastic çloka. Such stanzas figure in the Nala Episode of Mahābhārata, 16 and 17; Kathās. 20. 35, 212; Vāsavadattā (Gray's Translation, p. 93); Kathākoça, p. 28; Çatruṁjaya Māhātmyam (Indian Antiquary, xxx. 241); Jātakas 214, 338, 373. Love messages in çloka, Pārçvanātha 8. 8 ff.; Samarād. 2. 93 ff.; Jacobi, Ausgewählte Erzählungen, p. 12, l. 3. See for this entire theme, Benfey, Pañcatantra, vol. i, pp. 320, 598; Hertel, Das Pañcatantra, pp. 46, 142, 233, 297, 375; Charpentier, Paccekabuddhageschichten, pp. 3 ff., 25 ff., 35; the author in Proceedings of the American Philosophical Society, vol. lvi, p. 14, note 27; Gray in the Introduction to his Translation of Vāsavadattā, p. 35.

Additional note 19, to p. 64: *Josef and Potifar's wife.*

This motif is one of the stock of incidental and progress making devices of Hindu fiction. It takes three forms: either the woman tempts and the man rejects her; thus particularly in the impressive Mahāpaduma Jātaka (472). Or, a woman, out of hatred, pretends that a man has made overtures to her, so as to get him into trouble. Or, finally, more rarely, the woman tempts, and the man succumbs. A preliminary bibliografy of the subject is as follows: Mahābh. 1. 103. 1 ff.; 13. 19. 1 ff.-20 end; Kathāsaritsāgara 7. 57; 20. 118; 49. 30; Pārçvanātha 3. 400; 7. 44; Jātaka 472; Samarād. 2. 91 ff.; 5. 98 ff.; Kathāprakāça, in Gurupūjākāumudī, p. 125; Ralston, Tibetan Tales, pp. 102, 206, 282; Steel and Temple, Wide-Awake Stories, p. 222. Cf. W. A. Clouston, The Book of Sindibād, pp. xix ff.

Additional note 20, to p. 65: *Pañcadivyādhivāsa.*

This subject receives additional light from several passages of our text. The theme has been treated a good deal recently, especially by Edgerton in his article, 'Pañcadivyādhivāsa, or Choosing a king by Divine Will,' JAOS. xxx. 158 ff.; by J. J. Meyer, Hindu Tales, pp. 131, 212; and by Hertel, Das Pañcatantra, p. 374 (cf. pp. 144, 148, 155, 372, 373, 382, 385). Edgerton's explanation is unquestionably correct; that of the other two scholars, obviously conceived independently, is not very different.

The gerund adhivāsya occurs in 8. 26. A merchant Sāgara has become rich, therefore, wishes to set up a jeweled ikon (ratnabimba-cikīḥ). He requests the dharmatīrthikas to tell him what god will confer salvation. They tell him to invest with divine or divinatory power a precious jewel (sadratnam adhivāsya), and to think of some divinity who would then tell him. Sāgara does so, whereupon a certain divinity places before him a golden image of the Arhat.

There are two passages in which the pañcadivyādhivāsa is employed to choose a king. In 2. 826 ff. king Sundara, who has gotten low down in the world, goes to sleep under a mango tree, and is thus chosen, to wit:

> tadā tatra pure rājñi vipanne putravarjite,
> hasty-açva-cāmara-chatra-kumbhākhyam adhivāsitam,
> bhramat tatrāyayāu divyapañcakaṁ yatra sundaraḥ.
> çīlena sundaraṁ çīghram upaviṣṭaṁ vilokya tam,
> hayena heṣitaṁ hastipatinā vṛṅhitaṁ kṛtam,
> duritakṣālanāyevāpatat kumbhāmbu mastake,
> upariṣṭāt sthitaṁ chatraṁ lulitaṁ cāmaradvayam.
> sa karīndram athāruhya divyaveṣadharo niçi,
> mantryādibhir nato nītyā praviṣṭaḥ puram utsavāiḥ.

'Then there in the city (Çrīpura) the king died, leaving no son. The divyapañcakam ('oracle-pentad'), infused with divinatory power (adhivāsitam), and having the designation, 'Elefant-horse-chowrie-umbrella-pitcher,' roaming about, arrived at the spot where Sundara was. On account of his (Sundara's) virtue the oracle soon noticed him (lying under a tree). The horse neighed; the elefant-prince roared; the water of the pitcher poured itself upon his head to wash away misfortune; the umbrella stood over him; and the pair of chowries fanned. Sundara mounted the prince of elefants, and, dressed in divine (magic) garments, revered by the ministers and other dignitaries, was conducted by night with festive doings to the city.'

The other passage, 7. 111 ff., concerns the exiled prince Amarasena who has reached Kāñcanapura:

tasmiñç ca samaye tatra pure rājā mṛto 'sutaḥ.
tato hasty-açva-kalaça-chatra-cāmaralakṣaṇam,
bambhramīti pure devādhiṣṭhitaṁ vastupañcakam.
naraṁ rājyadharaṁ kaṁ cit tenānveṣayatā bahiḥ,
gatvā so 'marasenākhyaḥ kumāraḥ sahasāçritaḥ.
ārūḍho 'tha gajaskandhaṁ divyaveṣadharo nṛpaḥ,
praṇamya mantrisāmantanāgarāir abhinanditaḥ.
upariṣṭād dhṛtachatraḥ çvetacāmaravījitaḥ,
puraḥ kāutukibhir lokāiḥ kṛtasaṁgītamañgalaḥ.
çṛṇvan jayajayārāvaṁ janād īkṣitum āgatāt,
pure praviçya çobhāḍhye nītyā rājyaṁ karoti saḥ.

'At that juncture the king there in the city died sonless. Then the five objects defined as elefant, horse, pitcher, umbrella, and chowries, inhabited by god (or, a god), roamed about the city. Seeking some man who should rule the kingdom, the oracle went promptly outside, where was Prince Amarasena. Dressed in divine (magic) garments, he mounted as king upon the back of the elefant, and was acclaimed by the ministers, vassals, and citizens who bowed down before him. The umbrella stood above him; the white chowries waved over him. In front went the admiring people, singing songs and uttering blessings. Hearing the repeated cry of victory from the people, who had come to look on, he entered the festively adorned city, and ruled with discretion.'

Here the word devādhiṣṭhitam, 'god-ridden,' (in a good sense) is perhaps the clearest explanation of adhivāsita, as yet available. But Pārçva, no more than other texts, tells precisely how the five royal insignia are imbued with their divinatory power. Pariçiṣṭaparvan 6. 236, pañcadivyāny abhiṣiktāni, seems to indicate consecration by water—the Hindu equivalent of coronation—as the method, or, perhaps better, one of the methods. This coincides with Prabandhacintāmaṇi, text, p. 288, where the elefant alone is mentioned, tatrāputriṇi nṛpatāu pañcatvam upāgate sati sacivāir abhiṣiktapaṭṭahastī nikhile pi nagare yadṛchayā babhrāma. But there is no reason why this should not have been accompanied, or diversified by the use of mantras, perfumes, etc.; see Edgerton, l. c., p. 163, top.

I would remark that, in the end, the attention of folk-lore, which frequently alludes to the practice, concentrates itself upon the elefant; see Parker, Village Folk-Tales of Ceylon, vols. i, pp. 65, 81, 90, 92, 99; iii. 381, 382 (here royal elefant and hawk).

Additional note 21, to p. 68: *Goddess Fortune.*

Thus Lacchī (Lakṣmī), the royal Fortune of the Vidyādhara Asaṇivega goes over to Sanaṁkumāra (Jacobi, Ausgewählte Erzählungen, p. 23, l. 37). See also Çukasaptati 6; Jātakas 284, 382; Neogi, Tales Sacred and Secular, pp. 102 ff. Cf. also Hertel, Das Pañcatantra, p. 55, bottom (with parallels on p. 56); Hertel, ibid. p. 125. Cf. for Çrī in general Kathākoça, p. 225; Vīracarita xix (Indische Studien, xiv. 131); Kathāprakāça in Gurupūjākāumudī, p. 126; Prabandhacintāmaṇi, p. 11; Hertel, ibid., p. 383.

Additional note 22, to p. 69: *Gold-man.*

The story of the 'gold-man' is familiar from the Pañcatantra on: e. g. Pañcatantra 5. 1; Pūrṇabhadra's frame story in the opening of the fifth book; or Kṣemendra's Bṛhatkathāmañjarī version 5. 2; see Benfey, Pañcatantra ii. 322 ff.; Fritze, Pañcatantra, p. 350 ff. Cf. Benfey, ibid. i. 478; Hertel, Das Pañcatantra, pp. 125, 281, 332. Aside from the present story, the 'gold-man' is mentioned very frequently: Vikrama Carita (Indische Studien, xv. 278, 436); Suvābahuttarīkathā 68 (Hertel in Festschrift an Ernst Windisch, p. 145); Prabandhacintāmaṇi, pp. 10, 276, bottom (cf. Tawney's Translation, p. 207, bottom); Alberuni (Sachau's Translation), vol. i, p. 192. Cf. the note on 'gold-spitting,' p. 148.

Additional note 23, to p. 69: *Barber and Potter.*

The barber is the stock-figure in fiction for the low-born, cunning rascal, and butt of fortune. He is among men comparable to the jackal and crow among the animals (Böhtlingk, Indische Sprüche 3400). 'Son of a barber by a courtezan,' in Pariçiṣṭaparvan exhausts the vocabulary of opprobrium. In Mahābh. 13. 27. 1 ff., Matañga finds out that he is the son of a barber, and tries by asceticism to become a Brahman, but he can only reach the station of wizard, cultivated by woman. In the place of the rascally Sajjana in the Lalitāñga story (p. 26 ff.) the Suvābahuttarīkathā, nr. 72, puts a barber; see Hertel, in Festgruss an Windisch, p. 149. In Suppāraka Jātaka (462) a stingy king is called 'son of a barber.' In Dhammapada Commentary 2. 3ᵉ the king's barber agrees to cut his throat for money. But in Kathās. 32. 147 ff. a barber, whose wife the king has seduced, gets the better of that king by a not too savory trick. For further illustrations see Jātakas 190, 421; Hertel, Das Pañcatantra, pp. 72, 125, 281, 287, 332; ZDMG. lxi. 25.

Curiously enough, occasionally, in Jain texts, the potter takes the place of the barber in these estimates: Bhojaprabandha, stanza 48 (Nirṇayasāgara Press, 1913); p. 75, edition of Jib. Vidyāsāgara; Pārçvanātha 1. 334; Kathākoça, p. 166. Cf. Stevenson, The Heart of Jainism, p. 213: 'One should therefore never be a blacksmith, a limeburner, or a potter, or follow any other trade in which a furnace is used, for in a fire many insect lives are destroyed.' Very dubious reason.

Additional note 24, to p. 83: *Childlessness.*

In fiction childlessness figures frequently, and rather mechanically. It is, of course, always obviated, children being procured by the merit of prayer and sacrifice; by magic, by asceticism; and by simples. Thus, by prayer to sundry divinities or saints, in Vikrama Carita (Indische Studien, xv. 320; Lescallier, Le Trône Enchanté, p. 106); Pariçiṣṭaparvan 2. 51; Jātaka 458; Daçakumāracarita i, p. 3; ii, p. 23; Samarād. 4. 1 ff.; Ralston, Tibetan Tales, pp. 51, 247. In Mahābh. 3. 127. 3 ff.; Kathās. 13. 57 ff. a king obtains thru sacrifice a boy, named Jantu; and as he wants more children, is told to sacrifice Jantu. The panacea asceticism procures children in Mahābh. 3. 106. 7; 3. 293. 1 ff. In Kathās. 55. 149 ff. austerities and endurance of danger have the same effect. Kathās. 39. 5 ff. employs a magic potion; the same text, 9. 10, an oblation of rice, milk, sugar, and spices; Neogi, Tales Sacred and Secular, p. 88, a drug; in Ralston, p. 21, Indra sends a drug. The mango fruit procures children in texts that are far apart: Mahābh. 2. 16. 29; Siamese Paksi Pakaranam (see Hertel, Das Pañcatantra, p. 349); Day, Folk Tales of Bengal, p. 117. The Kāmaçāstra literature catalogs a riotous welter of drugs, plants, and magic; see Richard Schmidt, Beiträge zur Indischen Erotik, pp. 891 ff. J. J. Meyer, in the Introduction to his Translation of

Daçakumāracarita, p. 54, refers to extreme cases in which sterile queens are proffered to the male world in general, in order to procure an heir to the throne.

Additional note 25, to p. 88: *Dohada, or pregnancy whim.*

This is one of the most constant and fruitful of fiction motifs. It ranges all the way from a desire on the part of the woman to eat her husband's entrails, in Pradyumnācārya's Samarādityasaṁkṣepa 2. 361, or to eat flesh off her husband's back, in Ralston, Tibetan Tales, p. 84, to the desire to hear the instructions of a great Saint, especially common in Buddhist and Jain texts; e. g. Pārçvanātha 6. 793. In Çatruṁjaya Māhātmyam (Indian Antiquary xxx. 299) Kuntī on the occasion of her third conception sees, in her dreams, Indra, and consequently longs to kill Dānavas with arrows. In the rebirths of the principal personages in the Samarādityasaṁkṣepa, as doubtless, in its Prākrit prototype, the Samarāïcca Kahā, pregnant women are afflicted with dohada in nearly every instance; see 2. 13, 361; 3. 15; 4. 444; 5. 10; 6. 388. A preliminary bibliografy, subject to indefinite increase is as follows: Kathās. 22. 9; 30. 46; 34. 31; 35. 117; 46. 27; Jātakas 292, 309, 338, 342, 389, 400, 445 [1]; Dhammapada Commentary 4. 3ᵃ; 5. 15ᵃ; 6. 5ᵇ; Pārçvanātha 6. 793; 7. 275; Kathākoça, pp. 43, 53, 64, 177; Çālibhadra Carita 2. 56, 60; Pariçiṣṭaparvan 1. 246; 2. 61; 8. 231; Māhārāṣṭrī Tales (Jacobi, Ausgewählte Erzählungen), p. 34, l. 26; p. 41, ll. 25, 27; Çatruṁjaya Māhātmyam (Ind. Ant. xxx.), pp. 297, 299 (pluries); Jülg, Kalmükische Märchen, p. 31; Ralston, Tibetan Tales, pp. 84, 247. See Benfey, Das Pañcatantra, vol. i, p. 539; Hertel, Das Pañcatantra, pp. 5, 108, note, 196, 284; Translation of Pariçiṣṭaparvan, p. 41, note 2. See the interesting article on 'Doladuk' = dohada, by Goonetilleke in The Orientalist ii. 81 ff. Schmidt, Beiträge zur Indischen Erotik, p. 393, discusses the etymology of dohada, citing opinions of Lüders, Jolly, Aufrecht, and Böhtlingk.

Additional note 26, to p. 89: *Horse with inverted training.*

This feature of narration is a great favorite with Jain writers. Such an animal does the unexpected, because its rider does not know its peculiarity: when he checks it with the reins the horse

[1] Here 'showing a fancy for sour and strange tastes.'

runs away and leads him into adventure. Thus explicitly Jātaka 546 (Fausböll, vol. vi, p. 408 bottom). Pārçva 3. 500 uses for inverse training the expression vāiparītyena çikṣita; in 4. 25, pratīpaçikṣitva. In Devendra's Māhārāṣṭrī stories the same idea is expressed by vivarīyasikkha = viparītaçikṣa; see Jacobi, Ausgewählte Erzählungen, p. 20, l. 21; p. 45, l. 6; p. 48, l. 27; p. 84, l. 12. The same sort of horse figures in Kathākoça, p. 102, and in Prabandhacintāmaṇi, p. 286, where the word, according to Tawney's reading in the Translation of that text, is viparyastābhyasta. See also the story in Lakṣmīvallabha's commentary on Uttarādhyayana Sūtra, quoted without citation of place by Charpentier, Paccekabuddhageschichten, p. 126. An elefant trained in a similar manner is mentioned in Jātaka 231. Otherwise runaway horses in general carry heroes into adventure: Kathāsaritsāgara 5. 80; 18. 88; 32. 106; 94. 13; Daçakumāracarita i, pp. 4, 5; Kathākoça, pp. 22, 23, 31; Pārçvanātha Caritra 6. 877, 896; Kathāprakāça, in Gurupūjākāumudī, p. 122. A runaway elefant in Jacobi, l. c., p. 35, l. 2. Related with this is the magic horse that carries to a great distance; see Gray's Translation of Vāsavadattā, p. 117 with note.

Additional note 27, to p. 100: *Human sacrifices.*

Human sacrifices appear in fiction in a variety of aspects, two of which are quite standard or stenciled. First, the wild folk of the mountains especially of the Vindhya range, namely, the Çavaras, Bhillas, Pulindas, Tājikas, etc., are in the habit of offering up men to Durgā (Caṇḍikā, Bhavānī) in the ordinary routine of their lives. Usually their chieftains, bearing ferocious names (e. g. Siṅhadaṅṣṭra, Kathās. 56. 22), instigate the sacrifice. Thus, Kathās. 10. 141, 189; 22. 64; 55. 220; 61. 158; 101. 300. Occasionally they have in view some particular end; see Pārçvanātha 8. 101; Samarād. 6. 91. Similarly, in Dhammapada Commentary 8. 9, thieves desire to make a votive offering of a man's flesh and blood to the forest divinity (cf. ibid. 8. 3). A cobra has to be propitiated by a human offering in Parker, Village Folk-Tales of Ceylon, vol. i, p. 58. Secondly, wicked Kāpālikas, worshippers of Çiva of the left hand, or wicked demons, need human sacrifices for magic practices, usually in order to obtain some vidyā, or 'Science' which confers supernatural power: Kathās. 38. 59; Vetālapañcaviṅçati 24; Pañcadaṇḍachatraprabhandha 2 (p. 24); Lescallier, Le Trône Enchanté, pp. 177 ff.; Pārçvanātha 3. 903 ff.; Neogi, Tales Sacred and Secular, pp. 93 ff. In Kathās. 20. 104 the statement is made quite explicitly that eating human flesh confers power to fly. In the present instance the Vidyādharī is noteworthy, because she is by nature already in possession of the vidyās.

But there are also human sacrifices by other persons, and for a variety of other purposes. In Kathās. 20. 53 a queen wishes to make a human sacrifice, in order to confer prosperity upon her lord. In Vīracarita xiii (Indische Studien xiv. 120) king Haryamara offers three men to Caṇḍikā, in order to get access to heaven. In Dhammapada Commentary 5. 1 the heir-apparent of the king of Benares vows to offer the blood of a hundred kings and hundred queens to a spirit, if he comes into the kingdom on the death of his father. In Mahābh. 3. 127. 3 ff.; Kathās. 13. 57 ff. an only son is sacrificed to obtain many children. In Pārçvanātha 7. 422 ff.; Kathākoça, p. 48 queen Rati asks the house divinity for a son, promising in return, to offer her, as bali-offering, her co-wife's, Jayasundarī's, son. In Kathās. 26. 140 some fishermen attempt to sacrifice a man to Durgā, in order to avenge the supposed murder of their father. In Kathās. 37. 39 men are sacrificed by the son of Muravāra, a Turuṣka, to be sent as companions to his dead father. In Kathās. 51. 101 even the great Rāma, in a fit of wickedness, desires to perform a human sacrifice with a man having auspicious marks—the latter qualification being expressed or implied elsewhere in these accounts.—For the subject as a whole see Tawney's note to his Translation of Kathāsaritsāgara, vol. i, p. 445, where it is discussed in connection with the Vedic reminiscence of a puruṣamedha, 'human sacrifice,' undertaken by gods with the body of the noble Asura Namuci.

Additional note 28, to p. 131: '*David and Uriah.*'

Hindu ethics extol the virtue of respecting other peoples' marital relations (sodaryavrata); see Pārçvanātha 2. 723 ff.; 5. 22. Such a person is called paranārīsahodara, 'he who regards the wives of others as sisters,' ZDMG. xxiii. 444; see the story of Veda and Uttaṅka in Mahābh. 1. 3. 90; Kathās. 34. 1 ff.; Prabandhacintāmaṇi, p. 234 (king Kumārapāla treats his neighbors' wives as sisters).

But the gods themselves have set a frightful example of unchastity, incest, and worse; see the catalog of their sexual crimes in Daçakumāracarita i. pp. 44, 71; and Gray's Vāsavadattā, p. 129. Men are no better; hence stories of the 'David and Uriah' variety. In addition to the present gripping account, king Vikramayaças, 'possessor of a hundred wives,' corrupts Viṣṇuçrī, the beautiful spouse of the merchant Nāgadatta, with baleful results that extend thru several rebirths; see the episode in the story of Sanatkumāra, Pārçvanātha 6. 1057 ff.; Kathākoça, p. 32 ff.; Jacobi, Ausgewählte Erzählungen in Māhārāṣṭrī, p. 24, ll. 14 ff.[1] See also Hitopadeça 1. 8; Kathās. 32. 147 ff.; 34. 10 ff.; Jātakas 120, 194, 314, 443; Dhammapada Commentary 5. 1; Kathākoça, pp. 13 ff. (cf. p. 235); Nirmala Çrāvaka, reported by Hertel, Das Pañcatantra, pp. 231 ff.; Benfey, Kleinere Schriften, vol. ii, p. 101.

---

[1] A variant of this story, briefly treated, in the Çatruṁjaya Māhātmyam, sarga 1; see Indian Antiquary xxx. 241; cf. p. 292.

APPENDIX I.

PROVERBS AND PROVERBIAL EXPRESSIONS.

The Pārçvanātha Carita is at the bottom, and in the main, a Jaina dharma and nīti text (religion and morals), therefore, abounds in proverbial stanzas and expressions. Quite a large number of them coincide with those incorporated in Böhtlingk's well-known collection, Indische Sprüche. But others, not less entitled to figure as didactic apophthegms, do not occur in Böhtlingk's lists. Indeed, Jaina texts contain so large a number of new nīti-stanzas, as to call for a renewed endeavor to assemble this class of compositions in one place. The Pārçvanātha contains presumably more than a thousand such stanzas, of which the following account aims to point out some of the more interesting.

Nīti consists not only of solid stanzas devoted to didactic or proverbial themes, but also to incidental statements woven into other discourse. These have not been collected at all, tho they are not less interesting than the set stanzas. Kathāsaritsāgara stops several hundred times to spice its narrative with wise saws and reflections which amount to proverbs. Proportionally the prose Kathākoça and Prabandhacintāmaṇi are even more lavish with such sayings, which are just as much proverbs as, e. g., Manwaring's Mahrattī Proverbs. They are a constant element in Jain narrative, both Sanskrit and Prākrit. A collection of such sayings, arranged thematically, would be a valuable contribution to nīti-literature. For they also will be found repeating themselves, as does, e. g. the proverb, 'Two swords do not go into one scabbard,' in Jacobi's Māhārāṣṭrī Tales, p. 58, l. 31, which recurs in Samarād. 3. 24.

In the following I point out, first, a considerable number of nīti stanzas which figure in Böhtlingk's corpus.[1] Next, by selection, some stanzas out of many, which will ultimately figure in the larger corpus of the future, especially after most of the Jaina Caritras shall have been edited and extracted for this purpose. Finally,

[1] Similarly the Prabandhacintāmaṇi contains 22 stanzas which recur in Böhtlingk's collection. They are indicated in the footnotes to Tawney's Translation.

there is a list of incidental proverbial passages which do not embrace an entire stanza.

1. Proverbs quoted in Böhtlingk's Indische Sprüche.

1. 102 = Bö. 6921.

sarvathā sarvakāryeṣu mādhyasthyaṁ çasyate nṛṇām,
dantapātaḥ kathaṁ na syād atikarpūrabhakṣaṇāt.

Böhtlingk's mss. read paçyate which he corrects to dṛçyate. Our çasyate is the true reading. He translates: 'Allerdings tritt bei dem menschen eine gleichgiltigkeit gegen alle sachen zu tage: wie sollten einem vom übermässigen genuss vom kamfer nicht die zähne ausfallen?' In this rendering the second ardharca is a *non sequitur*. Is not Böhtlingk mistaken? I would render: 'Ever in all concerns moderation is recommended for men: how can excessive consumption of camfor fail to result in the loss of teeth?' In this sense alone the second half hinges properly upon the first half. For the second half cf. Pārçva 1. 15. 3, çarkarām açnatāṁ dantavyathāyāi kiṁ na karkaraḥ. See Pañcadaṇḍachattraprabandha, pp. 45, 80.

1. 103 = Bö. 2504; Kathākoça, p. 161

tārudāho 'tiçītena durbhikṣam ativarṣaṇāt,
atityāgād anāucityam atiḥ kutrāpi neṣyate.

Böhtlingk has ati for our atiḥ: the latter seems rationalized. Böhtlingk's emendation of nekṣyate (so also the mss. of Kathākoça) is supported by our text. Yet neṣyate may be lectio facilior.

1. 105 = Bö. 3708.

nityaṁ kṛtavyayaḥ svāiraṁ merur apy apacīyate,
tejasīva gate vitte naro 'ṅgārasamo bhavet.

Böhtlingk's Mss. read in a: kṛtavyayasvāiram, which he corrects to kṛtavyayasvarṇo. Our reading is the best: 'Even (mount) Meru grows less because he ever freely wastes.' Böhtlingk emends in b aparīyate to apacīyate, thus brilliantly anticipating our text. Pārçva continues with two stanzas (106-107) which deal well with the different attitude of the world towards rich and poor; they seem to echo Cārudatta's stanzas on this theme in the opening of Mṛcchakaṭikā.

1. 118 = Bö. 1576; Kathākoça, p. 162, top

1. 123 = Bö. 6676; Kathākoça, p. 162, top

1. 179 = Bö. 6150

Our text reads pāpakarma for pāpaṁ karma. Böhtlingk notes the reading pāpakarmaṁ.

1. 181 = Bö. 3753

1. 379 = Bö. 7458

1. 688 = Bö. 2589

tṛṇāni bhūmir udakaṁ vāk caturthī ca sūnṛtā,
satām etāni geheṣu nocchidyante (text, no chidyante) kadā cana.

This form of the second ardharca is quoted by Böhtlingk; his version in the text is, etāny api satāṁ gehe nocchidyante kadā ca na.

2. 211: the opposite Bö. 1726

kiṁ karoti kusaṁsargo nijadharmadṛḍhātmanaḥ,
sarpaçīrṣoṣitaḥ kiṁ na harate 'hiviṣaṁ maṇiḥ

'What effect hath evil association upon him whose soul is firm in its own righteousness? Why does not the jewel that dwells in the head of the serpent absorb the poison of the serpent? Böhtlingk's stanza:

kiṁ kariṣyati saṁsargaḥ svabhāvo duratikramaḥ,
paçyāmraphalasaṁsargī kaṣāyo madhuraḥ kṛtaḥ

'What effect has association with others, since one cannot escape one's own nature? Consider how can acrid taste be rendered sweet by contact with the mango?'

2. 710 (cf. Pārçva 2. 794) : Bö. 5181 (cf. Bö. 2487, 3519)

2. 792-3: cf. Bö. 4226

3. 220: cf. Bö. 7518

3. 367: Bö. 2757

dānaṁ bhogas tathā nāçaḥ syād dravyasya gatitrayam,
yo na datte bhuñkte ca tṛtīyāsya gatir bhavet

Böhtlingk's version in the text (cf. bibliografy of the stanza in his note):

dānaṁ bhogo nāças tisro gatayo bhavanti vittasya,
yo na dadāti na bhuñkte tasya tṛtīyā gatir bhavati.

3. 415: Bö. 1831

3. 416: Bö. 5389.

3. 422: cf. Bö. 1618

3. 442: Bö. 1859. The same sentiment from an opposite point of view, Bö. 691

3. 452: Bö. 4933; cf. 5290, 5643

3. 511: Bö. 4186

3. 569: cf. Bö. 6147-9

Our text's pāda d reads ratnasaṁjñābhidhīyate for Böhtlingk's ratnasaṁkhyā vidhīyate.

3. 1042: Bö. 2922

Our text seems corrupt (cf. Böhtlingk's note):

bhūṣito 'pi cared dharmaṁ yatra tatrāçrame rataḥ,
samaḥ sarveṣu bhūteṣu na liñgaṁ tatra kāraṇam

6. 417: Bö. 97 (cf. 4912)

Our text reads bhavet instead of dahet, at the end of the stanza.

7. 301: Bö. 6826

Our text has pāda c in better form than Böhtlingk's emended form: kārye nyāyye 'pi na svecchā, 'no free will even in duty to be performed,' for Böhtlingk's, bālyakāle 'pi na svecchā, 'no free will even in childhood.' His text intends nāryye kāle, but even that is inferior to Pārçva.

8. 10: Bö. 7209

Our text has an expurgated version:

strī nadīvat svabhāvena capalā nīcagāminī,
udvṛttā ca jaḍātmāsāu pakṣadvayavināçinī.

'Woman, like a river, is by nature fickle and downward inclined; when she breaks her bounds, she foolishly destroys both sides' (her own and her husband's, with allusion to the banks of a river). The Jain writer dodges the touch of obscenity contained in the Subhāṣitārṇava. A stanza of similar import, Bö. 7561.

8. 118: Bö. 2793

8. 315 (phrase, yāti vañçaḥ samunnatim): Bö. 6681.

2. Stanzas which either are proverbs, or are, more or less, like proverbs.

The Pārçvanātha Caritra contains so large a number of didactic stanzas, as to approximate the text to a nītiçāstra. In a sense they are all of them proverbial. But there is, after all, a difference between purely religious stanzas and proverbial stanzas. It is the difference between dharma on the one hand, and nīti or artha or kāuṭilya on the other hand. In the following are quoted or cited a number of such stanzas, out of the great mass, as reflect or approach most closely to the popular proverb, in distinction from the religious stanza. These are wanting in Böhtlingk's collection, but they are not distinguishable in tenor from those that are there:

1. 48: aghāṭam api kalyāṇaṁ sughaṭād api kūṭataḥ,
yathā praçasyate tadvad mugdho 'pi sukṛtī naraḥ.

'As gold even unbeaten is esteemed more than the well-constructed counterfeit, thus the pious man, even tho he be foolish.'

1. 51: chinnamūlo yathā vṛkṣo gataçīrṣo yathā bhaṭaḥ,
dharmahīno dhanī tadvat kiyatkālaṁ laliṣyati.

'As a tree whose root is cut, as a soldier whose head is gone, thus is the rich man devoid of virtue. How long will he disport himself?'

1. 108: viçuddho 'pi guṇavrāto na vinā lakṣmīṁ çobhate,
unmīlati yathā citraṁ na vinā kṛṣṇatūlikām.

'The excellent devotee of virtue (with punning allusion to the bow in the words viçuddho and guṇa) does not prosper without fortune. A painting does not unfold itself without the painter's black brush.'

1. 119-131, all dāna proverbs (1. 123 = Bö. 6676): see Bö. under dāna.

1. 180-183 (1. 181 = Bö. 3754)

1. 184: svādusvādānabhijñaç ced drākṣāsu karabho mukham,
vakrīkuryāt tatas tāsāṁ mādhuryaṁ kvāpi kiṁ gatam.

'If the young elefant crooks (withdraws) his mouth, because he does not know the taste of sweet in grapes, is their sweetness therefore gone somewhere?'

1. 288: vyañjayanty agham anyeṣāṁ khalā galanavastravat,
adhaḥ kṣipanti santas tu mahāhradavad ambhasām.

'Rogues disclose the faults of others like a drip-cloth (shows water); but good men strike down (hide) them as a great lake (the impurity) of its waters.' Cf. also 1. 287

1. 300-304: descriptions of evil-minded persons. So also 1. 330.

1. 351: ṛjutā dhanvaguṇayor astu vastusvarūpataḥ,
kāryasiddhāu praçasyate vakratāiva tayoḥ punaḥ.

'Granting that bow and string are straight by nature of the object, yet it is desirable that they should bend, in order to accomplish their purpose.'

1. 376: gurutvaṁ ca laghutvaṁ(ca) çrībhāvābhāvato jaḍāḥ,
vadanti tat punar dakṣāḥ sadvivekāvivekataḥ.

'Importance and insignificance, fools say, depend upon the presence

: absence of fortune; clever folk say, upon the presence or absence : keen discernment.'

1. 377: nirvivekanaraṁ nārī prāyo 'nyāpi na kāñkṣati,
kiṁ punaḥ çrīr iyaṁ devī puruṣottamavallabhā.

ls a rule even another woman does not hanker after a man wantg in discernment. How much less Fortune (Çrī), the goddess, ›loved of noblest men!'

1. 398-403: stanzas inculcating support of parents by children, pecially 400:

mātṛpitror abharakaḥ kriyām uddiçya yācakaḥ,
mṛtaçayyāpratigrāhī na bhūyaḥ puruṣo bhavet.

He that does not support his parents; the beggar that prescribes hat is to be done (beggars must not be choosers); he that accepts ie bed of a dead person, he is no longer a human being.'

1. 412-13: two stanzas extoling helpfulness (upakāra).

1. 421; 3. 124; 6. 363; 7. 121: all four deal with the aspirations : men of different characters (nīcāḥ, madhyamāḥ, uttamāḥ).

1. 506: 'spare the rod, and spoil the child.'

1. 537-8: two stanzas describing ideal king.

1. 679: pradīpa-sarṣapāu çlāghyāu laghū api guṇojjvalāu,
mahāntāv api na çreṣṭhāu pradīpana-bibhītakāu.

he commentary pradīpana = viṣaviçesaḥ. Cf. Bö. 334. Here is trick: the small fruits (and small words) are better than the rge fruits (and large words); pradīpa seems to be some small 'ain.

1. 763: kiṁ jātikusume vahniḥ kṣipyate kiṁ mahākarī,
mṛṇāle badhyate kiṁ vā rambhā krakacam arhati.

)oes one throw fire on a jessamine blossom? Does one fasten a g elefant to a lotus fibre? Or is Rambhā (the heavenly nymph) : for the saw'(?), or 'fit for the krakaca hell'? Cf. krakacāyate ear like a saw,' 3. 620; see p. 231.

2. 177: kṛtās tāruṇyacāitreṇa ye sphurannavapallavāh,
çaṭatpatradrumāyante jarasā phālgunena te.

The bursting young shoots which are produced in the spring onth (cāitra) of youth become trees with falling leaves in the ıtumn month (phālguna) of old age.' The stanza is one of four, ustrating excellently the impermanence of life. For çaṭatpatraumāyante see p. 231.

2. 239: mohāndhānām sukhāyante viṣayā duḥkhadā api,
lohaṁ dhattūritānāṁ hi kathaṁ na kanakāyate.

'The senses of them that are blind with folly are pleasurable, tho they really give pain. For how does not the copper color of them that are poisoned by dhattūra appear golden?'

2. 367: raso lavaṇatulyo na na vijñānasamaḥ suhṛt,
dharmatulyo nidhir nāsti na krodhasadṛço ripuḥ.

'There is no taste like salt; no friend like knowledge; no treasure like virtue; no enemy like anger.'

2. 513: mattadviradasaṁkāçe yāuvane 'narthakāriṇi,
puruṣasyādhirūḍhasya na çāstrād anyad añkuçam

'The man who is mounted (in authority) over worthless youth, that is like a mad elefant, has no elefant's hook other than instruction.'

2. 540: taj jalaṁ yat tṛṣāṁ chindyāt tad annaṁ yat kṣudhāpaham,
bandhur yo dhīrayaty ārtaṁ sa putro yatra nirvṛtiḥ.

'Water is what quenches thirst; food is what drives off hunger; a relative is he who comforts the afflicted; a son is he with whom there is happiness.'

2. 596: uccārūḍhāir narāir ātmā rakṣaṇīyo 'tiyatnataḥ,
dūrārohaparibhrañçavinipātaḥ suduḥsahaḥ

'The soul of men of high station must be guarded with exceeding care. Hard to bear is a fall when one tumbles from a high place.'

2. 600: jalaṁ galanavastreṇa vivekena guṇavrajaḥ,
saddānena gṛhārambho vacaḥ satyena çudhyati.

'Water becomes pure by a drip-cloth; the multitude of virtues by discernment; the householder's state by kind gifts; speech by truth.'

2. 648: mastakasthāyinaṁ mṛtyuṁ yadi paçyed ayaṁ janaḥ,
āhāro 'pi na rocate kim utākṛtyakāritā.

'That person, at whose head stands death, does not take pleasure even in food; how much less in the performance of crime.'

2. 757: kiṁ kṛtaṁ vidhinā yāvat çīlam akhaṇḍitam,
gataṁ tat tu yadā kālaṁ saṁpady api vipattayaḥ

'What has been accomplished by (evil) destiny, as long as virtue is unimpaired? But when that (virtue) has perished, there is failure even in success.'

2. 792 repeats almost verbatim Samarādityasaṁkṣepa 6. 118. See the author in Proc. Amer. Philos. Soc. lvi. 33, note 74.

2. 833: varaṁ kārāgṛhe kṣipto varaṁ deçāntarabhramī,
varaṁ narakasaṁcārī na dvibhāryaḥ punaḥ pumān.

'Better for a man to be thrown into prison, better to wander in strange lands, better to dwell in hell, then to have two wives.'

3. 143: kalākalāpasaṁpannā upakartuḥ parāñmukhāḥ,
na bhavanti mahātmānaḥ sarasaḥ çikhino yathā.

'Noble men, after they have been enriched by a pack of accomplishments, do not turn their faces from their benefactor, like peacocks from the pool (from which they have drunk).' The point of the passage is the pun upon kalāpa, which means both, 'bundle,' and, 'peacock's tail' (noble men do not turn their backs upon their benefactors).

3. 229-233: see the author in Proc. Amer. Philos. Soc., vol. lvi, p. 35.

3. 265: satī patyuḥ prabhoḥ pattir guroḥ çiṣyaḥ pituḥ sutaḥ,
ādeçe saṁçayaṁ kurvan khaṇḍayaty ātmano vratam.

'A good wife, that doubts the command of her spouse; a soldier, that of his king; a pupil, that of his teacher; a son, that of his father, break their vows.'

3. 422, 423: two good stanzas, with familiar comparisons, on keeping good or evil company.

3. 493: bālye 'pi madhurāḥ ke 'pi drākṣāvat ke 'pi cūtavat,
vipākena kadāpīndrāvāruṇīphalavat pare.

What kind of plant or tree is indrāvāruṇī? Not in Lexs.

3. 557 ff.: praise of sattva, 'noble courage.'

3. 785: varaṁ mṛtyur varaṁ bhikṣā varaṁ sevāpi vāiriṇām,
dāivâd vipadi jātāyāṁ svajanābhigamo na tu.

'Better death, beggary, service with enemies, when destiny has brought misfortune, than appeal to one's relatives.'

3. 1104: upekṣya loṣṭakṣeptāraṁ loṣṭaṁ daçati maṇḍalaḥ,
siṁhas tu çaram apekṣya çarakṣeptāram īkṣate.

'A dog waits upon him that throws a clod, and bites the clod (retrieves), but a lion disregards the arrow, and gazes at him that discharges the arrow.' Here maṇḍalaḥ = çvā, hitherto quoted only by Lexicografers. Cf. Bö. 2087, 2184, 4979, 7322.

4. 95: guṇāiḥ sthānacyutasyāpi jāyate mahimā mahān,
api bhraṣṭaṁ taroḥ puṣpaṁ na kāiḥ çirasi dhāryate.

'Great glory arises thru virtue for a man, even if he has fallen from his station. The blossom even that has fallen from the tree, by whom is it not worn on the head?'

4. 156: ikṣo rasaṁ yathādāya kūrcakas tyajyate janāiḥ,
dharmasāraṁ tathādāya dehaṁ tyajati paṇḍitaḥ

'Just as people take the juice of the sugar-cane, and leave the stalk, so does a wise man take the essence of virtue, and disregard his body.'

5. 182: svayam āchidya gṛhṇāno mṛgendro viçruto hariḥ,
anyadattaṁ tu gāur ichan varākaḥ paçur ucyate.

'Because he himself tears and snatches (his food), the lion is celebrated as king of animals. But the cow, which desires what is given by others, is called a wretched beast.'

6. 67: labhate 'lpaṁ dhanaṁ sthūlagrāvoddhāre 'pi karmakṛt,
tad bahu (read, tadbahu) svalpabhāreṇāpy arjayed ratnakovidaḥ.

'A laborer gets small riches, even if he lifts heavy stones; a connoisseur of jewels, even if he carries the smallest weight, may profit much from it.'

6. 181: kāṣṭham aṅgāratāṁ yāti bhasmatāṁ gomayādikam,
vahnāu kīrṇaṁ suvarṇaṁ tu suvarṇotkarṣatāṁ vrajet.

'Wood becomes coal; dung and the like, ashes; but gold cast into fire attains to the highest quality of gold.'

6. 418: devānāṁ bhāṣate pūjāṁ karoti vividhāuṣadhān,
māntrikān āhvayaty ārto nimittajñāṅs ca pṛchati.

'He who is in trouble worships the gods, prepares many sorts of herbs, calls in magicians, and consults interpreters of omens.'

7. 82: gaṅgāyā vālukāṁ vārdher jalaṁ mānaṁ mahāgireḥ,
matimanto vijānanti mahilāyā manas tu na.

'Wise men can tell how much sand there is in the Gaṅgā; how much water there is in the ocean; the measure of a great mountain; but not the mind of a woman.'

This stanza in Prākrit, in the story of Agaḍadatta, stanza 322 (Jacobi, Ausgewählte Erzählungen, p. 86):

gaṅgāe vāluyaṁ sāyare jalaṁ himavao ya parimāṇam,
jāṇanti buddhimantā mahilāhiyayaṁ na-yāṇanti.

7. 97: ādityāya tamaḥ sṛṣṭaṁ meghāya grīṣmaçoṣaṇam,
mārgaçramas tu vṛkṣāya duḥkhinas tūpakāriṇe.

Against darkness the sun has been created; against the drouth of summer, the cloud; against the fatigue of the traveler, the tree; and against sufferers, the benefactor.'

7. 312: nārī svayaṁprabhā patyuḥ prasādāt syān naro na tu,
rātrir induṁ vināpi syād divaso na raviṁ vinā.

A woman must shine by the favor of her lord, but not the man (by the favor of a woman). Night can be without moon, but not day without sun.'

8. 18: dāivo 'pi çaṅkate tebhyaḥ kṛtvā vighnāṅç ca khidyate,
vighnāir askhalitotsāhāḥ prārabdhaṁ na tyajanti ye.

Even fate fears and weakens, after having created difficulties for those who endure difficulties unfalteringly, and do not abandon what they have undertaken.'

8. 247: cāuraç cāurārpako mantrī bhedajñaḥ kāṇakakrayī,
annadaḥ sthānadaç cāiva cāuraḥ saptavidhaḥ smṛtaḥ

A (straight-out) thief; a betrayer of thieves; a minister; one who knows how to instigate strife; a purchaser of stolen goods; one who feeds a thief; and one who gives him shelter, are reputed the seven-fold kinds of thief.' Neither arpaka, nor ārpaka is quotable; its translation is in the air. Kāṇakakrayī, literally 'blind-buyer'; cf. Gāutama 12. 50. The last two kinds of thieves are reprobated in Manu 9. 278; Yājñavalkya 2. 276. The stanza probably comes from a Smārta text.

3. Some proverbial expressions.

1. 75: jalāiḥ puṣṭo 'pi kiṁ vārdheḥ sukhāya vaḍavānalaḥ, 'Does the submarine fire, even tho tempered by the waters of the ocean, give pleasure?'

1. 135: uṣṇīkṛtam api svīyaṁ çāityaṁ yāti . . . payaḥ, 'Water, tho heated, returns to its own cool temperature.'

1. 153: çarkarām açnatāṁ dantavyathāyāi kiṁ na karkaraḥ, 'Does not a stone ruin the teeth of them that eat pebbles?' Cf. p. 209.

1. 167: atinindyo hi pāpasya kārakād upadeçakaḥ, 'He who teaches sin is more reprehensible than he who practices it.'

1. 320: nīcasaṁgaprasaṅgena mṛtyur eva na saṁçayaḥ, 'The

habit of associating with the low surely brings death.' Cf. Bö. 3795.

1. 323: çañkhaḥ . . . dhavalo bahir atyantam antas tu kuṭilasthitiḥ, 'A conch-shell is exceedingly white outside, but inside its condition is crooked (cunning, plausible rascal).

1. 326: karpūrasya kathaṁ na syād añgāreṇa samaṁ ratiḥ, 'How can there be wanting affinity between camfor and coals?' Cf. Bö. 7291: karpūraḥ pāvakaspṛṣṭaḥ sāurabhaṁ labhatetarām, 'Camfor touched by fire becomes much more fragrant.'

1. 561: aphalo 'pi tarus tāpaṁ harate mārgayāyinām, 'A tree, even tho it bears no fruit, shields wanderers from heat.'

2. 22: saṁpūrṇo 'pi ghaṭaḥ kūpe guṇachedāt pataty adhaḥ, 'Even a full bucket falls into the well, when the rope breaks.' (In relation to guṇa in the hackneyed double sense of 'rope,' or 'virtue').

2. 481: anyathā cintitaṁ kāryaṁ karmaṇā kriyate 'nyathā, 'The scheme planned one way is executed in another by karma.'

2. 781: paṭahaṁ vādayed dāivo yathā nṛtyet tathā kṛtī, 'Fate sounds the drum; the performer (man) dances to its tune.'

2. 848 (p. 136, last line): satyam ābhāṇakaṁ jātaṁ yato rakṣas tato bhayam, 'There is a good proverb: 'From the quarter from which protection is expected comes danger.' This is indeed a familiar proverb, imbedded in proper surroundings in the Kathākoça: amṛte viṣam utpannaṁ sūryād andhakāraṁ candramasaḥ añgāravṛṣṭiḥ yato rakṣas tato bhayam. . . . See Tawney's Translation of Kathākoça, p. 14, lines 12-16, and the note on that passage, p. 235. For amṛte viṣam utpannaṁ, see, in turn Pārçva 3. 220, viṣam apy amṛtāyate . . . anukūle vidhāu nṛṇām, and Pārçva 2. 792, pratikūle vidhāu kiṁvā sudhāpi hi viṣāyate.

3. 146: svachatvena gabhīro 'pi darçayaty udadhir maṇīn: 'The ocean, tho deep, because it is clear, displays the jewels (at its bottom).'

3. 425: açvaḥ kṛço 'pi çobhāyāi puṣṭo nāpi punaḥ kharaḥ, 'The lean horse, not the fat ass, is graceful.'

7. 447: kubjaḥ karoti kiṁ dṛṣṭvā tarūccaçikhare phalam, 'What can the dwarf do when he sees a fruit on the high crown of a tree?'

7. 659: tṛtīyoḍḍayane . . . mayūro 'pi hi gṛhyate, 'At the third

flying-up the peacock is sure to be caught.' ('If at first you don't succeed, try, try again').

7. 754: vṛkṣo 'py apakve pīḍyeta chidyamāne phale dhruvam, 'Even a tree, when a fruit is cut from it, surely suffers in its unripe part.'

8. 55: nīcāir uccāiç ca puṅsāṁ hi cakranemi kramād daçā, 'Up and down misfortune (and good fortune) come to men like the movement of the felly of a wheel.' (Caprice of quickly changing fortune).

2. 160: dugdhe çarkarāpātaḥ, 'Sugar dropped in milk'; 6. 1349; çarkarādugdhasaṁyogaḥ, 'Union of sugar and milk.' (Excessive good fortune). The opposite of this, 7. 448: kṣārakṣepaḥ kṣate kṛtaḥ, 'Throwing acid on a wound.'

7. 518: mahāvṛkṣā viçeṣeṇa grīṣmakāle hi çāḍvalāḥ, 'Great trees are especially verdant in summer time.' (Help by the great when one is in direst need).

APPENDIX II.

THE LANGUAGE OF THE PĀRÇVANĀTHA.

1. Prākrit influence.

Jaina Sanskrit texts, presumably, never quite escape Prākrit influences. This has been observed, e. g., by Jacobi, Pariçiṣṭaparvan, Preface to his Edition, p. 9; by Tawney, in his Translation of Kathākoça, pp. xxii ff.; and by Weber, in his Edition and Translation of Pañcadaṇḍachattraprabandha, p. 5. The Pārçvanātha, tho written in the main in excellent Sanskrit, has a number of Prākrit back-formations into Sanskrit which it employs with surprising regularity. Chief of these is the 'root' vidhyāi in the sense of 'go out,' 'be quenched' = Pāli-Prākrit vijjhāi, from Skt. vi-kṣāi, 'burn out.' Thus 3. 893:

ity uktvā paçyatām eva teṣāṁ gatabhayaḥ çukaḥ,
jhampām adāc ca vidhyāto 'gniç cāsthād akṣataḥ çukaḥ,

'So saying, the parrot, without fear, in the very sight of them, took a jump (into the fire): the fire was quenched, and the parrot stood unscathed.' Similarly the past participle in 6. 854, iti vākyāmṛtāis tasyā vidhyātaḥ krodhapāvakaḥ, 'thus the fire of his anger was quenched by the nectar of her words'; and 6. 1322, vidhyātam iva pāvakam, 'like an extinguished fire.' More figuratively, in 6. 609, vidhyātadhīḥ, 'one whose courage has gone out,' and, yet more secondarily, 3, 361, hitādeçasudhāvidhyātamānasaḥ, 'whose mind has become calm (quenched) by the nectar of wise instruction.'

The primary present active of the verb is vidhyāyati, in 3. 297, davo 'pi ghananīreṇa vidhyāyati, 'even a forest fire is quenched by heavy showers.' The causative in the sense of 'put out,' 'extinguish,' occurs several times: 1. 489, tāpaṁ pitur vidhyāpayan, 'quenching the wrath of his father'; 8. 385, citām vyadhyāpayan [1] kṣīrāmbhobhir meghakumārakāḥ, 'Cloud-youths quenched (Pārçva's) funeral pyre with fluid from the milk (ocean)'; and 8. 243,

[1] Here the composite character of 'root' vi-dhyāi comes to light, as the augment follows the preposition.

ıa megho vidyutaṁ vidhyāpayati (misprinted, vidhyāyapati), 'the loud does not quench the lightning.'

Outside the Pārçvanātha this verb is not rare,[2] but nowhere else s it employed as familiarly as here. Pārçvanātha knows genuine Sanskrit expressions for the same idea, as shows 2. 811, nirvāpita-aṁtāpa, 'whose sorrow has been extinguished.' But he has fallen nto the diction of Jaina Prākrit literary speech; e. g., Bambha-latta, in Jacobi, Ausgewählte Erzählungen in Māhārāṣṭrī, p. 3, l. 26, vijjhāvio kohaggī, 'the fire of his anger was quenched'; cf., in Pāli, Milindapañhō, p. 46, l. 5, aggim avijjhāpetvā, 'not having put out the fire.' See Pischel, Grammatik der Prākrit-Sprachen, § 326; Anderson, Pāli Glossary, p. 105. The whole business would come as a shock to a Pandit in Benares.

The root ut-tar in the sense of 'descend' is a doublet of ava-tar, chosen doubtless with a view to metrical convenience. Tho ut-tar, 'descend' occurs also in Vetālapañcaviñçati (see Pet. Lex.) it is hardly doubtful that it is a Sanskrit back-formation from Prākrit, where oyaraï and uttaraï are interchangeable; see Jacobi, Preface to Pariçiṣṭaparvan, p. 9. Thus Pārçva has, 2.132, uttīrya vāhāt; 2.269, uttīrya bhujāt; 7. 236, uttīrya gajāt; 7. 639, açvād uttīrya; 3. 899, udatārayat rāsabhāt; 3. 896, samuttārya rāsabhāt; 2. 76, svāñgād uttārya; 2. 449, çikyakād annam uttārya; 2. 802, sutam uttārya (skandhāt). But 8. 294, açokād avatīrya; 2. 320; 3. 935, vyomno 'vatīrya, or, 'vatatāra; 2. 432, avatīrya vimānataḥ; 7. 243, avatīrṇāu bhuvaṁ svargāt. In its more proper sense of 'bring up,' or, 'bring out,' ut-tar seems rare: 1. 309, uttārya nīrataḥ. It would seem, however, that ava-tar is preferred in the sense of 'descent from heaven, or from on high,' in distinction from ut-tar which means mostly 'dismount.'[3]

The root caṭ 'fall,' 'get into,' tho not restricted to Prākritizing texts, yet figures with notable frequency in Jaina Sanskrit. Thus

[2] See Hemacandra, Anekārthasaṁgraha 3. 201; and Johansson, IF. iii. 220, note; Zachariae, KZ. xxxiii. 446. Cf. Wackernagel, Altindische Grammatik, i, p. liii. The Samarādityasaṁkṣepa has vidhyātaḥ in 5. 196; vidhyāpyeta, passive of causative, in 6. 435; and the noun derivative from the causative vidhyāpana in 6. 434.

[3] Saramādityasaṁkṣepa, derived from the Prākrit Samarāïccakahā, similarly has, rathād uttīrya, 1. 163; vaṭād uttīrya 4. 235; uttara turaṁgamāt, 4. 45; uttīrya dvipāt 7. 202; on the other hand divaç cyutaḥ, avatīrṇaḥ, 6. 9, but also āsanād avatīrya, 4. 555.

also here: 1. 35; 2. 580, 633; 3. 506; 6. 1157, 1348; 7. 175, 222; 8. 354. Especially in connection with kare, 'get into one's hand,' e. g. 2. 633, cintāmaṇir iva caṭito bhūpatiḥ kare, 'like a wish-jewel the king got into his hand,' sc., so that he could serve under him.' Similarly, e. g., Pañcadaṇḍachattraprabandha, p. 37, l. 15, 'asmatkare caṭati; Rāuhiṇeya Carita, stanza 173, haste caṭiṣyati. See Kathākoça, p. xxii; Hertel, Das Pañcantantra, p. 327.

The 'root' vi-kurv is clearly a Sanskrit back-formation of Prākrit viuvvaï, viuvvaë (past participle viuvviya; gerund viuvviūṇa); see Pischel, Grammatik der Prākrit-Sprachen, § 508. The verb means everywhere, 'produce by magic.' Thus in 1. 601 a thief who has, by means of a certain rite, gone up in the air produces by magic a big rock, vikurvya mahatīṁ çilām, wherewith he threatens his pursuers. Similarly 2. 352, vikurvya siṅharūpam, 'having assumed magically the form of a lion'; 2. 411, suvimānaṁ vikurvya, 'having created by magic an excellent car'; 5. 101, caturvṛṣīṁ[4] vikurvya tadviṣāṇotthāiḥ snapayāmāsa vāribhiḥ (prabhum); 6. 1129, vidyāvikurvite sāudhye muktvā (mām), 'having left me in a palace, constructed by magic science'; 8. 384, vikurvya vahniṁ vātaṁ ca vahnivāyukumārakāḥ, 'Fire and Wind Kumārakas (divine beings) having created by magic fire and wind.' Examples from Prākrit in Leumann, Die Āvaçyaka-Erzählungen, p. 35, l. 6, kālasuṇagarūvaṁ viuvvai, 'he assumed the form of a black dog'; in Jacobi, l. c., p. 53, l. 8, pāsāyaṁ viuvviūṇa, 'calling forth by magic a palace'; p. 26, l. 21, viuvviyaṁ maṇipīḍham, 'a jewel-floor created by conjury'; p. 44, l. 5, viuvviyaṁ varavimāṇam, 'a car created by magic.'

Pārçvanātha has a 'root' ava + lag in the sense of 'serve,' or 'cultivate.' Thus 7. 35, tena nṛpam avalagatā (gloss, sevamānena), 'by him who was serving the king'; 7. 42, rājño 'valagāyām, 'in the service of the king'; 7. 591, bhūpasyāvalagāyam 'in the service of the king.' Avalag is a Sanskrit back-formation from Prākrit olagga, past participle in the sense of 'following,' Jacobi, Ausgewählte Erzählungen, p. 66, l. 8. From this there is an infinitive olaggium, ib., p. 35, l. 3. Jacobi derives this 'root' olagg from Skt. anulagna 'attached to,' which is sufficiently doubtful

[4] Some sort of a horned animal: 'having produced by magic a caturvṛṣī, he bathed the Lord in the water coming out of its horns.'

om the point of view of sound. But there need be no question out the provenience of avalag from olag, abstracted from olagga, the like.

The word visaṁsthula 'lax,' 'flaccid,' occurs in 1. 188; 3. 574. ccording to Zachariae, BB. xi. 320 ff., it is a Sanskrit back-formation from Prākrit visaṁṭhula = Skt. viçranthula; cf. Wackernagel, ltindische Grammatik, i, p. liii. The word is late; its occurrences e largely in the drama and in Jaina texts.

The instrumental imāiḥ for ebhiḥ is firmly established in Prā-itizing Jaina Sanskrit texts. It occurs here in 1. 805; 6. 767; 398. The same Prākritism in Samarādityasaṁkṣepa 4. 508, 19; 6. 385; 8. 520; I seem to remember having seen it also in ariçiṣṭaparvan.

Further, sa as a latent positive prefix, contrasted with a, negative privative: sa-jñāna, 'knowledge,' with a-jñāna, 'ignorance,' 6. 77 (frequent both in Pāli and Prākrit). Similarly, hī = dhik, las,' 4. 78 (dhik, e. g., in 4. 81).[5] ucchanna for utsanna, 8. 347, probably a mere matter of Prākritic writing, as often in Sanskrit anuscripts. Similarly proper names occasionally show Prākrit unds: Javana, for Yavana, 5. 192; Jasāditya, or Jaçāditya, 2. 53, 496;[6] Deviṇī (Samarād. 7. 505, Deïṇī), 2. 453, for Devinī, 488. Duplications like jaya-jayā-rāva, 6. 1103; 7. 115; hā-hā-va, 6. 1131; kila-kilā-rava, 6. 1100; utkila-kilā-rava, 3. 905, are so of popular origin; see Speijer, ZMDG. lxv. 316.[7] There are so a few inverted compounds, in accordance with a marked tenency of popular diction, both in Pāli and in Prākrit[8]: narāika = anara, 'a certain man,' 1. 317; dṛṣṭi-bhraṣṭa = bhraṣṭa-dṛṣṭi, having lost sight,' 1. 397; karṇa-durbala = durbala-karṇa, 'weak-ered,' i. e., 'accessible to calumny,' 2. 348. In 6. 154 kaṣāyākṣa eems to mean 'sins of sight' = dṛṣṭi-kaṣāya.

Finally Prākritic influence is at the back of an occasional hyper-anskritism; see the words kṣātra = khātra, p. 225; and pulindra = pulinda, p. 230; and davaraka and davara = Skt. doraka and ora, p. 239.

[5] hī and dhik alternate in the drama.

[6] Perhaps, Skt. Yaçāditya.

[7] See, however, kuhā-kuhā-rava in Vāsavadattā (Gray's Translation), 204.

[8] See last Pischel, Grammatik der Prakrit-Sprachen § 603.

2. Lexical matters.

The text contains a considerable number of words which are quoted in native lexical or grammatical works, but have not, up to date, been found in literature; their rareness is made evident by glosses which the editors think it necessary to add in almost every case. Thus, kalyāṇam (kanakam), 'gold,' 1. 48, 782 (see under proverbs, p. 212); çulbam (tāmram), 'copper,' 1. 782; kalāda (suvarṇakāra), 'goldsmith,' 1. 79;[9] pāṇigṛhītī (vadhū), 'wife,' 1. 570;[10] kiçala (pallava), 'shoot (of plants),' 1. 623; ardaka (yācaka), 'beggar,' 1. 626; prājya (bahughṛta), 'having much ghee,' 1. 627; pradīpana (viṣaviçeṣaḥ), 'some sort of poison,' 1. 679; gantu (pāntha), 'wayfarer,' 1. 818;[11] durgā, 2. 309, 'name of a bird'; caṇḍila (nāpita), 'barber,' 2. 988; kaliñja (kaṭa), 'mat,' 3. 79; khalūrikā (çramasthānam), 'grounds for military training,' 3. 487; krāyaka, 'buyer,' 3. 821; pheraṇḍa (çṛgāla), 'jackal,' 3. 904; maṇḍala (çvan), 'dog,' 3. 1104; udaraṁ-bhari, 'nourishing one's belly,' 5. 6; agañjitaḥ (abhītaḥ), 'unterrified,' 6. 376;[12] arthāpayati, 'expound,' 3. 364 (quoted only by grammarians); aṭṭahāsa, 'loud laughter' (of Vetālas).[13]

In 2. 124 occurs a root cukk, apparently in the sense of obtain (gloss, cukkitāḥ, samāptāḥ). An animal, pursued by a king, afraid for its life, addresses the king:

> cukkitās tava kiṁ koçe 'ntaḥpure nagare 'pi vā,
> dīnān açaraṇān evaṁ yad asmān haṅsi bhūpate,

'Why are we gathered (alive) into your provision house, zenana, or city, if you thus slay us wretched, unprotected (animals), O king?' Dhātupātha has, cukk, cukkayati: vyathane, ārtāu, vyasane, implying that the otherwise unquoted root means, 'injure,' or, 'oppress,' in addition to the sense assumed here.

Other words, explained by glosses of the editors, are not mentioned in the Lexicons: Of especial interest in the nonce-formation ehireyāhira, 'servile,' 6. 82. Adjective from the expression ehi re

[9] Pet. Lexs. only from Lexicografers. Mon. Will., Jaina.

[10] Lexicografers, also pāṇigṛhītā.

[11] In this sense only Uṇādi-Sūtra 1. 70.

[12] Dhātup. has a root gañj, 'roar,' in the sense of garj.

[13] Both atta and attatta, in the sense of 'loud,' or, 'very loud,' are cited only by Lexicografers.

yāhi re, 'come here sirrah, go sirraḥ!' Used with kriyā 'work!' Glossed, ehi re, yāhi re, yasyāṁ kriyāyāṁ sa ehireyāhirā, tām. Further, kaççola, in abhrakaṁ kaccolamukhamātram, 'a little cloud of the size of the mouth of a jar,' 2. 155; glossed, kaccolaṁ pātraviçeṣaḥ, 'some kind of vessel.'—vyāpa, 'extension,' in ṛddhi-vyāpa, 'extension of prosperity,' 3. 123; glossed, vyāpo vistāraḥ.—tvatya, 'thine,' 3. 465; glossed, tvatyas tvadīyaḥ; cf. Whitney, Skt. Gramm. § 1245[bd].—caturī, 'pavillion in which marriage is solemnized,' 6. 1345; glossed, pāṇigrahaṇamaṇḍapaḥ, 'corī' iti bhāṣāyām.—lallī, 'flattery,' 'cajolery,' in lallīṁ kṛtvā, 7. 122, where lallīṁ is parafrazed by cāṭūni.—andhala, 'blind,' 7. 141; glossed, andha.—nirgādha, 'bottomless,' 2. 83; glossed, atalaspṛç.—abharaka, 'non-supporter,' 1. 400; glossed, apoṣaka (sc. mātṛpitroḥ).—akamaṭha, 'dwelling in grief,' 1. 701. In pun on the proper name Kamaṭha, sadāiva Kamaṭho 'py evam abhūd akamaṭhas tathā. Gloss, akaṁ duḥkham, tasya maṭhaḥ sthānam, akamaṭhaḥ. In the sense of 'pain' aka (= a-ka) occurs in TS. 5. 3. 2. 1. Lexicografers cite it in the sense of 'sin.'—oṣita, 'dwelling,' 'settled' = ā + uṣita, 1. 828; glossed, sthita.—mahādivya, in the sense of divya, 'ordeal,' 2. 350; glossed, agnipātādinā çuddhipradarçanaṁ divyam.—aghaṭa, 'incongruous,' 'paradoxical,' 2. 663, 664; glossed, aghaṭam, aghaṭamānam.—atijaras, 'superannuated,' 3. 1083; glossed, jarāṁ atikrānta.—tuchaçravas, 'small-eared' (of a horse), 4. 23; glossed, tuchakarṇa.—rāja-viḍvara, apparently 'internecine war,' 4. 54; glossed, rājyakleçaḥ.—atirati, 'of exceeding loveliness,' 4. 118; glossed, atiratayaḥ, ratim atikrāntavatyaḥ.—apratichanda, 'the like of which is not,' 6. 230; glossed, anupama.—kṣātra,[14] 'offal,' 6. 513, glossed, kṣetrakṣepyo malaḥ.—jalabha, 'water elefant,' 6. 869; glossed, jalahastin. The word is the equivalent of nīra-hastin in st. 866. In Devendra's Prākrit version of this story, jalakarī, and jalagaa; see Jacobi, Ausgewählte Erzählungen, p. 43, ll. 16 and 21. Kathākoça (Tawney's Translation), p. 21, has 'water elefant,' in its version of the same story. To be added to the list under suffix abha in Whitney, Skt. Gramm.,

[14] I suspect that kṣātra is a hyper-Sanskritism for khātra. In Rāuhiṇeya Carita 155, 156, 178, 325 kṣātra is clearly used in the sense of khātra 'breach made by a thief,' 'tunnel': ārakṣakagṛhe kṣātraṁ pradāya sarvasvaṁ jagrhe (155); kṣātraṁ dvāre (156); pātitaṁ kṣātraṁ mandire (178); kṣātraṁ pātitaṁ janagrhe (325).

§ 1199ª.—sarvaṁsahā-ruha, 'tree,' 7. 67, glossed, vṛkṣa. For sarvaṁsahā see Indian Antiquary, ix. 185.

The following words are new, or rare; their meaning apparent from the connection:

akṣatra-kṛt, 'performer of unknightly deeds,' 1. 177.

dogundaga, or dogunduga, a 'kind of god': dogund*a*ga ivāmaraḥ, 1. 267, 'like a Dogundaga god'; dogund*u*ga-surābhāsaṁ vidhāpya, 6. 495, 'having created the semblance of a Dogunduga god'; dogund*u*ga ivāmaraḥ, 7. 163, 'like a Dogunduga god.' The word is identical with doguṇḍika, Kathākoça, p. 63, 'a god in the Doguṇḍika heaven.'

galanavastra, 'drip-cloth,' 'sieve,' 1. 288; 2. 600.

dhanurgulikā, 1. 317; and dhanurgolikā, 3. 189, 'sling-shot.'

cūrṇi, 'flour' (= cūrṇa), 1. 386, 823; 3. 191; 7. 351 (here misprinted cūṇi, for cūrṇi).

bāhya-ruṣ, 'superficially gruff,' 'of stern demeanor,' 2. 18: tvayā . . . bhāvyaṁ bāhyaruṣā, 'you must adopt stern demeanor.'

asaṁmād, 'taking no pleasure,' 2. 76. Neither saṁmād, nor its negative are cited in the Lexicons.

indra-vāraṇa, 'Indra's elefant,' 2. 105. Referring to Airāvaṇa.

cāturgatika, in cāturgatikaduḥkhadaḥ . . . bhavaḥ, 'existence which causes pain to them that pass thru the four states' (apparently, the four āçrama, or stages of religious life), 2. 136. Cf. cāturāçramika, cāturāçramya, and caturāçramin.

bhadraka, 'a certain grade of Jaina lay devotee,' 1. 618; 2. 190; 7. 819, 822. In 7. 822 it figures by the side of çrāddha, another grade in the development of devotees.

mahābhujā, fem., 'great serpent,' 2. 256; bhujā, fem., 'serpent,' 2. 259; bhuja, masc., 'serpent,' 2. 269.

kāvalika, derivative of kavala, 'consisting of morsels,' 2. 292. Prince Bhīma is converting Kālikā (Durgā) from her practice of eating the flesh of corpses: kiṁ te kāvalikāhāravikalāyā mahāmiṣāir bībhatsāiḥ. Gods do not eat morsels (devāḥ kavalāhāriṇo nahi), 2. 326; see the note there.

karṇa-durbala, 'weak-eared,' i. e. 'accessible to calumny,' 2. 348.

piṣṭakurkuṭa, 'cock made of dough,' 2. 523, 524; see the note to that passage.

ūrjasvinī, 'name of a Magic Reputation' (prasiddhi), 2. 557.

dramaka, 'designation of a kind of hell inhabitant,' 2. 505.

Occurs also, in a different sense in Rāuhiṇeya Carita 18, in a passage reported under viçopaka, p. 233.

dhanuṣkikā, 'little bow,' 2. 785. In the compound, dhanuṣkikā-çara-vyagra-kara, 'with hands busy with little bow and arrow'; cf. dhanuḥ-çarān in 786.

bahu-dhava, 'having many husband,' 'wanton,' 2. 798. In double entente, 'having many dhava trees.'

divyapañcakam, 'the five ordeals by which a king is chosen, 2. 827. See the note on p. 199 bottom.

dharaṇī-dhava, 'husband of the earth,' 'king,' 2. 856. Perifrasis of mahī-pati, etc. Cf. dharaṇī-dhara.

danta-çakaṭa, 'tooth-wagon,' 'set of teeth,' 2. 899. In danta-çakaṭaṁ baddhvā, 'keeping his mouth shut,' ἕρκος ὀδόντων.

parakāyapraveça, 'art (vidyā) of enterting another's body,' 3. 119 ff. For other designations of the same magic practice see Proc. Amer. Philos. Soc., vol. lvi, p. 6.

paṭṭa-kuñjara, 'state elefant,' 3. 150 = paṭṭa-hastin, Prabandhacintāmaṇi, p. 288.

rāja-pāṭī, 'royal procession,' 3. 174. Tawney, p. 179 of his Translation of Prabandhacintāmaṇi, p. 286, l. 1, renders rājapāṭika by 'king's circuit.' The latter form also in Pañcadaṇḍachattraprabandha 1 (Weber, p. 11, l. 4, where the treatment is erroneous).

gūḍha-caturthaka = gūḍha-caturtha-prahelikā, 'a charade in which the fourth verse of a stanza has to be guessed,' 3. 219 ff. Cf. dodhaka, 'charade in which two verses have to be guessed,' Prabandhacintāmaṇi, p. 157. See Proc. Amer. Philos. Soc., vol. lvi, p. 32.

trikapālī-parīkṣaṇa, 'test of the three skulls,' 3. 234. See Proc. Amer. Philos. Soc., vol. lvi, p. 36, note 81; Hertel, Das Pañcatantra, p. 46.

divyaghāṭa, 'divine workmanship,' 3. 327:

> bhojye vacasi dānādāu sadvivekān naraḥ parām,
> pratiṣṭhāṁ labhate loke divyaghāṭād ivopalaḥ.

'In eating, speaking, bestowing of alms and other acts, shrewd discernment confers upon a man the highest position in the world, as a jewel thru divine workmanship.'

kaṭare, 'particle of surprise or admiration,' 3. 492; 8. 48. Gloss, adbhutārtham avyayam, 'an indeclinable, expressing wonder.'

Also in Çālibhadra Carita 2. 58, glossed by āçcaryabhūtam; in Hemacandrasūriprabandha, çloka 63 (Edition of the Prabhāvaka Carita, p. 300), kaṭare jananībhaktir uttamānāṁ kaṣopalaḥ, 'Behold, devotion to one's mother is the touchstone of noble men!' The word occurs also in Kathākoça, in a stanza printed in Tawney's Translation, p. 234, in a note on p. 3, lines 25-28, kaṭare karma-lāghavam, 'strange to say, my karma is light!' Pischel, Hemacandra's Grammatik der Prākritsprachen, vol. i, p. 157 (anent iv. 350), prints a doubtful and unexplainable word kaṭari, of which he cites a variant kūṭare in vol. ii, p. 187. This, presumably, is the same word.

ḍhāukanīya, 'to be given as a present,' 3. 499. Derived from ḍhāukana, 'present.'

heḍāvitta, apparently, 'horse-owner,' 'horse-dealer,' 3. 499. Cf. heḍāvuka in Mitākṣarā to Yājñav. 2. 30, and heḍāvukka in Lexicografers.

kāutastya = kutastya, 'coming whence,' 3. 618.

antarālāpin, 'he who interrupts by talking'; slang, 'butts in'; German 'dreinredner,' 3. 690.

çuddhi-tālikā, 'clapping of hands, or sign with hands, that a person tried by ordeal is innocent,' 3. 894.

vijijñapayiṣu, 'desiring to report or communicate,' 3. 1010. Glossed, vijñapayitum ichuḥ.

uttapti, 'act of plaguing, tormenting,' 3. 1021.

rakṣā-poṭṭalikā, 'some kind of protecting mark, or amulet,' 5. 75. Cf. rakṣā-paṭṭolikā.

samāsphālaya-, causative, in samāsphālayāmāsur mithaḥ pāṣāṇagolakāu, 'throw at one another,' 5. 76. See ā + sphal.

caturvṛṣī, 'some kind of an horned animal,' 5. 101.

puṣkali-çrāvaka, 'a kind of Jain lay disciple,' 6. 156.

trivaprī, 'triple mound, or wall,' 6. 225.

ujjhikā, 'the kitchen maid who throws offal from the kitchen on the garbage pile,' 6. 399. Gloss, tyāginī. Four wives have duties assigned them, each more important, or dignified than the preceding:

> ujjhikā bhasmapuñjādāu rasavatyāṁ ca bhakṣikā,
> bhāṇḍāgāre rakṣitā tu gṛhasvāmye ca rohiṇī.

'(The first) threw the garbage on the ash-pile and other (garbage) piles; (the second became) the tastress in the kitchen; (the third) k charge of the storehouse; but (the fourth) Rohiṇī was placed charge of the household.' As regards the gloss tyāginī, above, marādityasaṁkṣepa 4. 421 shows tyajantī in the sense of 'female ep.'

aṅgiman, or, caṅgima, 'discernment,' or 'discerning,' in the npound caṅginekṣaṇa, 'with discerning look,' 6. 448.

nimajjiṣu, 'desiring to dive,' 6. 455.

rasthānaka, 'expediting,' 6. 457.

ṛṣnākṣaravidhi, seemingly, 'some thieves' magic,' 6. 458.

numṛti, 'act of following to death,' 6. 593.

nukta-bāṇa, 'one who has shot his arrow,' apparently in the se of, 'having done one's utmost.' Describes physicians (mukāṇeṣu vāidyeṣu) 6. 609.

aha-mṛta, 'a man who enters the pyre with a woman,' 6. 707. s. only saha-mṛtā, 'a woman performing suttee.'

āyasa, 'body,' in mano-vāk-kāyasa, 6. 762. The word has a ier intricate history. Intermediate between itself and kāya lies s-stem kāyas which is sure to result on the analogy of manas, vacas which often accompany it; see the author in Amer. Jour. Philol., xvi. 415. After that kāyasa still further imitates mā-. The word may be of Prākritic origin.

ad-āgraha, 'evil inclination, or whim,' 6. 787.

īpa-kalikā, 'flame of a torch,' 6. 857. Lexs. only as name of a mentary on Yājñavalkya.

aṁ-vāc, 'so speaking,' 6. 898.

āmla, 'a kind of penance,' 6. 1180 (ācāmla-vardhamānākhyaṁ s). According to Hoernle, Indian Antiquary xix. 239, note it means eating dry food simply moistened or boiled in water. word occurs also in Kathākoça, p. 84. For its Prākrit corondent āyambilabaddhamāna see Glossary to Jacobi's Ausgelte Erzählungen, s. v.; and Meyer, Hindu Tales, p. 87, note, e explanation of the word is very doubtful. Leumann, Āupaa-Sūtra, p. 101, has the word in the form, Prākrit āyambilahamāṇaga = Sanskrit āyāmāmlavardhamānaka, the latter a doubtful construction on the part of the author.

bara-vāidya, 'a certain class of (low born) physicians,' 6. ; Samarād. 6. 402; Prākrit savara-vejja, Jacobi, Ausgewählte hlungen, p. 28, l. 4.

ımūrṣaka, 'about to die,' 6. 1306. Ordinarily, mumūrṣu.

kopa-gṛha, 'anger-chamber' ('swearing-room'), 7. 42.

ati-kūjita, 'great howl,' 7. 176.

āupayācitaka, 'fond prayer,' 7. 180 = upayācitaka, 3. 171; Samarād. 4. 645. Neither in the Lexs.

saṁjīvanī-ṅasya, masculine, 'errhine to resuscitate with,' 7. 332. Cf. nasya, 7. 316.

gophaṇī, 'some sort of cannon-like war instrument,' 7. 681.

pulindra and pulindraka = pulinda, 'designation of a rude forest-dweller,' 7. 756, 759. Hypersanskritism, as tho pulinda were Prākrit for Sanskrit pulendra. Cf. govinda = gopendra.

gokulinī, 'shepherd's wife,' 8. 3.

dharma-tīrthika, 'designation of a Jain religious,' 8. 25.

bhṛgu-pāta, 'suicide by throwing one's self down a precipice,' 8. 98.

nikācitam, sc. karma, 'loathed,' 'loathsome,' 8. 155. So also Samarādityasaṁkṣepa 2. 363 (nikācitakarma). In the latter text, 1. 196, nidānaṁ nikācayam, 'loathing the fetter of existence, or sin'; and, 8. 521, nyakācayat, 'treated with contumely.'

divya-māntrika, 'manager of ordeals,' 8. 266.

punaççyava, 'rebirth downward in the scale of reincarnations,' 3. 1060. Cf. punarmṛtyu.

pratīpa-çikṣatva, 'inverted training (of a horse),' 4. 25 = viparītya-çikṣatva. See note on p. 204 bottom.

bhavanādhipāḥ (viṅçatiḥ), 'Lords of natal stars,' 5. 92.

kurkuṭoraga, 'cock-serpent,' 1. 859. See note on p. 21.

anaṅgabhara, perhaps kenning for 'female breast.' See the author in Proc. Amer. Philos. Soc., vol. lvi, p. 23, note 48.

-kṛmika, in sadguṇakṛmika, 'practicing,' 3. 322. Perhaps for karmika, quoted by Lexicografers.

There are a number of new onomatopoeic words: bumbā-rava, 'noise of echoing thunder,' 2. 157; 'battle-cry,' 7. 680; ciliciliscara, 'sound of the bird called durgā,' 2. 309; utkilakilā-rava, 'noise made by a Ḍākinī (witch),' 3. 905 (cf. kila-kilā); kiṅkilli (text, ṅkikilli), perhaps, 'cry of joy,' 6. 253; kila-kilāyita, neuter, 'sound made by ghosts (preta),' 7. 145; bhūt-kṛ, 'sound bhūt, made by an ass,' 7. 203 (cf. phūt-kṛ).

The text shows a considerable number of new denominal (denominative) verbs, as well as denominal participles and abstract nouns, which are formed directly upon a primary noun, omitting intermediate verbal stage: kamalāyate, 'be as a lotus,' 2. 52; akāyate, 'shine as gold,' 2. 239; prāyaçcittayati = prāyaçcittī-, 'undergo penance,' 2. 599; viṣāyate, 'turn poison,' 2. 792; āyate, 'grow dark,' 2. 793 (gloss, tama iva ācarati); kūṭāyate, ›w false,' 2. 793; arthāpayati, 'expound,' 3. 364 (quoted by mmarians); anaçanīyati, 'desire to commit suicide by starva-,' 3. 608 (gloss, anaçanam ichati); bhṛtakīyati, 'act as a hired ı,' 3. 788; divasāyate, 'play the part of day,' 6. 354; çaraṇīyati, ort for protection,' 6. 1128 (gloss, çaraṇam ichati); arṇavāyate, ; as an ocean,' 6. 1280; vratīyati, 'desire to take the vows,' 8. 64 ›ss, vratam abhilaṣ); karabhāyate, 'become an elefant,' 8. 74.

[ore problematic are the following: çaṭat-patra-drumāyate, 'act tree with falling leaves,' 2. 177. The root çaṭ carries on a pre-ous existence in Dhātup., but not in the sense assumed (cf. caṭ, 21). The stanza is translated on p. 213.

:akacāyate, 'tear like a saw'(?), 3. 620 (krakaca, 'saw'). The za reads:

> vañcanā tv āha māṁ tāta citām āroḍhum ādiça,
> kiṁ na vetsi mamāiṇyā hi maraṇaṁ krakacāyate.

ñcanā however said: "Father, order me to mount the pyre; ⁊ou not know that the death forsooth of my doe tears like a ?' Cf. 1. 7631, kiṁ vā rambhā krakacam arhati; see p. 213.

enominative participles and abstract nouns: dhattūrita, 'poı-d by the dhattūra plant,' 2. 239; kalakalāyita, 'confusedly y,' 3. 1077; tanmayāyita, from tan-maya, 'permeated with,' ntified with,' 6. 518 (gloss, tammayāyitam, tanmayam ivācari-); mālāyita, 'wreathed,' 'garlanded,' 6. 926; niçumbhita, in,' from niçumbha, 'slaughter,' 8. 219 (gloss, mārita); dha-na, from dhavalaya-, 'illumination,' 3. 286; anakūlana, from ɩūlaya-, 'act of making favorable,' 3. 338.

uite a number of words occur with more or less form change, ›mpared with their correspondents in the Lexs. Thus:

luṇṭha in solluṇṭhavacana, 'ironic speech,' 1. 194. The Lexs. ulluṇṭhā, but the quotations show ulluṇṭhā only (always in position). Also, ulluṇṭhana, in ulluṇṭhanāiḥ (plur. tant.), ckery,' 3. 436.

'aḥpati = svarpati, 'Indra,' 3. 403.

.jyadhūr, in composition = rājyadhurā, 'burden of govern-t,' 3. 272.

anumodanā, fem. = anumodana, neut., 'joy with,' 'sympathy 3. 284.

bhūmī-gṛha = bhumĭ-gṛha, 'underground chamber,' 3. 364.

granthaphala, probably = granthiphala, 'designation of a tree,' 1. 608.

kaṣapaṭṭa = kaṣapaṭṭikā, 'touchstone,' 3. 1022.

vimṛṣṭar, for vimārṣṭar, or vimraṣṭar), noun of agency, 'reflecting,' 'conservative,' 3. 653. Perhaps to be corrected (vimraṣṭāraḥ). See also the list of words with suffix -ka, below.

There are some very rare words, and words which occur only in Jain texts. Thus:

ḍittha and ḍavittha, 'X and Y, as names of irrelevant persons,' 3. 58:

> sa eva puruṣaḥ sārthanāmā çeṣās tu bibhrati,
> svākhyāṁ ḍitthaḍavitthādiçabdā iva nirarthikām,

'That man alone (namely, he who carries perfection to the highest point) has the name 'Successful' (Sārtha); the rest carry their names senselessly, like names of the class Ḍittha and Davittha.' Cf. Weber, Ind. Stud. xiii. 421.

jalāçaya = jaḍāçaya, 'foolishness,' in tyaktākhilajalāçayaḥ, 'having given up all foolishness,' 1. 29; jalāçaya = jaḍāçaya occurs once or twice in Kathās.

ajanani, 'non-birth' (curse word), 1. 182.

hīlanā, 'injury,' 6. 434. Cf. hīlayate, 'be wroth at,' 6. 1322.

çrī-karī, 'easy-chair,' 6. 519. Glossed, sukhāsanam.

rāura, 'laborer,' 8. 221. Pariçiṣṭaparvan 8. 72, 291 has rora in the same sense.

nīrañgikā, 'veil,' 8. 185. The word occurs in Pariçiṣṭaparvan 2. 8, 144, 496, and is listed in Hemacandra's Deçīnāmamālā 2. 20, and 90 (here nīrañgī); Samarād. 4. 555 also has nīrañgī. Tawney, Translation of Kathākoça, p. xxiii, quotes nīrañgī as a Prākrit word.

chuṭ, 'escape,' 1. 175, in tava bāṇaprahārataḥ kathaṁ chuṭye, 'how shall I escape from the blow of thy arrow.' The word occurs in the expression, saṁkaṭāc chuṭitaḥ (or chuṭṭitaḥ), 'escaped from danger,' in Prabandhacintāmaṇi, p. 20; see Tawney's Translation, p. 13, note 4; in the same sense in Samarād. 9. 234, and in Rāuhiṇeya Carita 365. Weber, Pañcadaṇḍachattraprabandha, p. 26 emends effectively budhyate to chuṭyate: kathaṁ chuṭyate tasyāḥ kālarātryāḥ sakāçāt, 'how is one released from the presence of this (witch) Kālarātrī'; see his note 130, and p. 66, note 2. The root is listed in Dhātup., and seems to mean literally, 'cut off' (choṭana, 'act of cutting off').

A number of words remain unclear, or altogether unintelligible:

avasvāpanikā, 5. 85. and avasvāpinī, 5. 113. Clearly from root svap. Would seem to mean 'sleeping-charm,' or the like. Indra gives it to a queen with child (85), and later on (113) takes it away again. Followed in 5. 85 by pratirūpa, and in 5. 113 by pratirūpaka. All four words not in Lexs.; avasvāpanikā, 'sleeping charm' in Pariçiṣṭaparvan 2. 173; avasvāpinī, apparently in the same sense, in Rāuhiṇeya Carita 14, to wit:

> kathayitvā khaned gartaṁ dattvāvasvāpinīm api,
> yāti jāgarayitvā so 'kalanīyaç ca duḥsahaḥ.

viçopaka, in the expression, tāvad viçopakāikasyāmelato lekhyake kaliṁ kurvantam, 2. 620. Here a thief, about to rob a rich merchant's house, sees that merchant quarreling with his son because a single viçopaka does not meet (does not agree?), amelato, in a letter, lekhyake; see p. 60. The word also in Rāuhiṇeya Carita 18, which reads thus:

> tasya grāsaḥ kṛtaḥ kīdṛk bhuktahaṭṭe viçopakaḥ,
> vasann eko varo grāmo dramakaç ca gṛhaṁ prati.

The word dramaka in this passage does not tally with 'hell-inhabitant' in Pārçvanātha 2. 505; see p. 56.

nidāyaka, glossed, ucchedaka, apparently in the sense of 'weeding,' 6. 348:

> mahatāṁ dūṣaṇoddhārād upakārī khalaḥ khalu,
> mudhā nidāyakaṁ sasyakṣetre ko nābhinandati,

'A rogue, verily, who removes the faults of noble men, is a benefactor. Who does not praise him that weeds vainly in a field of grain?' Neither nidāyaka nor ucchedaka is in the Lexs.; the sense of this nīti-stanza is not clear.

māṣa-tuṣādibhiḥ, glossed by, muniviçeṣāiḥ, 'by distinguished Munis,' 6. 410: vināivādhyayanaṁ siddhir lebhe māṣatuṣādibhiḥ, 'without any kind of study the Sages so designated have attained to perfection.'

çironyuñchanaka, 6. 1188, possibly, 'some kind of arrangement of the hair of the head':

> pṛṣṭāu ca cakriṇā kiṁ bho ihāgamanakāraṇam,
> kevalaṁ tāu dhunītaḥ sma çironyuñchanakaṁ kila,

'And when the emperor asked them: "Why, gentlemen, have you come here?" they merely shook. . . .' This passage is wanting in the corresponding places, Kathākoça, p. 35, middle, and in the Prākrit version, Jacobi, Ausgewählte Erzählungen, p. 27, l. 5. Rāuhiṇeya Carita, stanza 122, describes the following little ceremony which the mother of the thief Rāuhiṇeya undertakes in honor of his first theft:

> nyuñchanāni vidhāyāçu pradīpaṁ saptavartibhiḥ,
> vidhāya tilakaṁ mātā putrāyety āçiṣaṁ dadāu.

utpāṇika, apparently, 'open-handed,' 'liberal,' 2. 913.

kaṇālīka, in darçanīya-kaṇālīka, 1. 627. Glossed,' kaṇālīkam uccaçilpam api. Seems to refer to some part of a Jaina temple.

herayitvā, in herayitvā ṣaṇmāsām, perhaps, 'waiting.'

niropa, apparently, 'instruction,' 'advice,' 7. 171.

mahīyasya kāurikasya(!) sutaḥ, 1. 334. Apparently 'the son of some man of lowly occupation.' In the corresponding passage, Kathākoça, p. 266, l. 5, 'son of a potter,'; see the note 23, on p. 33.

çāurārpaka, and kāṇakakrayin, 8. 247. Two of the seven kinds of thief, listed in a versus memorialis, see p. 217.

kāndavikāyate, apparently from kāndavika, 'baker,' 6. 362. Unintelligible in its connection.

pradīpa, in the compound pradīpa-sarṣapāu seems to be the name of some small useful grain, 1. 679; see p. 213.

indrāvāruṇī-phala, 'some kind of fruit,' 3. 493. See p. 215.

3. Proper names.

The text abounds in new proper names of all classes: names of gods, goddesses, Vidyādharas, Yakṣas, and Rākṣasas; names of kings, princes and queens; names of Saints, male and female, Brahmans, Purohitas, ministers; names of merchants, and other gentlemen, and their wives and children; names of low-born men and courtezans. Geographical and topical names repeat, in general, those that are current in other Jain chronicles; yet there are many

7 ones: names of countries, cities, villages; of mountains, forests, l parks; of lakes and rivers; of tīrthas, cāityas, and other holy ces; names of heavens, and abodes of delight. As in other nar- ive texts, beginning with the Epic, domestic animals and inani- te objects of utility receive names; thus Abdhikallola, 'a horse,' 1024; Pālaka, 'a chariot,' 5. 81.

The following lists contain words which are not in the Lexs., but te a number occur in published Jain texts, and others are very ely to turn up in future publications of the same class. It is rcely necessary to point out that here, as in other fiction, a good t of the names are symbolic of the character of the persons or alities named.

Names of divine or demonic beings: In 5. 51, 56, 60, 62, 64, 66, 68 are listed 56 heavenly maidens, called Jyotiṣkumārikās, or ierwise defined, many of them new, and doubtless products of ıcy, for the nonce. Gods like Maṇiprabha, 3. 1012; Varadāna, 105; Ṇāṭyamāla, 4. 414; Saṁgama, 6. 1177, need not to be ken too seriously, or regarded as permanent members of the Jain ympus. The Yakṣas, Asitākṣa, 6. 1092; and Sundara, 7. 639; the kṣasas, Sarvagila, 2. 351; and Kelīkila, 7. 398, are conventional oducts of free fancy. Nāigameṣin is added, 5. 80, to Nāigameṣa, meso, 'a demon that afflicts children,'; see Winternitz, JRAS., 95, pp. 149 ff. Taṇḍula is the name of a fabulous fish. New dyādharas and Vidyādharīs are: Vidyudgati, 2. 5; Candravega d Bhānuvega, 6. 1138; Açanivega, 6. 1139; Mahājāina, 1. 573; adanāñkura, 7. 442; Saṁdhyāvalī, 6. 1135; Mṛgāñkalekhā, 8. . Caṇḍasenā, 8. 101 is another name for Caṇḍā, Caṇḍikā (Dur-) in 8. 101.

Names of kings and princes: Kiraṇavega, and Kiraṇatejas, 2. .; Gupila, 2. 88; Naladharma, 2. 115; Bhuvanasāra, 2. 137; arivikrama, 2. 181; Abhicandra, 2. 508; Mānamardana, 2. 616; ajravīrya, 3. 6; Hemaratha, 3. 485; Suvarṇabāhu, 4. 15; Kṛta- ila, 4. 107; Kurudeva, 6. 286; Sevāla (= Çevāla), 6. 287; Maṇi- tha, 6. 773; Yugabāhu, 6. 774; Maṇiprabha, 6. 873; Nami, 6.)2; Surabhi, 6. 1125; Varasena, and Amarasena, 7. 37; Susthita, 504; Caṇḍasena (Bhilla chieftain), 8. 87; Kurumṛgāñka, 8. 210. aṇḍaratna is the name of a general, 4. 107.

Names of queens and princesses: Tilakāvatī, 2. 8; Madanarekhā,

6. 774; Sahadevī, 6. 1013; Bakulamatī, 6. 1041; Vijayādevī, 7. 36; Jayasundarī, 7. 377.

Names of Brahmans and other religious, Purohitas, ministers, and teachers: Viçvabhūti, 1. 28; Kṣirakadamba, or °dambaka, 2. 511, 519; Parvata, or °taka 2. 544, 570; Añgāramukha, 3. 610, or Añgāravaktra, 3. 682, or Añgāra, 3. 692; Kāuṭilya, 3. 639; Vajrahṛdaya, 3. 878; Satyavasu, 3. 832; Kaṭha (= Kamaṭha) and Rora, his father, 5. 1, 3; Vinayaṁdhara, 6. 1210; Mugdhaka, 7. 750, or Mūḍha, 7. 785; Yogātman, 8. 151. In 6. 1352 ff. note the list of Pārçva's ten Gaṇabhṛts; see p. 144.

Names of merchants and gentlemen: Nandaka and Bhadraka, 1. 798; Sadvaḍa, 2. 440; Sarga, 2. 441; Īçvara (hypocoristic of Maheçvara), 2. 456 (cf. 455); Aruṇa (hypocoristic of Aruṇadeva, 2. 459, cf. 452); Jasāditya (also Jaçāditya), 2. 453 ff.: Çrīsāra, 2. 776; Dhanasāra, 2. 893; Dhanāḍhya, and Gṛhasaṁbhūta, 2. 931; Lobhanandi, 3. 450; Hemala, 6. 127; Dhanaçarman, 6. 414; Manorama, 6. 663; Jinadharma, 6. 1075; Abhayaṁkara, 7. 70; Hitajña, Yogya, and Cāru, 7. 785; Bāndhavānanda, 8. 186; Supratiṣṭha, 6. 128.

Names of lowly persons: Kāladaṇḍa, name of a Niṣāda, 3. 825; Prakṛti, name of a servant, 7. 11.

Names of Brahmans' wives and daughters, nuns, and hetaeras: Anuddharā, 1. 30; Devinī (also Deviṇī), 2. 453; Vāñcanā, 3. 608; Viṣṇuçrī, 6. 1058; Kuçalamatī, 7. 10; Suvratā, 6. 921; Bālacandrā, 8. 223; Gaṇinī, 8. 223; Anañgasundarī, 3. 841; Maghadhā, 7. 126.

Names of countries: Sukaccha, 2. 1; Sukacchavijaya, 3. 1094; Tamisrāguha, 4. 107; Maṇḍalāvatī, 4. 108; Sīmāla, 6. 287; Puṇḍradeça, 8. 1; Kopakaṭa, 'locality,' 6. 114; Harimela, 'island,' 1. 393.

Names of cities: Tilakā, 2. 1; Kamalapura, 2. 52; Vardhanāgapura, 2. 440; Pāṭalāpura, and Pāṭalāpatha, 2. 453; 8. 21; Mahākṛpaṇa, 'Stingytown,' 2. 915; Çrīviçālapura = Viçālapurī, 2. 959; Çubhaṁkarā, 3. 1; Kukkuṭeçvara, 'city and cāitya,' 6. 167; Viçvapura, 6. 666; Ratnāvaha, 6. 873; Priyasaṁgamā, 'Vidyādhara city,' 6. 1109; Ṛṣabha, or Ṛṣabhā, 7. 8; Garjana, or Garjanā, 8. 150; Cakrapurī = Cakrapura, 8. 210; Kuçalasthala, 5. 146; Kṣitipratiṣṭhita, 7. 502 (also in Samarādityasaṁkṣepa 1. 48).

Villages: Sukara, 7. 36; Hillara, 8. 354.

Mountains: Jvalanādri, 3. 1095; Kṣīragiri, 3. 145; Sukūṭa, 7. 89; Pūrṇa, 7. 776; Kaligiri, 6. 125.

Forests and parks: Çakrāvatāra,[15] 3. 573; Kṣīravaṇā, 4. 145; Campaka, 'park,' 2. 75; Nalinīvana, 6. 1243.

Rivers: Nimagnā, and Unmagnā, 4. 109.

Lakes: Kuṇḍa, or Kalikuṇḍa, 6. 125, 140. For other occurrences of this important locality see above, p. 22.

Tīrthas: Kāmuka, 6. 570; Prapāta, 6. 635.

Designations of heavenly abodes: Sahasrāra, 1. 867; 8. 345; Jambūdrumāvarta (vimāna), 2. 1057; Sarvārthasiddha (vimāna), 6. 1322; Nirmalānandasāgara, 3. 1106; Mahāprabhavimāna, 4. 157; Sanatkumāra (kalpa), 8. 322.

4. Grammatical matters.

The list of novelties in grammatical forms is not inconsiderable. It includes some forms cited by Grammarians, but hitherto unquoted in the literature. Thus, as regards verbal inflection the present sthagati, 'cover,' 8. 131; the nā- present dhunītaḥ, 'they two shake,' 6. 1188. The unaccented a-class participle a-gaṇan. 'not counting,' 2. 663, is new, being glossed by a-gaṇayan, regular. The third plural iyrati, 'they go,' from iyarmi, 7. 824, is rare (Pariçiṣṭaparvan 1. 14). The aorists adhāviṣṭa, 'he ran,' 4. 25; and ahvāsta, 'he called,' 1. 341 (also Samarād. 5. 96), are known only to Grammarians. The form ā-tathās, injunctive from root aorist of ā + tan, 1. 177, is new. The corresponding augmented form is quoted only by Grammarians. The passage reads: tad evaṁ kathyate te yan mā pāpamatim ātathāḥ, 'this story is thus told thee, that thou mayest not spin thy evil designs.' There are two new aorist passives 3d sing.: agrāhi, 'he was taken,' 8. 58; and asthāpi, 'he was placed,' 2. 398.[16] The reduplicated aorist causative samaciskarat, 'he prepared,' 3. 935, is novel, both as regards the verb category and the propagation of the s.

More anomalous are: bibharāṁcakre = bibharāṁbabhūva, 'he carried,' 2. 638; and the perifrastic active participle kathayāmāsivān, 'he narrated,' 2. 958. The latter novelty is paralleled by dāpayāmāsivān, 'he caused to be given,' Samarād. 4. 67; cinta-

[15] Name of a tīrtha in Vikrama Carita (Ind. Stud. xv. 362); Prabandhacintāmaṇi, p. 100.

[16] Samarādityasaṁkṣepa has the following unquoted corresponding forms: aprachi 6. 42; 7. 152; āpi 4. 120; acinti 7. 51; ārpi 7. 302; vyajñapi 2. 408. Cf. Whitney, Roots of the Sanskrit Language, p. 240.

yāmāsivān, ib. 5. 294; jñāpayāmāsivān, ib. 5. 478.[17] Anomalously, vyaktī-syāt = vyaktī-bhavet, 'shall be unfolded,' 6. 725.

As regards syntactic usage the causative gerund vismārya, 'forgetting,' in the sense of vismṛtya, occurs 3. 179, 321. Imperatives in prohibitive expressions with mā are perhaps unusually frequent: mā pṛcha, 3. 759; mā kuruṣva, 3. 929; mā vilambasva, 3. 492; mā vikreṣṭāstu(!), 'let him not sell,' 3. 771; mā bhava, 5. 213; mā kuru, 6. 298; 7. 328; mā brūhi, 6. 904; mā vada, 7. 89, 410.

In noun inflection the anomalous combination yaty ūce = yatir ūce, 'the ascetic said' (yaty glossed by muniḥ), 6. 158. In noun-formation the desiderative participle cikīḥ, 'desiring to do' (gloss, kartum ichuḥ), occurs 8. 25. The word is reported by the Grammarians, being probably a Jaina word, as it occurs also Pariçiṣṭaparvan 7. 9; 8. 453. Stem rāi, 'wealth,' in the compound ratnarāi-rūpyāiḥ, 6. 225, is otherwise authenticated only by rāi-kṛ, 'convert into property,' reported by Grammarians. The comparative suffix -tarām is very frequently added to finite verbs; e. g., akārayattarām, 1. 430; cf. Whitney, Skt. Gramm. § 473[c].

The suffix ka shows occasionally its latent diminutive or pejorative function:[18] mayakā, 'by wretched me,' 1. 478; 2. 409, 874; anyakat, 'other mean thing,' 1. 419;[19] abhraka, 'small cloud,' 2. 155 (gloss, kaccolamukhamātram). In 3. 296, 420, dāivakam means 'wretched fate' = durdāivam 7. 723. In 3. 79 sraṅsatkaliñja-gṛhaka seems to mean, 'a little hut made of tumble-down mats' (gloss, kaliñjaḥ = kaṭaḥ). In 3. 171 upayācitakam, and in 7. 180 āupayācitakam seem to mean 'fond prayer'; in 7. 80 alīkaka, 'wretched falsehood.' In 2. 785 dhanuṣkikā seems to mean 'little bow.' In a case or two words with -ka alternate with the same word without -ka, apparently with diminutive intention: Pulindraka, 'common Pulindra,' 7. 756; Vasantaka, 'poor Va-

[17] These occurrences show predicative usage, as is to be expected. The words are really substitutes for the past active participle in -tavant which is employed regularly, indeed practically without exception, as a finite predicate thruout Sanskrit literature. This point of syntax is ignored by Western grammars.

[18] Edgerton's searching study on these functions of -ka does not, unfortunately, include the post-Vedic period; see JAOS. xxxi. 93 ff.

[19] Such pejorative pronouns carry on a rather lively existence in Samarādityasaṁkṣepa, to wit takam 2. 278; mayakā 2. 185; 4. 201, 330; asakāu 4. 141, 513.

santa,' 6. 469. In other cases this differentiation is much less pronounced, or altogether undeterminable: Kṣīrakadamba, or, Kṣīrakadambaka, 2. 511, 519, 'name of a teacher'; gṛha-godhaka, 3. 289 = gṛha-godha, 3. 304, 'house-lizard'; avasvāpanikā, 5. 85 = avasvāpinī, 5. 113, apparently 'sleeping charm or draught'; see p. 233. In 3. 365 davaraka = davara, means 'string'; in 1. 304 guṇa is glossed by davaraka: both are rare Jain words, hyper-Sanskrit for dora, or doraka, rare Sanskrit words of the same meaning (dora occurs in Rāuhiṇeya Carita). In a few other words with superadded -ka, not listed in the Lexicons, the suffix is probably simply formative, in the maner of the Prākrits: srastaraka, 'couch,' 3. 340; 6. 1335; āṇḍaka, 'egg,' 7. 349, 350; çastrīka, 'knife,' 1. 198; sṭhaṇḍilaka, 'mound,' 6. 705 (cf. Kathākoça, p. 105).

A few ku- compounds are wanting, perhaps intentionally, in the Lexicons: ku-saṁga, 'evil association,' 1. 481; ku-vikalpa, 'false determination,' 1. 805; ku-maṇi, 'false jewel,' 4. 2.

CORRECTIONS IN THE TEXT OF THE PĀRÇVANĀTHA CARITRA

1. 56: sphūrtimatī, for sphŭrtimatī
1. 75: vārdheḥ, for vārddheḥ; printed correctly vārdhi, e. g., 1. 404
1. 167: atinindyo hi, for atinindyo 'hi
1. 169: vyādha, for vyādhaḥ
1. 246: vardhāpyase, for varddhāpyase
1. 341: yatkṛtyādeça,°, for yat kṛtyādeça°
1. 343: ma iti, for me iti
1. 376: insert ca after laghutvaṁ
1. 600: viṣvagvyāhārakā, for viṣvag vyāhārakā
1. 636: vāirājya° for vāi rājya°
1. 666: vārddhakam, 'old age,' for vārdhakam. So also 2. 822
1. 688: nocchidyante, for no chidyante
1. 781: in the gloss on udvase correct girjane to nirjane
1. 884: jātu cit, for jātucit
2. 10: çrītilakāvatyā, for çrītilakāvalyā
2. 213: bhīmo, for bhībho
2. 232: aṣṭāpadam aham, for aṣṭāpadag aham
2. 307: tittirī toraṇe, for tittirītoraṇe
2. 316: nijapṛṣṭhe, for nijapṛṣṭe
2. 319: sphuṭam, for sphūṭam
2. 327: nahi, for nahiṁ
2. 350: çaṇāiç, for saṇāiç
2. 369: adyaprabhṛty, for adya prabhṛty
2. 518: parasparam, for parasvaram
2. 268: çunā, for khunā (thru ṣunā)
2. 674: vidhāya, for vidhāyaṁ
2. 741: uktā, for uktvā
2. 759: kaṇikādi, for kaṇikkādi; also 2. 917
2. 802: skandhe, for skandhaṁ
2. 881: muditāsyāḥ, 'with joyous faces,' for muditāsya
2. 894: deçāntaravaṇijyayā, for deçāntarvaṇijyayā
2. 938: °bāndhavāt, for °vāndhavāt

2. 978: spraṣṭavyo, for spṛṣṭavyo
2. 1001: maharddhikaḥ, for mahardhikaḥ
3. 124: tasyāçu, for yasyāçu
3. 129: tathānyad, for yathānyad
3. 155: prāvartyanta, for prāvartanta
3. 215: yayā, for yathā
3. 217: kāulika°, for kolika°
3. 220: change arrangement and punctuation: see Proc. Amer. Philos. Soc., vol. lvi, p. 32, note 72
3. 309: deçāntaryeṇa, for deçāntareṇa
3. 364: divide after bhūmīgṛhasthasyopari
3. 380: tathā chātrasya, for tathācchātrasya
3. 436: ulluṇṭhanāis, for ullaṇṭhanāis
3. 864: sa caṇḍāla, for saccaṇḍālo
3. 884: rākṣasīkarma, for rākṣasī karma
3. 890: ām iti, for āmeti
3. 891: prati, for pratim
3. 988: putram, for putra
3. 989: agāt, for agāḥ
3. 1072: çrīvajranābho, for çrī vajranābho
4. 51: rājarakṣyaṁ, for rājarakṣaṁ
5. 51: puṣpamālā tv°, for puṣpamālātv
5. 64: navamikā, for navamiāka
5. 147: °pravartanāt, for prarvatanāt
5. 192: yavanas, for javanas (Prākritism)
6. 64: kaṭha, for kaṭa
6. 67: tadbahu, for tad bahu
6. 132: cārupadmāni, for cāru padmāni
6. 187: teṣāṁ, for keṣām
6. 215: dhātakītale, for dhātakī tale
6. 237: nāirṛtyāṁ, for nāiṛtyāṁ
6. 253: ñkikillir, probably for kiñkillir, 'cry of joy'(?)
6. 313: vijayo, for vinayo
6. 719: hṛdi, for hradi
6. 1181: yathā rūpaṁ, for yathārūpaṁ
6. 1352: vasiṣṭho, for vaçiṣṭho
7. 34: çūrasenākhyaḥ, for sūra
7. 279: jīvitaniḥspṛhaḥ, for °nispṛḥaḥ
7. 351: cūrṇihetor, for cūṇi°

7. 435: dāivena, for devena
7. 634: dele the interrogation mark at the end of the first ardharca
7. 828: pārçve, for pārçvo
8. 9: pratiçlokaṁ, for prati çlokaṁ
8. 108: niḥsvo, for nisvo
8. 243: vidhyāpayaty°, for vidhyāyapaty°
8. 246: me 'parādhinaḥ, for me parādhinaḥ
8. 379: 'rudan, for rudan

INDEXES

The following abbreviations are used: B. = Brahman; Ci. = city; Co. = country; F. = forest; G. = god, or goddess; K. = king; M. = merchant; Mi. = minister; Mo. = mountain; P. = prince or princess; Pu. = pupil; Q. = queen; R. = river; S. = sage; T. = teacher.

1. Index of Names

2. Index of Subjects